Customers and Thieves

An Ethnography of Shoplifting

DANIEL J. I. MURPHY

Gower

Published by

Gower Publishing Company Limited
Gower House,
Croft Road,
Aldershot,
Hants GU11 3HR,
England.

Gower Publishing Company,
Old Post Road,
Brookfield,
Vermont 05036,
U.S.A.

British Library Cataloguing in Publication Data

Murphy, Daniel J.I
　　Customers and thieves: an ethnography of
　　shoplifting.
　　1. Shoplifting — England
　　I. Title
　　364.1'62　HV6665.G7

Library of Congress Cataloging in Publication Data

Murphy, Daniel J.I., 1950 —
　　Customers and thieves.
　　Bibliography: P. Includes index.
　　1. Shoplifting — England
　　2. Retail trades — England — security measures
　　I. Title.
　　HV6665.G7M87　1986　364.1'62　85-31694

　　ISBN 0-566-00882-3

Printed in Great Britain by Blackmore Press, Shaftesbury, Dorset

Contents

List of tables

List of figures

Acknowledgements

I would like to thank the following for their assistance and cooperation: Baroness Phillips of APTS; Peter Jones of IPSA; the store detectives and chief security officers who so freely gave me their time; the many shops and stores that provided me with access and information; and the police officers who allowed me to interview them and observe the way they arrested and processed shoplifters. Unfortunately, for reasons of confidentiality, it is not possible to name the very many people who provided the basic data for the research.

I would like also to express my appreciation to the editors and journalists of the following newspapers for their kind permission to let me reproduce extracts from their journals: *Daily Mail; Daily Mirror; Daily Star; Daily Telegraph; Evening News; Evening Standard; The Guardian; News of the World; Sun; Sunday Express; Sunday Mirror; Sunday People; and Sunday Telegraph.*

Thanks go to Paul Rock, David Downes and particularly Terence Morris of the London School of Economics. I would also like to express my appreciation to the Home Office for all their assistance, to Tony Marshall and especially to Susan Iles for their help and encouragement during the research. Needless to say, the views expressed are solely those of the author and should not be taken as representative of the Home Office.

Lastly, I would like to thank the many shoplifters who were the passive subjects of the research, and hope that this report goes some way to prompt a reconsideration of the offence and its control.

DANIEL J.I. MURPHY

1 Introduction

This book is concerned with the offence of shoplifting or, more correctly, theft by customer. Although there is no specific offence of shoplifting as such under the Theft Act 1968, this offence is nevertheless recorded by the police as shoplifting, and throughout this study the term 'shoplifting' will be used for ease of reference and because that is how respondents referred to it.

The book itself reports on research conducted in shops, police stations and magistrates' courts to provide a 'criminological ethnography of shoplifting'. It was decided to adopt such an ethnographical approach for two reasons. The first was simply that there has been no empirical observational study of how shoplifting is controlled in England. Although there have been several interview surveys of store detectives and retailers' shoplifting policies, there has been no academic research which has investigated the day-to-day organisation of store detectives and shop security in practice. Moreover, even the American studies which approximate to this type of research, besides being conducted in a different legal framework, are now over 20 years old. This study, then, is the first empirical investigation of shoplifting on the shopfloor, in the police station and the court to be carried out in any systematic and academic way in England.

The legal and historical background to shoplifting is traced in Chapter 4, while Chapters 5 and 6 outline the interviews with chief security officers and how store detectives operate. Chapters 7 and 8 examine how shoplifting affects the police and the courts.

1

The second reason for adopting an ethnographical approach to the investigation of shoplifting was theoretically and methodologically based. It will be argued subsequently that the meaning of offences can only be understood by examining the decision-making processes of the agents of social control in the context in which they make them. For most offences these agents are the police, but for shoplifting, they are the store detectives. Studies of officially recorded offenders are thus eschewed in favour of analysing how shoplifters are 'produced' and managed. These issues are addressed in Chapters 1 and 2.

Chapter 1 examines the methods criminologists have propounded to repair the deficiencies of officially recorded offenders. The purpose of this is twofold. First, the various studies of shoplifting outlined in Chapter 2 mostly reflect attempts to perfect research on officially recorded offenders. Secondly, an exposition of the problems of official statistics provides a theoretical perspective for the analysis of other shoplifting research and a framework for the present study. How the research was conducted is discussed in Chapter 3. To understand fully the ethnographic approach to the study of crime, then, it is first necessary to outline its development through studies of criminal statistics. This is the focus of the rest of this chapter.

Criminal statistics

History

Paul Wiles states that, 'in popular debate about crime as a social problem one question always dominates all others: how much crime is there in our society and is it increasing or decreasing? To answer these questions people usually turn to the criminal statistics.'[1] These days media reports of crime rates are often eagerly awaited as indices of serious crime, crimes with violence and, inevitably, police efficiency. The production and significance of criminal statistics have become accepted as part of our everyday lives and yet they are a comparatively modern phenomenon. The collection and processing of criminal statistics only really began in the nineteenth century, after the introduction of the census and with statistics on birth and death rates. Sellin, however, reports that in the last quarter of the eighteenth century, Jeremy Bentham advocated the introduction of registers of court convictions for use as a political barometer by parliament:

> The ordering of these returns is a measure of excellent use in furnishing data for the legislators to work upon. They will form altogether a kind of political barometer, by which the effect of

every legislative operation relative to the subject may be indicated..
They may be compared with the bills of mortality published
annually in London: indicating the moral health of the country...
as the latter do the physical.[2]

In discussing the *Petty Papers,* Sellin and Wolfgang cite Petty as saying,
'by the number of people, the number of corporal sufferings and
persons imprisoned for crimes,[is] to know the measure of vice and sin in
the nation'.[3] Thus criminal statistics were to be used as guides for
legislators and administrators to deal with criminality by discovering
its 'causes', and as a means of gauging the moral and political welfare
of the nation.

In a paper on the interpretation of criminal statistics presented before
the Royal Statistical Society, the Rev. Morrison commented that
national criminal statistics were a product of the nineteenth century:[4]
they were first introduced in France in 1825 and first published there
in 1827; they date from 1850 in the Austrian Empire, 1880 in Italy
and 1882 in Germany. Sellin thought that Guerry de Champneuf took
much responsibility for this, as he believed that the statistics would
'assist in determining the circumstances which co-operate in increasing
or diminishing the number of crimes'.[5] Morrison was of the opinion
that criminal statistics dated from 1857 in England, but McCabe and
Sutcliffe[6] show that crime statistics of a sort were collected from 1820,
with the bills of indictments to quarter sessions and assizes, which were
published. Additionally, the Metropolitan Police were able to provide
figures on crimes known to them, but it was not possible to generalise
from these to the whole country.

Lodge discusses the legal basis for the collection of criminal statistics;
and this is still relevant today.

> For England and Wales the statistics of crime and court criminal
> proceedings are contained in the Criminal Statistics, published
> annually after presentation to Parliament by the Home Secretary.
> Nearly all the statistics contained in this volume are collected by
> the Home Office from the police under the County and Borough
> Police Act of 1856, though some information is also obtained
> from the Court of Criminal Appeal, the Director of Public
> Prosecutions, coroners and other sources. Information about
> criminals, though not directly about crimes, is also contained in
> the Annual Report of the Commissioners of Prisons.[7]

In addition, information is provided in *Supplementary Statistics,* the
report of Her Majesty's Inspectors of Constabulary and the report of
the Commissioners of the Police of the Metropolis. Criminal statistics
are, then, by no means homogeneous.

In the *Criminal Statistics,* an important distinction was made between indictable and non-indictable offences, which corresponded to serious and non-serious crimes. Although this distinction was clear at the beginning of the twentieth century, it has now become somewhat obfuscated. Lodge explains that an indictment was simply an accusation of an offence which was read out to a prisoner brought before a court of assize or quarter sessions, at which a jury decided on the suspect's guilt or innocence.[8]

In magistrates' courts, on the other hand, this procedure did not obtain and the prisoner was charged with an offence by means of information laid before the magistrates, who then determined guilt or innocence. (There are no juries in magistrates' courts.) The confusion arose between those indictable offences which could only be tried on indictment (i.e. in front of a judge and jury—for example, for murder) and those offences which could be dealt with either in this way or summarily by the magistrates' courts. The power of magistrates to deal with indictable offences stemmed from the Criminal Justice Act 1925, but only when both the magistrates and the accused person agreed to this — the so-called, 'scheduled offences'. When magistrates believed their powers of sentencing to be insufficient the defendant could be referred to a higher court for a more appropriate sentence. A number of indictable offences (e.g. driving a car while under the influence of drink or drugs) could be tried either on indictment or summarily, provided the court agreed. The permission of the accused was not required in these cases.

Non-indictable offences are those which could only be dealt with summarily (e.g. many traffic offences) or summarily or on indictment where the accused elected for trial by jury under the Summary Jurisdiction Act 1879 (and other Acts). These latter were referred to as 'hybrid offences' as they transcended the barriers and distinctions between the two types of offence. Such offences included e.g. cruelty to children and unauthorised taking of a motor vehicle.[9] Shoplifting as an offence of theft, was an indictable offence, but one which, subject to the usual provisions, could be tried summarily before magistrates or on indictment.

The position was confused by a revision of classification in the 1979 edition of *Criminal Statistics,*[10] when the term 'serious offence' was introduced to cover those offences which had to be tried by jury and also indictable offences which were triable summarily with the consent of the accused by virtue of the Magistrates' Courts Act, s.19. This was necessitated by the redefinition of the coverage of 'indictable' offences in the Criminal Law Act 1977. Under Part III (implemented 17 July 1978) three methods of trial were introduced:

1. offences which could only be tried on indictment at the crown court;
2. offences which could be tried either at the crown or at a magistrates' court; and
3. offences which could only be tried summarily at magistrates' courts.

The first offence grouping in the statistics is a combination of (1) and (2), and although the Act refers to the combination of these two groups as indictable offences, in the statistics... they are [now] described as 'indictable/triable-either-way', in order to differentiate them more clearly from what were previously 'indictable offences'.[11]

More recently, they have been reclassified as 'notifiable' offences. Shoplifting, then, was an indictable/triable-either-way offence of theft but can now be termed a 'notifiable' offence.

Problems with criminal statistics

Criminal statistics include records from the police, the courts, prisons and other sources, such as coroners, borstals and remand homes.[12] Beattie argues that a prime function of criminal statistics was to produce precise information about individual criminal offenders, their motivation, background and personalities. He believes that 'little progress will be made in the prevention of crime either in its initial stages or by means of rehabilitation until a great deal more is known about the individual offender... and the factors relating to his criminal conduct'.[13] Cohen succinctly summarises this perspective when he says, 'in the field of juvenile delinquency, for example, the bulk of research is directed towards the taxonomic tabulation of the delinquents' traits (or attitudes, or values) in an attempt to see how delinquents differ from non-delinquents'.[14]

The comparison of officially recorded offenders and non-offenders is not without problems, however. Criminal statistics are based on recorded criminality. As Sellin observes, 'this criminality consists of offences which, having come to the notice of public authorities through complaints lodged by private citizens or directly as a result of police patrol, etc., are registered by such authorities.'[15] Critically, recorded criminality is only a sample of total criminality, the latter being an unknown quantity. Sellin believes that early statisticians and criminologists always considered that the sample of recorded criminality maintained a constant ratio to the total criminality, regardless of offence or time of year. Consequently, it did not matter that researchers did not know the total population of offenders and offences as they believed that their sample was representative of the total: by examining officially recorded offenders they could accurately predict what was occurring in the population as a whole. This naive view of criminal statistics that Sellin ascribes to early researchers has been criticised by others, but nevertheless the point made is vital — criminal statistics represent but samples of offences and offenders.

Wiles contends that 'what we are analysing when we examine "crimes known to the police" is merely a selection of all the behaviour which would be defined as criminal if it were reported'.[16] Appreciation of this fact does not necessarily mean that it is either accepted or near to being solved. He points out that many criminological studies persist in comparing known offenders with the characteristics of assumed non-criminals and thus ignore the possibilities of the non-criminals being equally or even more deviant than the sample of offenders: 'The contamination of control groups by dark figure crimes (that is crimes which have not come to the attention of the police or are not recorded) is all too frequently ignored.' [17]

Criminal statistics describe samples of offenders, not the total delinquent population itself, and these samples can sometimes be very unrepresentative. Studies based on official statistics, where these statistics are taken to represent actual crime, suffer from the fact that police records only contain a sample, produced in unknown ways, of a population which has unknown characteristics. Following this argument, then, the initial problem with criminal statistics is the degree of accuracy or reliability of those statistics: that is, how large the sample is, how representative it is, and whether it changes over time and by offence.

Sellin and Wolfgang[18] divide crimes into three categories: (1) crimes that directly harm people; (2) victimless crimes, in which participants freely engage in some 'criminal' act; and (3) crimes which affect society in general, e.g. acts of pollution, tax evasion, etc. They argue that police statistics are not a reliable measure for the second two categories since people either do not realise that they have been offended against or have a vested interest in keeping matters secret. Even with the first category, it is only with the more serious crimes (particularly those where insurance claims are involved) that we can talk with any degree of certainty about the number of offences coming to the attention of the police.

Perhaps an even greater problem is with the validity of criminal statistics — that they actually do measure what they purport to measure. Robertson and Taylor, for example, point out a profound fault with criminal statistics:

When we begin to unpack such terms as fraud, sexual offences and larceny, we find that they do not refer to a clearly identified, readily circumscribed behaviour. They are not sociological categories with pretensions to universality, but rather legal or statistical categories which reflect historical and contemporary attitudes towards particular behaviour in their titles — fraud, embezzlement, grand larceny, dangerous driving and in their differentiation — misdemeanours and felonies, indictable and non-indictable.[19]

Short and Nye point out, in addition, that much of criminological research is founded upon statistics about crime, class, family status, etc., but argue that the statistics rarely deal with the dependent variables. They believe that criminologists 'are concerned with etiological variables and processes, having accepted the definitions of subjects as criminal, alcoholic, from broken homes or neurotic. The continuous distribution of the deviant behaviour is ignored'.[20]

Wiles argues that British criminologists, concerned with empirical research and data-gathering, treated criminal statistics as archetypal social facts, and consequently questions about their validity and what they really mean tended to be ignored until comparatively recently. Part of this new thinking meant that what traditionally had been accep - ted as obviously and manifestly criminal now became equivocal. 'The implications for criminal statistics were however profound,' he said, 'for it meant that rather than being seen as providing the parameters for the study, they now had to be seen as part of the problematic area comprising the processes by which people became criminals.'[21]

Taylor, Walton and Young,[22] in analysing the position of positivists, isolate three problems. First, criminal statistics are based on crimes known to the police, which are but a sample of the total population of criminal acts (the problem of reliability). Second, the statistics are couched in a legal framework and reference structure and might not be appropriate for sociological investigation (the problem of validity). Third, and introducing a new aspect to the discussion, they argue that statistics define crime in terms of deviance and conformity to laws and that these laws might 'reflect only the caprice of lawmakers or the interests of powerful groups'.[23]

The new criminologists introduce a further aspect to the discussion on statistics — the political — and this is taken up by others. For example, Pearce [24] and Chapman [25] argue separately that the crimes of the powerful, although infractions of the law, often escape detection and, if discovered, are treated leniently. (The National Deviancy Conference and the Conference of Socialist Economists discuss this more fully.)[26]

The 'dark figure'

Appreciating the problems criminal statistics have with accuracy and reliability, criminologists have supplemented them by examining other sources in an attempt to discover how great the number of offences and offenders 'really' are, and how complete a picture criminal statistics provide. Antilla believes that the term the 'dark number' of criminality or the 'dark figure' was originally coined by the Japanese criminologist, Oba.[27] He includes in the term all the criminality in a particular area, at a particular time, which is not recorded by the police. Antilla opines that a useful distinction can be made when considering dark figure crimes between those offences which are not reported to the police and other types of unrecorded criminality.

McClintock urges a more sophisticated classification of the dark figure, and subdivides the concept into four distinct classes:[28] (1) there are those crimes which are neither reported nor recorded by the police and which consequently do not figure in official police statistics as 'crimes known to the police'. McClintock calls this category, the 'dark figure' in crime. (2) he isolates those offences which are registered by the police but for which no person is apprehended: he terms this the dark figure of criminality in the population. Category (3) he classifies as the 'grey figure' of criminality and includes in this those people who are arrested for crimes known to the police but who, for various reasons, are not found guilty of the offences charged. And (4) McClintock isolates the section wherein offenders are convicted of certain crimes but for whom not all offences are known. He calls this the dark figure of criminality in the criminal record of convicted persons. Most investigations into the dark figure of crime are concerned with the first two areas identified by McClintock, with perhaps most attention going to the first.

There have been a number of studies which have attempted, among other things, to assess the dark figure of crime by concentrating on an organisation and its context. Ditton [29], for example, looked at a bread factory; Cameron [30] studied a department store; and Martin [31] discussed offenders as employees. Most investigations explicitly concerned with the dark figure, however, have tended to take one of two forms: the victim or victimisation survey, and the self-report of delinquency study.

Victim Surveys

The purpose of victim surveys is to remedy the defect in official statistics resulting from the police having to wait to be informed of (possible) crimes. To overcome this, researchers interview people and ask them

directly what crimes have happened to them. A number of such victimisation surveys have been conducted. Ennis with the National Opinion
Research Center in the USA asked respondents if they had ever been
the victims of crime, whether they had reported those crimes to the
police, and their reasons for doing so or not. The conclusions reached
were that twice as many offences appeared to have been committed as
reported to the police.[32] In another study, Decker found that with the
major exceptions of car theft and burglary, there were large discrepancies
between the experiences of victims and official records.[33] Sapsford[34]
summarises the results of several studies, and argues that the general
figure for unreported crimes varies around 65 per cent (65 per cent for
the studies carried out by Hindelang et al.[35] and Decker,[36] and 61 per
cent for Hawkins[37]). In an English study, Sparks et al. found a much
lower proportion of 1 in 12 crimes coming to the attention of the
police, but here the comparision was not with official records of crimes
but with the victims' claims of reporting to the police.[38] The Sparks
study demonstrates that the ratio of reported crimes varies with the
offence, and is related to such factors as the perceived seriousness of
the crime, the victim's role in the offence, the relationship with the
offender, the visibility of the offence, and the victim's awareness of
the offence. Again burglaries and car theft have higher reporting rates,
presumably because they lead to insurance claims which require police
referral. More recently, the British Crime Survey found that

> taking crimes of violence together (sexual offences, robbery and
> wounding), there were on the basis of the survey estimates five
> times as many incidents as were recorded; for incidents involving
> loss or damage to property the figure was four times. The overall
> ratio for incidents which had been compared was one in four.[39]

Hood and Sparks believe that victimisation surveys are helpful in that
they provide information on the processes and decision-making which
prompt people to report to the police.[40] In addition, they think that
such surveys are useful in demonstrating the volume and nature of all
the criminal events occurring in a particular area for a particular time.
    There are considerable methodological problems with victim surveys,
however. Skogan argues that official records of criminal activity and
surveys of victimisation have similar defects in that they both tend to
underestimate certain types of offences, i.e. those which are difficult to
identify, and those of a consensual nature.[41] Box well illustrates the
problems with this type of survey.[42] The surveyors tend to ask questions
of one person in a household as a representative of all the members of
that household's victimisation experiences and, as Hood and Sparks
point out, this type of household sampling results in an over-represent-
ation of older people and women, as they are more likely to be at home,

and under-represents commuters, as they are not.[43] In addition, people can only talk about offences if they are aware that they have been victimised, which results in a bias in the type of offences reported.

On a more technical basis, Biderman identified two psychological components which need to be considered: the demand characteristic of the interview, and the temporal mnemonic effect.[44] The demand characteristic implies that, as in many other experimental social situations, the respondent replies to the assumed wishes of the interviewer. As a consequence of this psychological accommodation, 'time-telescoping' may occur; that is, events which occurred before or after the period under question may be included in the responses. 'The second broad class of time distortions to which incident interviewing is subject includes those confusions and distortions of recall associated with the passage and accumulation of experiences by the person through time.'[45] To combat this second defect, Biderman advocates the use of such mnemonic devices as 'Since Christmas has this occurred?', rather than asking open-endedly, 'Has this occurred to you in the last six months?'[46]

Biderman believes that victim surveys point out that far more offences are occurring than a review of criminal statistics would suggest, but these offences are not greatly significant happenings in people's lives, a finding supported by the *British Crime Survey.*[47] Typically, experiences of victimisation are infrequent and soon forgotten. Biderman still believes that victim surveys are useful in that they demonstrate the wider experience of harm suffered by citizens. In addition, they show that there is a large 'weeding-out' process of citizens' complaints by the police before they are recorded in the criminal statistics. This would suggest not that studies such as Decker's and Sparks' are incompatible, but that police willingness to record complaints is a critical factor in the processing of events into offences. Biderman shows that a quite high proportion of offences become known to the police and, if this is true, then the dark figure of crime may be due more to police organisational procedures than to the non-reporting of crime by victims. In the *British Crime Survey,* for example, of the incidents which were known to them, the police recorded as separate notifiable offences about two-thirds of incidents which involved property loss or damage and rather less than half of those involving violence.[48]

We discussed earlier criminal statistics in terms of their accuracy and their validity, and both these are relevant for analysing victim surveys. In terms of their accuracy, Levine argues that the methodological considerations of crime over-reporting are as important as the factors which emphasise the omission of crimes, such as sampling biases and memory fading.[49] He believes that victim surveys also

> present certain validity problems which proponents have tended to overlook.... The so-called unreported crime uncovered in the

surveys may well include many 'crimes' that never took place at all, and the 'gap' between reported and unreported crime may be more aptly interpreted as the difference between two fallible measurement techniques rather than a showing of a massive failure of victims to notify the police.[50]

What is understood by a criminal event varies from respondent to respondent and what one citizen interprets as a criminal victimisation may, in fact, have no legal status. This is substantiated in Ennis's study where evaluators examined 3,296 incidents of reported crimes and discounted over a third of them as failing to meet the legal requirements to constitute an offence.[51]

Self-report studies

The second approach to establishing the size of the dark figure has been self-report studies of delinquency, where samples of respondents admit to any of a number of offences in confidential interviews. The advantages of this type of study are fairly apparent. Instead of relying upon assumed non-delinquent control groups for comparison with delinquent control groups (which, as has been argued earlier, ignores the possibility of deviance in the control group), the self-report study permits examination of the extent and variety of criminal behaviour in the population as a whole (or some sample of it).

The main advantage of this approach is that it does not rely upon biased samples of respondents, which reflect the predominance of lower-class, male youths in institutions and official records. Indeed, the major finding of self-report studies is that criminal activity is not restricted to members of the lower socio-economic groups. As Short and Nye state:

> for the purposes of etiological enquiry, such data have the advant-age that they can recognise the existence of institutionalisation and in fact study its influence as an etiological process. That is, a frequent criticism of past studies has been that some of the process-es studied e.g., emotional instability, strained family relations, and school maladjustment, may result from institutional experiences, or the fact of institutionalisation, rather than being the cause of the delinquency being studied.[52]

Hood and Sparks summarise the advantages of self-report studies:[53] They make possible an estimate of the number of people who commit deviant acts of various kinds and the frequency with which they do it; they allow the comparison of official with unknown delinquents; they facilitate longitudinal studies of the delinquent careers of individuals over time; and finally, they are indispensable for any study that attempts to compare delinquents with a control group of supposedly non-delinquent people.

One such self-report study was conducted by Wallerstein and Wyle, who interviewed over 1,000 men and 700 women living in New York City.[54] The respondents were presented with a list of 49 offences, and 99 per cent of the sample confessed to having committed at least one of them. Similarly, in England Belson substantiates the high proportion of youths who have been involved in some form of criminal activity.[55]

As with victim surveys, however, this type of research is not without its methodological problems. First, self-report studies rely upon volunteers responding to the interviews and there is a consequent danger of bias here. Short and Nye, however, are of the opinion that the possibil - ities of bias can be overcome;[56] this is substantiated by Wallin[57] and Locke.[58] Box, however, is more critical of self-report studies and is less sanguine about their validity. He argues that there are three questions which can be asked of this type of research:

1. Are the data from self-report studies a valid measure of deviant behaviour?
2. Are the items in self-report schedules consistently relevant to the issue of delinquency, and are they comparable between different studies?
3. Have the research samples for self-report studies been adequate for the purpose of generalising to the whole population? [59]

The answers, he believes, are usually in the negative.

The first problem with this form of research concerns the honesty of the respondents; that is, whether they answer the questions truthfully. There is a danger that individuals may over-report their involvement in criminal activities in boastful attempts to be seen as delinquents; or alternatively, they may under-report for fear of being considered bad or criminal.

In a self-report questionnaire, administered to test the predictive validity of confessed delinquency, Farrington considered that self-admissions of deviance were predictively viable and reflected deviant behaviour 'rather than, for example, merely acquiescent response bias, boastfulness or deviant self-image'.[60] On the other hand, Blackmore, in a study which examined the response rates for officially recorded delinquents, found that respondents admitted to just over 75 per cent of their known offences.[61] Gold, however, points out that respondents' honesty cannot be equated with the validity of their replies.[62] In other words, precautions taken to ensure that interviewees reply truthfully do not guarantee that what is honestly believed to be a delinquent act necessarily is.

There are obvious parallels here with the problems of victim surveys. Gold's research shows that half of the acts of damage and vandalism would not be classified as criminal offences and that there are similar incongruities for other offences. Realising these difficulties, Gold believes that a useful classification could be made between perceived delinquent behaviour, actual delinquent behaviour and officially record-ed delinquent behaviour.[63]

Again, as with victim surveys, self-report studies are not easily comparable with each other and with official statistics because there has been a failure to standardise the response items and categories in the interview. Also, it is apparent that there are manifest biases in the samples of respondents, the most extreme of which is that, with the exception of the Wallerstein/Wyle study, the people interviewed were children and adolescents.

Comparing official statistics with self-report studies and victim surveys, it appears that criminologists have appreciated the methodological defects of criminal statistics, but in their attempts to remedy them by investigations into the dark figure of crime they have generated other problems of bias, accuracy and validity. It seems that criminologists are moving away from the self-report study. They have been useful in demonstrating that delinquency is not bound by considerations of socio-economic class, but their methodological difficulties make them a suspect research instrument. McClintock, for one, is of the opinion that victim studies might now be a more fruitful direction for research as the results are 'obviously more directly connected with practical questions of social prevention and law enforcement'.[64]

By means of victim surveys and self-report studies criminologists have attempted to repair the deficiencies of criminal statistics. If their intentions were to demonstrate the ubiquity of deviance and the bias of official records, then their efforts have been advantageous. If, however, they have attempted to fix a definite size to the dark figure then they are inexorably doomed to failure. Offences and offenders cannot be considered without the judgemental, legal and constitutive processes which go into their making. This is not to say that incidents of perceived harm, damage or victimisation have not occurred; on the contrary, victim and self-report studies are not necessarily erroneous from the perspective of the respondent, but they register events which may or may not be differently construed as harmful or wrong by different people according to their knowledge of the situations and their interpretations of complex legal rules. No act is, *per se,* an offence, it is only such in the judgement of particular people. If the attempts at measuring the dark figure of crime profess no more than to demonstrate that there is more perceived harm and there are more perceived delinquents than recorded in the criminal statistics, then there can be little argument. There is, however, a tendency for such research to equate perceived harm and self-reported acts with 'offences'.

The police role in the production of criminal statistics

At the same time as criminologists turned to analyses of the dark figure of crime there was a growing interest in the role of the police as agents in the production of official records. This stemmed partly from a desire to discover whether the police or the public played the more significant role in detecting crime, and whether disparities between dark figure statistics and official records resulted from public apathy in referring 'crimes', or police refusal to classify incidents as offences. There was also an emerging approach in which the organisational procedures for managing official records became significant, thus making police activity interesting in its own right. According to Bottomley and Coleman,

> a crucial distinction lies in whether the situations that are eventually recorded in police files, and subsequently in the official crime statistics, result from some sort of *police* initiative, or from the action of *a member of the public* who feels that an incident 'is something that the police ought to do something about'. This distinction corresponds to whether the police role in the discovery of a crime situation is a '*proactive*' or a '*reactive*' one.[65]

McCabe and Sutcliffe discovered in two studies of police activity that 73 per cent of all offences in Oxford were notified to the police by members of the public. For the other city, Salford, the proportion was even higher at 83 per cent.[66] Bottomley and Coleman's study showed that in 45 per cent of indictable offences citizens took the initial action and, taking all offences as a whole, there was a preponderance of public-initiated crime complaints.[67] Similarly, Chatterton found that almost half of all arrests for crime were cases in which the public had provided the police with a suspect.[68] Moreover, Bottomley and Coleman demonstrated that the police in one city only discovered 14 per cent of offences,[69] a figure which was duplicated in Mawby's study.[70]

These studies suggest that the police in England and Wales follow a largely reactive policy, and that the traditional view of police officers detecting crime is largely a myth. Further, information gained from these studies is illuminating for considering whether the dark figure is largely the responsibility of citizen failure to refer incidents to the police, or the inability of the police to record citizen complaints, either through lack of evidence, or because of a desire to keep reported crime low.

In discussing the dark figure of crime, Biderman and Reiss isolate two competing hypotheses: the 'realist' and the 'institutionalist' perspectives.[71] They argue that the realist hypothesis concentrates on how well official statistics record the 'real' or actual crime which occurs in a given society. The institutionalist perspective emphasises that criminal statistics are best understood in terms of the organisation and practices of the police and the criminal justice system. Ultimately, the institutional perspective believes that an offence has not occurred until a person has been found guilty. Biderman and Reiss argue that only when a person has been found guilty is there an irrevocable decision on the offence, but even here there is room for discretion, as a first decision ignores the possibility of a successful appeal.

It is apparent that the strengths of one hypothesis are the weakness of the other, and vice versa. Realist theorists would concentrate on the reduction of institutional processing and discretionary decision-making in criminal statistics; whereas those following the institutional approach would concentrate on the organisational parameters of official records as worthy of study in themselves.

The two approaches give two different answers to the question of how much crime there is. The realist position, by the use of dark figure research and official records, argues that the extent of crime in society is something like three to four times that indicated by the official statistics, with some offences having higher ratios to official statistics and some lower. On the other hand, for the institutionalists the extent of crime in society is exactly defined by criminal statistics. It is apparent that the concept of 'crime' means two different things for the two different perspectives. For the institutionalists, a crime is anything for which there is an offence and an offender; for the realists, a crime is anything included in criminal statistics, *plus* all those incidents in society which are not discovered, reported and processed by the police which could possibly be. As Biderman and Reiss show, 'the crux of the traditional realist vs. the institutionalist controversy involves questions of validity rather than reliability'. [72]

Bottomley and Coleman on the other hand, believe that Biderman and Reiss have confused the issue by equating the realist perspective with what they term the 'instrumental' approach. [73] By 'instrumental' they understand a traditional concern with the problems of validity and reliability in official statistics as a means of discussing criminality and attempts to combat it. Like the realist perspective, the instrumental hypothesis is intended to produce as accurate as possible a picture of crime — the 'real crime' problem. Bottomley and Coleman believe that statistics

> ought to be studied as social phenomena in their own right, rather
> than from an 'instrumental' point of view in which an external
> 'crime reality' is envisaged, of which the official statistics are
> seen as a more or less accurate reflection; instead they should
> be viewed from an 'institutional' perspective, according to which

they may be seen as indices of social and organisational processes, in the context of a community's social response to crime and suspected criminals.[74]

Wiles similarly considers that criminal statistics do not represent an external reality of crime but instead are constructed by a number of processes such as police organisation, legal codes and public willingness to become involved and report crime. He states that 'to understand precisely what the criminal statistics mean we must have a detailed knowledge of the organisations involved in the collection process and how they relate to, and are influenced by, the wider social structure'.[75]

Wheeler believes that problems with criminal statistics are not necessarily related to questions of reliability and validity, but are also due to the way in which the problem was defined in the first place. He advocates that criminologists ignore the technical deficiencies of official records, as ordinarily construed, and redefine the problem. His reformulation has three features: (1) an offender who performs a socially proscribed act; (2) the public, who constitute the victims and reporters of offences; and (3) the police who respond to illegal acts. Wheeler believes that by making police organisation a feature to be explained and investigated (as with the other two features) our knowledge of criminality will be enhanced.[76]

These various arguments follow from Kitsuse and Cicourel's seminal work, in which they analysed criminal statistics in terms of three models.[77] The first accepts that delinquency and criminality as measured by official records, are differentially dispersed among the socio-economic groups, with a preponderance in the lower categories, and attempts to explain this phenomenon; the second investigates how individuals came to be involved in deviant acts; and the third examines behaviour systems and delinquent sub-groups. They argue that although all three lines of inquiry stem from the same sources, they have not been theoretically integrated because of a failure to appreciate the distinction between units of behaviour which can be termed deviant, and the activities of agencies which produce units in the rate of delinquency. (A distinction between the 'behaviour-producing process' and the 'rate-producing process' — a distinction which is reflected in the dichotomy between instrumental and institutional.) Kitsuse and Cicourel advocate concentrating on the rate producing process. 'Our primary aim,' they say,

> is to explain the *rates of deviant behaviour*. So stated, the question which orients the investigation is not how individuals are motivated to engage in behaviour defined by the sociologist as 'deviant'. Rather, the definition and content of deviant behaviour are viewed as problematic and the focus of enquiry

shifts from the forms of behaviour ... to the 'societal reactions' which define various forms of behaviour as deviant .... Thus the explanation of rates of deviant behaviour would be concerned specifically with the processes of rate construction.[78]

A number of consequences follow from this argument. First, all statistics, whether they are official or informal, are of interest in the investigation of the processes by which records are produced. Secondly, by viewing delinquency in terms of organisational reaction and process and not as traditional units of behaviour, means that the problem of the reliability of official statistics in representing the total picture of crime disappears; deviance now is that which is processed by the agency. 'Thus, rates can be viewed as indices of organisational processes rather than as indices of the incidence of certain forms of behaviour.'[79] In summary, 'the search for the etiological factors and variables involved in crime is abandoned in favour of an examination of the social organisation of labelling and processing of perceived deviants.'[80]

There is a shift in focus of investigation here from that advocated by Becker's aphorism, 'deviant behavior is behavior that people so label'.[81] The possibilities of hidden delinquency are recognised by Kitsuse and Cicourel. Indeed, they do not deny that deviant acts exist, whether as construed by examination of official statistics or by investigation of the dark figure, but rather, they are interested in the ways certain deviant acts are processed by legal agencies to form official records. More technically, the change in emphasis is achieved by treating the methods of rate production and categorisation as the topic of research in its own right, rather than a resource for producing the sociologists' description of the world. (For a fuller discussion of the question of topic and resource see Bittner,[82] Zimmerman and Pollner,[83] and Murphy.[84])

Black agrees with Kitsuse and Cicourel, arguing that criminologists have viewed official statistics of crime in two ways.[85] The first treats official records as an index of the real amount of crime in society; the second abandons the search for an actual yardstick of existing criminality. The second approach has usually been achieved either by defining deviance by the reactions of official agencies, or by treating criminal statistics not as rates of delinquent behaviour but as indicators of social control. Black, and Kitsuse and Cicourel, then, make the important distinction that official records can be seen either as an index of deviant behaviour or as an index of organisational behaviour and social control. They believe that the latter perspective is potentially the more promising.

Black argues that criminal records are social facts in their own right and should be treated as such; they merit investigation for themselves rather than as a means to some etiology of deviant behaviour.

Viewed from this perspective, criminal statistics cannot be inaccurate or unreliable; in Black's words, 'they are an aspect of social organisation and cannot, sociologically, be wrong'.[86]

Douglas criticises traditional social theorists in general for their use of social statistics and the points he makes are useful for the present argument.[87] He believes that 'macro analysts', as he terms them, have used social rates as independent evidence for assessing and supporting descriptions about society. He argues, however, that social statistics are not scientific facts but the products of the commonsense interpretations of officials and agents responsible for their processing. Consequently, social theorists in unquestioningly using statistics, rely upon the commonsense understandings of others, rather than their own. Secondly, Douglas believes the meanings of those social statistics cannot be interpreted by macro analysts without recourse to their everyday commonsense understandings. Macro analysis *per se*, according to Douglas, is not necessarily to be discontinued but its reliance on commonsense interpretations should be realised and its spurious 'scientificity' should be acknowledged. Douglas stresses that the critical problem in using official statistics is that of validity, and this is reiterated by Atkinson.[88] Concentration on questions of reliability and accuracy implicitly assume that there is a 'real' amount of an offence or social event such as suicide, which can be determined independently of the social situations in which they occur.

Cicourel argues in similar vein that official statistics are used to support theories which have been derived from commonsense understandings of the world, that such facts reflect the perceptions, decisions and interpretations of unknown agents, and consequently the many varied processes by which such records are constituted are lost to the investigator.[89] He returns to the question of validity and reliability:

> Pointing out that the rates discernible from official statistics are worthless or contain errors that can be corrected, or distortions that can be balanced with tempered inferences, is to overlook the heart of the matter: the use of such data to document conventional theories of individual delinquency obscures the view that official statistics reflect socially organised activities divorced from the sociological theories used retrospectively for explaining the same statistics.[90]

The argument is that considerations of technical matters which concentrate on how reliable statistics are and how representative they are, detract from the basic validity problem that statistics are not independent of the social world from which they are produced, and should not be viewed as such.

Atkinson believes that the phrase 'official statistics' is misleading, perpetuating as it does matters of technical reliability, whilst obscuring the social context of official records.[91] He advocates the term 'data derived from official sources', which would have a twofold purpose: to remind us that the sample to be analysed is predetermined by the decisions of official agents and second, 'the main body of data on which analyses are based may be obtained from records made available by such officials'.[92] Atkinson's phrase is useful in pointing out the derivation and constraints on rates which are intrinsically and inexorably socially determined. Unfortunately, the phrase is somewhat cumbersome, and so the more traditional 'criminal statistics' will be used.

To conclude, this chapter has looked at criminal statistics, what they are, how they are produced and collected, and their history. Problems of validity and reliability have been discussed and the investigations into the dark figure by victim surveys and self-report studies were analysed in terms of their success in overcoming these problems. There was then a theoretical shift with the message that criminal statistics must be treated as events themselves, and that consequently researchers should analyse rate-producing practices. As Douglas says, 'the only valid and reliable evidence concerning socially meaningful phenomena we can possibly have is that based ultimately on systematic observations and analyses of everyday life'.[93] What this means, in effect, is that investigators should concentrate their energies on the agents who produce and process criminal statistics. For most purposes, this is usually the police. However, we have seen that the public can play a significant part in bringing crimes to the attention of the police, and their role should constitute an important component in any study of police organisation. Secondly, for some offences such as employee theft and shoplifting, the police have little to do with the discovery of offenders.

Bottomley and Coleman have pointed out in their study that store detectives were directly or indirectly responsible for generating the majority of reports of shoplifting, which in numerical terms amounted to a greater proportion of the sample than the total of all crime reports discovered by police activity.[94] Consequently, as this study is concerned with the investigation of shoplifting, it will focus on the role of shop assistants and security officers who discover the offence and thus generate the criminal statistics on shoplifting.

Notes

1. Wiles, P., 'Criminal Statistics and Sociological Explanations of Crime', in *The Sociology of Crime and Delinquency in Britain*, ed. Carson, W.G. and Wiles, P. (London: Martin Robertson, 1975), Vol. I, pp. 198—219.
2. Sellin, T., 'The Significance of Records of Crime', in *The Sociology of Crime and Delinquency*, ed. Wolfgang, M.E., Savitz, L. and Johnston, N. (London: Wiley, 1962), pp. 59—68.
3. Sellin, T. and Wolfgang, M.E., *The Measurement of Delinquency*, (New York: John Wiley, 1964; reprinted 1978), p. 7.
4. Morrison, W., 'The Interpretation of Criminal Statistics', *Journal of the Royal Statistical Society* (1897), Vol. LX, Part I, pp. 1—24.
5. Sellin, *op. cit.*
6. McCabe S. and Sutcliffe, F., *Defining Crime: A Study of Police Decisions* (Oxford University Centre for Criminological Research Basil Blackwell, 1978)., pp. 2—3.
7. Lodge, T.S., 'Criminal Statistics', reprinted from the *Journal of the Royal Statistical Society* 1953., series A, Vol. CXVI, Part III, pp. 283—97.
8. Ibid.
9. Ibid.
10. Home Office, *Criminal Statistics: England and Wales* London: HMSO, 1979, pp. 31—5.
11. Ibid., p. 35.
12. Sellin, T, *op. cit.*
13. Beattie, R.H., 'Problems of Criminal Statistics in the United States', in *The Sociology of Crime and Delinquency*, ed. Wolfgang, M.E., Savitz, L. and Johnston N. (London: Wiley, 1962), pp. 37—43.
14. Cohen, S., 'Mods, Rockers and the Rest: Community Reactions to Juvenile Delinquency', in *The Sociology of Crime and Delinquency in Britain*, ed. Carson, W.G. and Wiles, P. (London: Martin Robertson, 1975), pp. 261—73.
15. Sellin, *op. cit.*
16. Wiles, *op. cit.*
17. Ibid.
18. Sellin and Wolfgang, *op.cit.*, p.33.
19. Robertson, R. and Taylor, L., *Deviance, Crime and Socio-Legal Control* (London: Martin Robertson, 1973), pp. 32—3.

20. Short, J.F. and Nye, F.I., 'Reported Behaviour as a Criterion of Deviant Behaviour', in *The Sociology of Crime and Delinquency*, ed. Wolfgang, M.E.,Savitz, L. and Johnston, N. (London: Wiley, 1962), pp. 44—9.

21. Wiles, *op. cit.*

22. Taylor, I., Walton, P. and Young, J., *The New Criminology* (London: Routledge & Kegan Paul, 1977), p. 11.

23. Ibid., p. 11.

24. Pearce, F., *Crimes of the Powerful. Marxism, Crime and Deviance* (London, Pluto Press, 1978).

25. Chapman, D., *Sociology and the Stereotype of the Criminal* (London: Tavistock, 1968).

26. National Deviancy Conference/Conference of Socialist Economists, *Capitalism and the Rule of Law* (London: Hutchinson, 1979).

27. Antilla, I., 'The Criminological Significance of Unregistered Criminality', *Excerpta Criminologica* (1964), 4, pp. 411—14.

28. McClintock, F.H., 'The Dark Figure', *Report of the Sixth Conference of Directors of Criminological Research Institutes* (Strasbourg: Council of Europe, 1968), pp. 9—34.

29. Ditton, J., *Part-time Crime: An Ethnography of Fiddling and Pilferage* (London: Macmillan, 1979).

30. Cameron, M.O., *The Booster and the Snitch* (New York: Free Press, 1964).

31. Martin, J.P., *Offenders as Employees* (London: Macmillan, 1962).

32. Ennis, P., *Criminal Victimisation in the United States: A Report of a National Survey* (Chicago: National Opinion Research Center, 1967).

33. Decker, S.H., 'Official Crime Rates and Victim Surveys: An Empirical Comparison', *Journal of Criminal Justice* (1977), Vol. 5, pp. 47—54.

34. Sapsford, R., *Crime and its Growth* (Milton Keynes: The Open University Press, 1980), p. 19.

35. Hindelang, M.J. *et. al.,Sourcebook of Criminal Justice Statistics* (Washington, D.C.: US Government Printing Office, 1975).

36. Decker, *op. cit.*

37. Hawkins, R.O., 'Who Called the Cops? Decisions to Report Criminal Victimisation', *Law Society Review* (1973)., Vol. 17, pp. 427—44.

38. Sparks, R.F., Genn, H. and Dodd, D.J., *Surveying Victims* (London: Wiley, 1977), p. 152.

39. Hough, M. and Mayhew, P., *The British Crime Survey* (London HMSO, 1983), p. 10.

40. Hood, R. and Sparks, R., *Key Issues in Criminology* (London: Weidenfeld & Nicolson, 1978), pp. 23–34.

41. Skogan, W.G., 'Measurement Problems in Official and Survey Crime Rates', *Journal of Criminal Justice* (1975), Vol. 3, pp. 17–32.

42. Box, S., *Deviance, Reality and Society* (London: Holt, Rinehart & Winston, 1981, 2nd edn), pp. 62–3.

43. Hood, and Sparks, *op. cit.*, p.28.

44. Biderman, A.D., 'Time Distortions of Victimisation Data and Mnemonic Effects', unpublished paper for the Bureau of Social Science Research Inc.

45. Ibid.

46. Ibid.

47. Biderman, A.D., 'Surveys of Population Samples for Estimating Crime Incidence', *The Annals of the American Academy of Political and Social Science* (1967), Vol. 374, pp. 16–33.

48. Hough, and Mayhew, *op. cit.*, p. 17.

49. Levine, J., 'The Potential for Crime Over-reporting in Criminal Victimisation Surveys', *Criminology* (1976), Vol. 14, pp. 307–30.

50. Levine, *op. cit.*

51. Ennis, *op. cit.*

52. Short,and Nye, *op. cit.*

53. Hood, and Sparks, *op. cit.*, p. 13.

54. Wallerstein, J.S. and Wyle, C., 'Our Law-Abiding Law Breakers', *Probation* (April 1947), pp. 107–12.

55. Belson, W.A., *Juvenile Theft: The Causal Factors* (London: Harper & Row, 1975).

56. Short, and Nye, *op. cit.*

57. Wallin, P., 'Volunteer Subjects as a Source of Sampling Bias', *The American Journal of Sociology* (1949), 54, pp. 539–44.

58. Locke, H.J., 'Are Volunteer Interviewees Representative?', *Social Problems* (April 1954), pp. 143–6.

59. Box, *op. cit.*, p.66.

60. Farrington, D.P., 'Self-reports of Deviant Behaviour: Predictive and Stable?', *The Journal of Criminal Law and Criminology* (1973), Vol. 64, No. 1., pp. 99–110.

61. Blackmore, J., 'The Relationship Between Self-reported Delinquency and Official Convictions amongst Adolescent Boys', *The British Journal of Criminology* (1974), Vol. 14, No. 2, pp. 172–5.

62. Gold, M., 'Undetected Delinquent Behaviour', *Journal of Research into Crime and Delinquency* (1966), Vol. 3, pp. 27–46.

63. Ibid.

64. McClintock, *op. cit.*

65. Bottomley, A.K. and Coleman, C.A., 'Criminal Statistics: The Police Role in the Discovery and Detection of Crime', *International Journal of Criminology and Penology* (1975), 3, pp. 1—9 (emphasis added).
66. McCabe, and Sutcliffe, *op. cit.*, p. 38.
67. Bottomley, and Coleman, *op. cit.*
68. Chatterton, M., 'Police in Social Control', in *Control Without Custody* ed. J.F.S. King, Papers presented to the Cropwood Round Table (1975), pp. 104—22.
69. Bottomley, A.K. and Coleman, C.A., 'Police Effectiveness and the Public: the Limitations of Official Crime Rates', in *The Effectiveness of Policing,* ed. Clarke, R.V.G. and Hough, M. (Aldershot: Gower, 1980).
70. Mawby, R., *Policing the City* (Farnborough, Hants: Saxon House, 1979), pp. 90—108.
71. Biderman, A.D. and Reiss, A.J., 'On Exploring the Dark Figure of Crime', *Annals of the American Academy of Political and Social Science* (1967), No. 374, pp. 1—15.
72. Ibid.
73. Bottomley and Coleman (1975), *op. cit.*
74. Ibid.
75. Wiles, *op. cit.*, p. 212.
76. Wheeler, S., 'Criminal Statistics: A Reformulation of the Problem', *Journal of Criminal Law, Criminology and Police Science* (1967), Vol. 58, No. 3, pp. 317—24.
77. Kitsuse, J.I. and Cicourel, A.V., 'A Note on the Use of Official Statistics', *Social Problems* (1963), Vol. 11, pp. 131—9.
78. Ibid.; original emphasis.
79. Ibid.
80. Ibid.
81. Becker, H.S., *Outsiders: Studies in the Sociology of Deviance* (New York: Free Press, 1963), p. 9.
82. Bittner, E., 'The Concept of Organisation', in *Ethnomethodology,* ed. Turner, R. (Harmondsworth: Penguin Books, 1974), pp.69—81.
83. Zimmerman, D.H. and Pollner, M., 'The Everyday World as a Phenomenon', in *Understanding Everyday Life,* ed. Douglas, J.D. (London: Routledge & Kegan Paul, 1971), pp. 80—103.
84. Murphy, D.J.I., 'Theft From Stores by Employees and the Public — An Everyday Perspective', *Abstracts on Criminology and Penology* (1979), Vol. 19, No. 3, pp. 243—8.
85. Black, D.J., 'Production of Crime Rates', *American Sociological Review* (1970), 35, pp. 733—48.
86. Ibid.

87. Douglas, J.D., 'Understanding Everyday Life', in *Understanding Everyday Life*, ed. Douglas, J.D. (London: Routledge & Kegan Paul, 1971) pp. 3—44.

88. Atkinson, J.M., 'Societal Reactions to Suicide: The Role of Coroners' Definitions' in *Images of Deviance*, ed. Cohen, S. (Harmondsworth: Penguin Books, 1977), pp. 165—91.

89. Cicourel, A.V., *The Social Organisation of Juvenile Justice* (London: Heinemann, 1976), pp. 26—37.

90. Ibid., p. 37.

91. Atkinson, J.M., *Discovering Suicide — Studies in the Social Organisation of Sudden Death* (London: Macmillan, 1978), pp. 33—4.

92. Ibid., p. 34.

93. Douglas, *op. cit.*, p. 12.

94. Bottomley, and Coleman, (1980), *op. cit.*

2 Review of shoplifting research

Introduction

The organisation of this chapter reflects that of the preceding one so that the different methods of investigating shoplifting can be readily classified within the wider context of criminology.

It was stated in Chapter 1 that criminologists have looked to criminal statistics for information on the extent and size of the crime problem as well as data on offenders. Research into shoplifting has also adopted this approach. However, attempts to gauge the cost of shoplifting by reference to the value of the goods recovered from prosecuted or cautioned offenders alone grossly understates the extent. No one seriously believes that the official statistics on the cost of shoplifting reflect anything but a small percentage of the total (without even considering the costs of security personnel and the burden on the criminal justice system). Consequently, researchers have looked to other data sources to assess the *total* cost of shoplifting. These are examined in the first section of this chapter.

Considerable effort has been expended on the investigation of officially recorded shoplifters. These studies have been based on large samples of offenders as well as on the small groups treated by psychiatrists and the medical profession. The second section of this chapter, then, examines the studies of convicted offenders.

Official statistics on offenders, it was argued earlier, are composed of samples drawn from an unknown total of offenders. Consequently, comparisons with control groups of assumed non-shoplifters become questionable when one considers the number of people who have shoplifted but have not been apprehended, and the numbers who have been apprehended but not referred to the police. Shoplifting is one of the least reported (or discovered) offences and is one of the most frequently committed. The problem of reliability is apparent. Realising the problems posed by criminal statistics for analyses of shoplifters, researchers have tended to supplement or replace them with data derived from other sources. This again parallels attempts in dark figure research to discover, among other things, the reliability of official statistics and the 'real' number of offences and offenders. The two principal approaches to dark figure research were identified in Chapter 1 as the victim survey and the self-report study. Self-report studies on shoplifting, or where shoplifting is one of a number of listed offences, have been popular as they do not rely on biased samples of recorded offenders. They do suffer, however, from similar problems experienced in other self-report studies, tending to rely on students and adolescents for their samples. Nevertheless, they demonstrate the prevalence of the offence in all classes. The third section thus concentrates on the work of self-report investigators.

Section 4 correspondingly examines the data provided by victim surveys. Obviously, these differ from surveys of individuals or households as they relate to business organisations, but the principle remains the same. Realising the deficiencies of criminal statistics in representing the total picture, criminologists have turned to the site of the criminal activity to assess the degree to which individuals (or organisations) have been victimised and their reasons for referring suspects to the police, or not. The discussion on victim surveys is subdivided into an analysis of the suspects who are apprehended in shops, and the examination of the factors which determine referral of those suspects to the police.

It was argued in Chapter 1 that dark figure research was informative in demonstrating the ubiquity of deviance and bias of official statistics, but there were problems when attempts were made to set the size of an unknown — but theoretically knowable — totality of offenders. An interesting development in shoplifting research has been the introduction of 'following exercises', where customers are randomly followed to see if they take goods, precisely in order to 'fix' the limits of the shoplifting population. However, it will be argued in the section dealing with following exercises that a crucial distinction has to be made between 'taking' and 'stealing', and while such exercises are useful in demonstrating the number of people who take goods from shops they can tell us little about theft from shops.

Customer involvement in reporting suspected shoplifting is usually very low. Some interesting research has been conducted on this topic and this work is discussed later.

The penultimate section deals with the remaining miscellaneous shoplifting literature. Much of this will be alluded to throughout the book, but included here are such topics as store detectives' memoirs; consumer advice to shoppers; security advice on the prevention of theft; and community campaigns against shoplifting.

The last section discusses the general theoretical arguments which underpin the research. In summary, then, this chapter is divided into eight sections:

1. Total cost from official statistics and estimates of shrinkage.
2. Studies of convicted offenders: (a) general surveys, (b) psychiatric studies.
3. Self-report studies.
4. Victim surveys: (a) surveys of apprehended shoplifters, (b) reasons for referral.
5. Following exercises.
6. Customer involvement.
7. Miscellaneous.
8. Theoretical discussion of the present research.

1 The costs of shoplifting

The Home Office Working Party Report on Shoplifting and Thefts by Shop Staff estimated that the annual cost of shoplifting ranged from £56 to £300 million.[1] In practice, however, these figures are little more than estimates arrived at by assessing the 'shrinkage' figures for all shops and stores, and determining what percentage is due to shoplifting.

The Institute of Grocery Distribution Working Party defined shrinkage as 'the difference between the value at selling price of the stock supplied to the shop, and the cash or stock revealed at stock-taking, allowance being made for price changes'.[2] In the USA and the UK shrinkage is usually expressed as a percentage of the selling price, whereas in some other countries it is fixed in relation to the cost price. Cameron provides a fuller definition and explains the considerable variance in the figures of shoplifting losses provided by the stores.

> Losses due to theft become part of a general, undifferentiated figure composed of several factors and known as 'inventory shrinkage' or 'inventory shortage'. Inventory shrinkage is calculated by taking the difference between the retail price for merchandise, as assigned by store management, and the actual amount realised on the sale of the merchandise. It is usually reported as a per cent of gross sales volume.[3]

For example, if a store has an annual income of say, £1 million, either in cash or goods, and an inventory shortage of £10,000, then that store has a shrinkage rate of 1 per cent.

The Institute of Grocery believes that it is misleading to represent shrinkage as a percentage of annual turnover and would prefer it to be expressed in relation to total net profit. 'It is not always realised that when goods are lost, the loss is not just the profit on that article, but the cost of the article plus the profit that would have been made if the article had been sold.'[4] In this way, a 1 per cent shrinkage rate could be 20 per cent of net profit.

It is important to realise that not all inventory shrinkage is the result of theft and that there may be other, perfectly legitimate, explanations. For example, included in inventory shrinkage are such factors as lost or damaged goods, goods which have had their prices reduced because of shop-soiling, and simple administrative errors. Cameron continues,

> Inventory shrinkage, then, is the index regularly used by merchants as a general measure for many forms of loss. Unfortunately, it is seldom a specific measure of theft and never a measure capable of differentiating between the different kinds of theft. Therefore, it is impossible for store management, or anyone else, to specify accurately the amount of loss resulting from any particular component. Even if one is able to make some rough estimate of how much loss is due to theft and how much is due to markdown, it is impossible to give more than a semi-informed guess as to how much theft is the result of shoplifters and how much theft is the result of employees.[5]

Cameron cites the generally accepted ratio of employee theft costing three times as much as shoplifting, but believes it is impossible to delineate the percentages with any degree of accuracy.

Nevertheless, various authors have attempted to be precise about the relative size of losses due to shoplifting and employee theft. An Australian study by Bleakley estimated that 75 per cent of loss was attributable to dishonest staff.[6]

A special report for the Economist Intelligence Unit isolated three main areas responsible for unexplained losses: robbery by breaking and entering, shoplifting, and employee theft. It was thought that robbery accounted for 15 per cent of total shrinkage loss, employee theft for 60 per cent, and customer theft about 25 per cent of losses.[7]

The Home Office Working Party balanced the opinions of the larger retailers (who said they were unable to distinguish losses by shoplifting from those by staff and delivery men) against the views of the smaller retailers (some of whom blamed all their losses on customers), and concluded that the larger retailers were the more realistic. In the opinion of the Working Party:

> a high proportion of the losses attributed by some shops to
> shoplifting is due to staff thefts, and to losses on delivery
> either as a result of collusion between shop staff and delivery
> staff or by short deliveries which are undetected because of
> inefficient systems of checking.[8]

If it is difficult to decide whether losses are legitimate or not, it is far
more complex to determine the specific contributions made by employee
theft and shoplifting. For example, it may be obvious that thieves have
broken into a shop, but it becomes a matter of guesswork whether
customers or employees are responsible for other losses, unless they are
caught in the act. We rely, then, merely upon educated estimates of the
relative significance of the various losses.

The Institute of Grocers asked one chain of retailers to assess the
distribution of losses caused by shoplifting and employee theft and
received the following reply:

> Our experience in this area is not quantified in any precise way
> and in fact we are doubtful whether it could be. Our views
> therefore are really intelligent estimates based on our familiarity
> with day-to-day management in stores which have to face this
> problem all the time.[9]

It transpires, then, that the fixing of the costs of shoplifting are based
on estimates, formed in uncertain ways, from people's understanding
of the problem. There is little that can be said accurately, except perhaps
that staff thefts tend to be under-emphasised, and too much importance
placed on customer theft. However, whether or not shoplifting costs
more than employee theft, it is a significant crime involving as it does
over 200,000 offences per annum and being controlled almost exclusively
by private security officials.

2   Studies of convicted offenders

General Surveys

It was stated earlier that the analysis of convicted offenders would be
subdivided into two sections: the investigation of offenders in terms of
the time of offence, amount stolen, previous record, age, sex, etc.;
and the more intensive psychiatric analyses. This classification is some-

what arbitrary and there is some overlap between the two, perhaps no more so than in Gibbens and Prince's study.[10]

In a later article, Gibbens said,

> Shoplifting interests the professional student of crime because it is especially clear that a large number of selective processes go on between committing the crime and appearing in court. You have to be caught red-handed, in a shop which employs a detective, which has a policy of arresting and also charging those they detect. Each process makes a selection so that those who appear in court may not be representative in any way of the people who commit these crimes. This occurs to some extent in all fields of crime but it is much easier to forget or ignore than in the case of shoplifting.[11]

Gibbens reiterates here the points made in Chapter 1 that officially recorded offenders are not necessarily representative of all offenders and that the intervention of private security agents in the selection and decision-making processes increases the probability of bias. Nevertheless, Gibbens and Prince's research concentrates on the investigation of officially recorded offenders. In addition, they declare that the purpose of their research is to study a 'number of representative groups of shoplifters'.[12] The use of the word 'representative' is misleading here, particularly considering Gibbens' earlier statement on representativeness, and presumably refers to their sample being representative of officially classified offenders and not to an assumed total shoplifting population.

Gibbens and Prince's sample comprised 532 women offenders, the total number of female shoplifters in three courts in Greater London for the year ending in August 1960. As they were also interested in the question of recidivism among female shoplifters, the authors examined the criminal records of about 100 women shoplifters convicted in the same three courts ten years previously. They also examined records of all the juveniles who were found guilty in the three courts and, in addition, looked at the records of 218 men who were prosecuted in 1949 and 234 who were prosecuted in 1959. The final part of the study was conducted by Epps at Holloway Prison where 200 women who had been arrested for shoplifting were interviewed, as well as 50 other women arrested for a variety of other property offences.[13]

Of the whole group of women offenders in 1959, 80 per cent were of previous good character and had no criminal record, and this was also true of the 1949 sample. Of those recidivists who had previous convictions, 40 per cent stole goods valued at £5 or more, whereas only 25 per cent of the total sample took similar amounts. Thirty-six per cent of the total female offenders stole goods valued at less than £1; and interestingly so too did a third of the recidivists. Even for recidivists, then, the value of the goods stolen was not particularly high. The authors believe shoplifting for women was offence-specific and that if women aged over 40 were to commit further offences they were likely to be shoplifting ones.[14]

One of the most significant features to emerge from the research was the predominance of immigrant women in the shoplifting population: 29 per cent of the women were foreigners (mostly from Europe) and were young. This represented a startling change from the 1949 sample.[15]

Gibbens and Prince collected their social demographic data on the offenders from three sources. First, they took the domestic situation, income and occupation as a measure of social status; second, social stress was identified by problems in relationships and financial difficulties; and third, an historical picture of the offender was composed by reference to her education, work record, etc. Curiously, Gibbens and Prince discovered that caretakers and housekeepers stood out in the data, and they could offer no explanation for this finding.[16]

The authors stated that 'the relatively superficial information obtained in many cases did not allow firm psychological conclusions' to be made, but nevertheless they proceeded to interpret the psychological motivations of their sample.[17] They thought that the personalities and the motivations of the offenders were age-specific. For the teenage girls and those in their early twenties there were no overt signs of psychological disturbance, but, Gibbens and Prince argued, underlying tensions were signified by the unusual and pointless nature of the offence. Because there was no need for the person to steal, and because the item stolen was not particularly useful or valuable, Gibbens and Prince believe that this was a manifestation of some inner disturbance, an explanation shared by other psychologists.

The non-recidivist female shoplifter aged 25—40, was subject to obvious frustrations, particularly sexual ones. The most significant group, the 40—55-year-olds, were characterised by depression which was often accompanied by physical ill-health. Gibbens and Prince found the older age groups of 55 and over, and especially those in their sixties, exhibited least obvious psychological manifestations and were difficult to classify.[18]

Of the total sample, 18.9 per cent exhibited an obvious psychiatric disturbance, and 9 per cent had some form of physical ill-health, though Gibbens and Prince thought that low intelligence, low income, or unhappy marriage were not directly related to shoplifting. The authors considered that greed (i.e. the desire for goods without paying), was a factor in most of the offences but believed that this was precipitated by other underlying motives. The most significant predisposing factor to emerge in their study was that of depression, and Gibbens and Prince conclude that shoplifting is a form of para-suicide or a 'cry for help'.[19]

During the period of the research in the three courts 175 juveniles under 17, 88 boys and 87 girls, were found guilty of shoplifting offences. The girls demonstrated the same characteristics as the women — they rarely had previous convictions, and where they did it was usually for shoplifting. The boys, on the other hand, more often had previous convictions, although not for shoplifting, and they began their criminal activities earlier than the girls. Like the convicted men, boys tended to steal books. Between 50 and 60 per cent of the men stole books, whereas only one woman offended in this way.[20] Nearly half of the sample were categorised as 'disturbed' in some way, and Gibbens and Prince identified three different motivations for the theft: an act of defiance; an appeal for help; a feeling of worthlessness.[21]

Almost half of the adult male offenders had previous convictions, but only 4 per cent had previous convictions for shoplifting alone.

Information gathered by Epps in Holloway suggested that the links between pre-menstrual tension and shoplifting were tenuous. Similarly, the data did not support the convention that the menopause was a predisposing factor as there were over three times as many post-menopausal women as there were those in the menopause.[22]

To summarise Gibbens and Prince's study, 80 per cent of the women offenders had no previous convictions, and recidivists restricted themselves to shoplifting. Of the adult male offenders, on the other hand, almost half were recidivists but not necessarily for shoplifting. Of the female shoplifters, a startling feature was the large number of European immigrants in the sample. Traditional explanations, such as pre-menstrual tension and the menopause, were largely discounted, but there did seem to be an underlying common feature of depression, physical illness and frustration. Among the adolescents, patterns of criminal offending closely paralleled the sex differences of the adults, and nearly half of both boys and girls could be regarded as 'disturbed'.

Gibbens and Prince's study is important, partly because it was one of the first to investigate convicted shoplifters in England, and partly because of the size of the sample. There are a number of problems, however, and insight into them is provided by Gibbens himself. He appreciates that a critical factor in deciding who is prosecuted is the presence of store detectives and their policy on police referral. Because of the relative smallness of the numbers of people prosecuted for shoplifting during their study, the actions of a few shops with store detectives could easily bias the 'representativeness' of the sample. For example, Gibbens and Prince explain the significance of immigrants in terms of their isolation and youth. It could equally well be, however, that this section of the population were more noticeable to store detectives and more regularly followed. Typically, the authors are at a loss to explain the presence of housekeepers and yet there is no logical reason why they cannot be subjected to similar interpretations as the immigrants.

Bennett, in her study of a Midlands town ('Midtown') collected data from police records of arrests for shoplifting in 1966. On this occasion women did not dominate the figures, forming the bare majority shoplifters (56.6 per cent). In addition, while boys aged 11 to 14 and middle-aged women tended to be the main offenders, they did not overwhelm the equivalent groups of the other sex. Nearly half of the men arrested for shoplifting were aged under 21, and of all the sample, nearly 40 per cent were in this age group. The low value of goods stolen was confirmed in this study as 43 per cent of thefts were valued at less than 10 shillings, and only 7 per cent of offences involved goods valued at over £5. Interestingly, having spoken both to store personnel and the police, Bennett concluded that 'it was generally agreed that, for the first offence especially, the sentence imposed was of little importance. The shock of arrest, prosecution, and above all the fear of publicity in the newspapers were the real punishments and deterrents.'[23]

Ten years later Davidson set out to test the validity of what he termed the myth of the middle-class, middle-aged women among shoplifters. The annual prosecutions for shoplifting in Hull provided a sample of 514 offenders, of whom only 44 were women in the 41–55 age range. Eighteen of these women lived in high-status areas and so, Davidson argued, the middle-class, middle-aged woman myth was constructed in the Hull case on only 3.5 per cent of the total sample. He goes on to suggest that a far more fruitful area of inquiry would be the majority of shoplifters who were males in the younger age group. Of all shoplifters in Hull 52 per cent were under 17 and 66 per cent of this group were males, who were also more likely to be recidivists and to live in low-status areas.[24]

Redding's survey, conducted in Plymouth at the same time included all the people appearing before the courts on charges of shoplifting, a total of 479, (252 men, 227 women), of whom 417 were convicted and sentenced in the magistrates' courts. He found that young people were more likely to commit shoplifting — 152 of the 417 sentenced offenders were between the ages of 17 and 29. Interestingly, Redding's data revealed that more men were convicted than women during the age when the menopause might be occurring. Redding also found that 63 per cent of men had previous convictions, compared to only 33 per cent of women. Again, the amount stolen by each was relatively small, averaging only £5.30.[25]

As part of a wider study Walsh looked at the records of all shoplifting offences known to the police in Exeter for the year 1975, and constructed a 10 per cent sample of all offenders. He discovered that just over 32 per cent of this sample had previous convictions, though not necessarily for shoplifting. Of the recidivists, 66 per cent were males and 34 per cent females.[26] These figures on recidivism closely match Redding's and correspond to the national criminal statistics for shoplifting.[27]

We conclude this section with a consideration of an article by Harris. Like Davidson, Harris is concerned with disputing the myth of the depressed menopausal woman predominating among shoplifters, and he believes that a wide range of people actually shoplift. To illustrate his hypothesis, he took as his sample fourteen offenders convicted at Poole magistrates' court in a six-week period. Despite the size of his sample, his findings were similar to Redding's. Both sexes were equally represented, (7 men and 7 women), of whom three were under 21, five were in their fifties and sixties, and the average age was 38. Only two of his sample had previous convictions for shoplifting, and in six cases the offenders exhibited medical or psychiatric symptoms.[28]

Although these studies of officially recorded offenders vary in terms of sample size, location and year(s) of research, a number of similarities can be noted. The menopause as a contributing factor tended to be discounted in all the studies, and the younger age group was isolated as being important. Males tended to be recidivists more often than females: in Gibbens' study, 80 per cent of women had no previous convictions, whereas almost half of the men had criminal records. Redding and Walsh both identify similar male — female recidivism rates, with about two-thirds of men having criminal records and women only one third. Depression, ill-health and frustration were identified in some, but not all, of these studies.

Psychiatric studies of convicted offenders

In some aspects, this section is disparate, taking studies which span continents and decades; however, in other respects, the underlying assumptions are similar.

Badonnel belives that shoplifting is a form of delinquency which is specifically female, and that the offence is precipitated by weakness of character and lack of a sound moral code. He considers that shop-lifting could be like illness (i.e. an escape from reality), possibly the initial symptom of incipient schizophrenia with an underlying general depression.[29] Versele continues in a similar mode, arguing that female delinquency which manifests itself in shoplifting is the result of inner emotional conflicts. He thinks that the need to shoplift has an under-lying motivation of frustrated love, emotional insecurity and inferiority.[30]

Arieff and Bowie conducted a survey in Chicago. They found that only 5 per cent of shoplifters apprehended in stores were referred to the courts and of that 5 per cent, between a quarter and a third were referred for psychiatric investigation (i.e. approximately 1.8 per cent of all apprehended shoplifters). The majority of their patients were women (313 out of 338) and were mostly young or middle-aged/menopausal. Arieff and Bowie believe that marital disharmony, low economic level and low intelligence level are not precipitating factors. Of the 338 patients they examined, however, '77% had some definite mental or emotional disorder. The diagnosis for a large percentage of patients was acute anxiety state with mental depression.'[31]

In all the cases referred to Neustatter in England, 'there was a degree of tension and depression: in three of them it was brought to a climax by some special event' e.g. the death of a friend, an accident to the husband, or an emotional conflict within marriage. In most of the cases he examined the patients showed evidence of an hysterical personality.[32]

Meyers thinks that the drastic and pervasive effects following apprehension and prosecution for shoplifting are related to some equally strong personal motivation. He argues 'the most important and pervasive of personal values are those related to one's psycho-sexual nature, and it may be reasoned that accordingly there must be a relationship between shoplifting and the psycho-sexual values of the individual.'[33] These psycho-sexual values are not manifested solely in sexual intercourse but as a background to a person's whole emotional and sensuous life. According to Meyers, 'each person is endowed with sensuous needs that demand fulfilment, which can only happen by contact with another person — usually of the opposite sex.'[34] If these needs are not satisfied in some way, they are not sublimated but find expression in other forms, for example, shoplifting.

Meyers' survey was based on a sample of 95 offenders, of whom 28 were men and 67 were women referred for psychiatric examination. The author found that there were no special characteristics among those referred, save over half of the women weighed over 125lb (8 stone, 13lb). Also of significance for Meyers was the presence of other symptoms, including headaches, backaches, gastro-intestinal disorders, nervousness, surgical operations and the tendency to be accident-prone.[35]

Meyers provides a few case studies to support his theories. Shortly after her second marriage and for the next 15 years, Mrs X shoplifted, and continued to do so apart from the long periods when she was away from her husband. She complained that her husband ignored her and as she was very affectionate, with 'strong needs', she found her husband's occasional approaches for sexual release disturbing. Meyers believes that Mrs X began to shoplift because her sensuous needs were not being fulfilled.

Again, for Mrs Z, the physical relationship with her husband was poor; he ignored her sexually for periods of up to seven years. The shoplifting was Mrs Z's first offence and after therapy she began to realise that there was a relationship between her offence and the lack of fulfilment in her marriage. The case of Mrs Y was similar. Her husband paid her little attention and Mrs Y began to steal. During therapy the lack of fulfilment of her sensuous needs became apparent to her. Her husband became enthusiastically involved in the therapy, and fortunately Mrs Y no longer needed to steal. Meyers concluded that the element of unfulfilled sensuous needs was apparent, but the connection between the act of stealing and sensuous frustration was not clear.[36]

Russell likewise believes that unsatisfied emotional needs, matrimonial stress, loneliness and depression are all related to the motivation for shoplifting, and he too provides case studies to support his theory.

Mrs A was a young housewife with a forceful father, and a husband who tended to ignore her and give her little sexual satisfaction. After an emotional conflict with her father, Mrs A stole a slip from a shop. During therapy, Mrs A

> was seen as an intelligent woman with many assets and talents who had been saddled with neurotic conflicts that had comprom- ised her sense of identity and identification, thus crippling her capacity for maturity. After a period of intensive psychotherapy, Mrs A was able to make a much more mature approach to her life problems and to utilise her assets in constructive self-realisation.[37]

In an earlier study, Rouke stated that 10 per cent of shoplifters were professionals, 3 per cent stole for their own purposes and the remaining 87 per cent shoplifted because of emotional disturbances. Rouke based his observations on over 80 referrals over a five-year period, of whom 65 saw him, and less than half of this latter group returned for subsequent visits. All the offenders referred to him were women, mostly between the ages of 18 and 25. Apart from two of the patients whom Rouke considered to be psychotic, he was able to classify the rest into four categories: (1) shoplifting precipitated by symbolic sexual gratification, exemplified by the woman who shoplifted after experiencing sexual temptation. (2) stealing as a means of gaining status or acceptance, either through the overt daring of the act or the ability to purchase seemingly good 'bargains'. (3) the person who shoplifted out of a desire for punishment. Rouke exemplified this by the case of a woman who was unfaithful to her husband absent on service, who divorced him and also had an abortion. Rouke considered that she stole because unconsciously she wanted to be punished. (4) there were those who stole out of defiance in order to bring humiliation and disgrace on the family.[38]

Arboleda-Florez *et al.* attempted to isolate the psychological characteristics of 32 shoplifters who were referred for psychiatric assessment: 20 were women, with ages ranging from 16 to 68. Of males 66 per cent were under 30, while only 50 per cent of women were similarly aged. Interestingly, the recidivism rates for the women almost match the figures presented earlier by Walsh and Redding: 40 per cent of female offenders had previous convictions (eight women), and of these 30 per cent had convictions for shoplifting only. Of the men, only four had no previous record.

The authors describe three types of shoplifter: the 'psychotic', where the offending was subject to delusions of various sorts; the 'snitch', who stole articles for personal consumption on a fairly regular basis; and the 'unusuals', where there did not appear to be any apparent motivation. Half of both men and women were categorised as 'snitches'; one woman and two men were thought to be 'psychotics'; and nine women and four men were considered to be 'unusuals'.[39] Arboleda-Florez *et al.* make an interesting observation on the classification of shoplifters:

> The problem may stem from the paradox involved in the very 'ordinariness' of shoplifting. It is such a common offence and it is committed by so many people that no specific characteristic or pattern arises to make a typology of an all-encompassing classification of the offenders.[40]

Ordway, basing his observations on shoplifters referred to the Cincinatti municipal psychiatric clinic, noted an apparently low rate of recidivism. He believes, in common with many other psychological researchers, that depression is an underlying feature of shoplifting, which might be precipitated by bereavement or as a means of gaining attention or sublimating sexual fulfilment.[41]

Before summarising and commenting on these studies into the psychological reasons for shoplifting, a fairly recent British study is examined, not for its insight into shoplifting, as it deals only with one person, more because it presents as an extreme in the 'treatment' of shoplifting.

Kellam describes the history of his patient, a 48-year-old married housewife. Her first offence of shoplifting occurred in 1951 when she was fined in court, as she was dealt with subsequently until finally she was sent to prison for three months in 1961. In the same year she was given a probation order for three years, and in 1963 she was given a further probation order for two years with a condition of treatment at Morgannwg hospital. Her depression was treated with electro-convulsive therapy and she also received electro-aversion therapy for shoplifting. The woman had experienced 19 sessions of this therapy when she was discharged as an out-patient. In 1967, after further periods of depression, shoplifting and electrical aversion, she was re-admitted after threatening suicide. At this point it was decided to use a film.

> The film was then edited so that the S (the psychologist) entered the shop's doors, the patient with her face visible appeared through the doors and appeared to enter the shop and the S then proceeded into the shop and stole the articles without her face appearing again. After each theft, during the secretion of the articles stolen, a shot of eight frames length of a disapproving face was inserted .... The final film showed the patient appear to enter the shop and proceed to nineteen thefts during a 10 min. film; the thefts were interrupted by 20 just-recognisable flashes of disapproving faces. This film was then shown to the patient in a darkened corridor equipped as a cinema. Electrical aversion was administered by an operator sitting behind the patient...
>
> After 5 weeks and 40 showings of the film she reacted with anxiety to every stimulus whether or not a shock was given, in addition she had a generalised fear of shops accompanied by a strong sensation of being watched whenever she entered a shop. She noticed she was avoiding large shops in favour of small ones and had to avoid going past the shop used in the film. At this stage she was discharged.
>
> At follow-up 3 months later she was able to shop but avoided it if she could. When she entered shops she felt anxious. She had felt an urge to steal ... on at least five occasions. This urge has resulted in anxiety, tension in the arm, and an overwhelming memory of seeing the film, especially the faces which 'loomed before her eyes'. Everyone in the shop seemed to turn to look at her and the urge disappeared. She felt that but for this reaction she would inevitably have stolen each time. She was given 4 further showings of the film and at present it is planned to repeat this every 3 months.[42]

Kellam concludes by suggesting that the techniques perfected on this patient 'would seem to have application in the treatment of other conditions using similar films'.[43]

Summarising the findings of the research into psychological reasons for shoplifting, it appears that nearly all of the authors dealt with only women or a majority of females. Versele and Badonnel believe shoplifting is solely a female delinquency caused by frustration. Arieff and Bowie dealing mainly with females isolated emotional or mental disorders as critical. Neustatter and Ordway both felt tension and depression were important background features. Rouke, treating only women, believed 87 per cent stole because of emotional disturbances.

Meyers emphasised that unfulfilled sensuous needs were a serious consideration and, peculiarly, he believes that headaches, nervousness, backache, a history of surgery and accident-proneness are all related. These 'symptoms' must be experienced by the majority of people and their relationship to shoplifting remains to be proven. Similarly, half of the female sample weighed over 125lb, but this does not seem particularly gross, particularly for older women.

A number of points can be made about these studies. First, all the samples were small. Secondly, overwhelmingly the people treated were women. This is not the place to delve into feminist literature, but there would seem to be operating here a dual standard whereby men are criminalised for their offences and women are medicalised. The question remains, would the woman seen by Kellam receive the same treatment if she were a male recidivist burglar? Does the punishment fit the crime? In addition, it could be argued that Mrs A, in Russell's research, was not the person who needed therapy but her husband and father. Underlying most of these studies is the assumption that if there is no obvious reason for theft (i.e. the article is not required for immediate consumption or is not useful to that person) then it is a symptom of hidden emotional conflict (which affects 87 per cent of shoplifters, according to Rouke). The exception here is the work of Arboleda-Florez *et al.*, who think that some people are obviously mentally disturbed when they shoplift, while for others it is simply greed for goods for which they are not prepared to pay. However, they believe there is a category of 'unusuals' who do not seem to have any apparent motive for theft. Obviously, some of the explanations put forward by the other researchers are perfectly valid interpretations, but the dangers in dealing with small samples of highly selected offenders (female) are that they generalise to the whole population of shoplifters. Perhaps arguments such as unfulfilled sensuous needs and emotional conflicts were more relevant when only relatively few people shoplifted. These days, when thousands of offences are committed, and, as we shall soon see, sizeable numbers of the population seem to have offended at some stage, it is perhaps better to take Arboleda-Florez *et al.*'s message, that shoplifting is an ordinary offence. Perhaps shoplifting should be treated in the same way as an offence such as drunken-driving. Explanations for this offence are many and varied, and are all with some degree of validity, but drunken-driving is not seen as an inherently psychological conflict: it is a serious offence and needs to be controlled, but there are few efforts to medicalise what is essentially a criminal act.

Realising the problems officially recorded shoplifters pose for representativeness, researchers have turned to dark figure research. Some self-report studies have been initiated, but the greater emphasis has been placed on the shop as a victim to provide information on the numbers of people apprehended but not referred to the police, the stores police referral policies, and the incidence of their victimisation. First, however, self-report studies are examined.

3 Self-report studies

There has been little direct concern in England with self-report studies of shoplifters alone — research such as Belson's demonstrates that shoplifting is a popular offence with adolescents and youths, and shows the ubiquity of the offence, with 70 per cent of boys admitting to having shoplifted.[44] Specific studies of shoplifting self-report are concentrated in the USA.

In a small, mid-western community, El-Dirghami attempted to measure the magnitude of shoplifting among two samples of students: a college sample with 106 usable questionnaires (from a stratified, random sample of 200, i.e. 53 per cent), and a high school sample based on 112 questionnaires (from a stratified, random sample of 178, i.e. 62.9 per cent). El-Dirghami wanted to compare the attitudes of shoplifters and non-shoplifters to the seriousness of the offence, and to investigate any common characteristics of shoplifters. He divided the sample into three categories: the non-shoplifter; the trier, defined as somebody who had shoplifted once; and the repeater. From the total sample combining the two sub-samples, 54.9 per cent were non-shoplifters, 19.72 per cent were triers and 25.69 per cent were repeaters. College students tended to be more law-abiding than high school students — 60.38 per cent of them had never shoplifted, compared to 49.11 per cent non-shoplifters at high school. There were 22.32 per cent triers in the high school sample and 28.37 per cent repeaters, while 16.98 per cent were triers and 22.64 per cent were repeaters in the college sample.

Non-shoplifters were slightly more disapproving of shoplifting than respondents who had shoplifted, but all agreed that the offence was a relatively serious form of theft. El-Dirghami isolated six factors that he found to be associated with shoplifting: sex, religion, smoking in forbidden areas, faking excuses, and lying to teachers. He believes, however, that social class, degree of extra curricular activities, disobeying parents, copying homework, swearing and drunken-driving are not associated with the tendency to shoplift.[45]

Wisher's study was based on a larger sample of 1,000 teenage respondents. Nearly half (472) had shoplifted at least once. The offence, however, was almost twice as common among boys, of whom 62.2 per cent had stolen, compared with 32.2 per cent of girls.

A later study by Kraut attempted to isolate the precipitating factors in the decision to shoplift, focusing primarily on the social — psychological variables suggested by the deterrence and labelling models of deviance. He sent out 1,500 questionnaires to a random sample of University of Pennsylvania students but received only 606 completed responses. Sixty-one per cent of his sample had shoplifted at least once, and of these, 16 per cent had been caught at least once. Unlike Wisher's study, Kraut found that men shoplifted only slightly more than women, and he believes that religion and race were not associated with shoplifting.

Those respondents who had shoplifted in Kraut's survey did so because they did not want to pay for the merchandise: they wanted the goods, and they saw little risk of apprehension. Non-shoplifters, on the other hand, would only steal if they were in straitened circumstances, or by accident. Students who had shoplifted saw least risk in their actions in terms of both official apprehension and possible prosecution, and informal sanctions from family and peers. Significantly, for Kraut, those respondents who had been apprehended for shoplifting believed that the risk of further apprehensions was higher, with subsequently more severe punishment. Kraut believes that his data support the deterrence model by confirming that respondents who had been caught once saw themselves more at risk than others. The informal sanctions for shoplifting, however, appear to be more significant than the official ones, but this is presumably based on the assumption that the conse-quent official sanctions were not severe.[47]

Kraut believes that shoplifting is not a bizarre offence with deep, underlying psychological motivations, rather, he considers it to be everyday and commonplace. In fact, he thinks that the motivation for shoplifting is the same for normal shopping: 'the acquisition of goods at minimum cost'.[48]

Another self-report study, this time in Australia, was conducted by Dingle using two samples of boys between the ages of 10 and 20, one from an institution, the other from a private school. Just over half of the respondents admitted shoplifting, with more shoplifters in the institutional sample.[49]

In Chapter 1, it was pointed out that self-report studies had a number of weaknesses, the most important of which was their reliance on youths and adolescents for their sample. The self-report studies on shoplifting are no exception. Indeed, some of the studies could be criticised for naivety and a low response rate. However, it is interesting to note that about half to two-thirds of adolescents questioned admitted to shop-lifting. Whatever qualifications are made about their methodological rigour, the self-report studies do tend to suggest that shoplifting is a common occurrence among many adolescents and it may also be 'normal' behaviour engaged in by a majority.

4 Victim surveys

This section is subdivided into two parts, the first deals with the analysis of apprehended shoplifters, the second concentrates on a discussion of the reasons for referral of suspects to the police. Again, this distinction is somewhat artificial and consequently some studies will appear in both sections.

Surveys of apprehended shoplifters

Robin obtained data on every person apprehended for shoplifting in three large department stores (A, B and C) in Philadelphia in 1958. 285 persons were apprehended in store A, 834 in store B, and 465 in store C. Of the total sample of shoplifters, 40 per cent were male and 60 per cent female. Of all shoplifters in store A, 33 per cent were aged between 14 and 17. This age group constituted 60 per cent of all shoplifters in store B. In store A, the median theft for adults was $14, whereas in store B it was slightly higher, at $14.84. In store B, the median for juvenile theft was $8.97, whereas in store A, it was $5.98. Of the total sample, only 14 per cent of shoplifters were referred to the police, with juveniles having a referral rate of 5.5 per cent and adults 25.8 per cent. Three-quarters of juveniles were apprehended in groups, whereas just over three-quarters of adults were apprehended alone.

The incidence of shoplifting apprehensions increased at Christmastime, but Robin warns that this increase might not necessarily be the result of greater activity on the part of shoplifters. Alternative explanations could be found in the fact that the stores stayed open for longer hours and also employed more part-time store detectives. A self-fulfilling prophecy could have been set in motion — because the stores expected more shoplifting at Christmas they took more precautions, and consequently apprehended more shoplifters.[50]

While Robin was engaged in his research in Philadelphia, Cameron was conducting her research in Chicago. Her study was based on a sample (the 'store' sample) of one out of four shoplifters apprehended in one store in Chicago during the eight years from 1943 to 1950. Cameron supplemented these data with the cases of all women charged with shoplifting in the City of Chicago for the period 1948–50.

Comparing the mean and median values recovered from all the shoplifters, Cameron concluded that a small number of adults were responsible for expensive thefts. The median value across all the sample was $6 (for women it was $6.74, for girls $5.00, for men $8.30, and for boys $3.71). The mean values were higher however, particularly for the adults, with women taking $16.40, girls $8.06, men $28.36, and boys $7.14. Half of the sample stole goods valued at less than $10 and two-thirds took goods valued at under $20.[51]

Of the total sample, 60 per cent were female, and this percentage increased to 83 per cent when considering adults only. For teenagers under 18 there was an equal distribution between boys and girls. In terms of race, whites were apprehended about nine times as frequently as blacks, which approximately paralleled the race distribution in the city. However, the sex distribution of black shoplifters differed from that of the white. Fifty-seven per cent of black shoplifters were males, while the corresponding figure for whites was 24 per cent. Moreover, almost half of the black adults apprehended were men (46 per cent) while only 15 per cent of white adults were male. Compared with their white counterparts, black women were considerably under-represented.[52]

Cameron concluded that most of the shoplifting carried out in the store was 'pilfering' (i.e. petty theft for personal consumption). In addition, she believes that the thefts were planned and rational because the extensive presence of techniques to dispose of incriminating wrappers and tags precluded impulsive and accidental thefts. As with other observers, Cameron's data revealed that most juvenile shoplifting was done in groups, whereas the adults tended to steal by themselves. The evidence from police files and unofficial store records suggested a low rate of recidivism — once shoplifters had been apprehended, they rarely repeated the offence.[53]

A later study by Won and Yamamoto attempted to analyse the relationship between shoplifting and class. Taking all the apprehensions for the major supermarket chains in Honolulu, Hawaii, gave them a total of 493 shoplifters, of whom about 60 per cent were women and approximately a third were aged 19 or under. An overwhelmingly large proportion of the cases involved thefts of less than $5. The authors classified the neighbourhood of the offenders in terms of its income and educational levels. 'The median income typing of the neighbourhood of the offender was designated as his income class of orientation and reference category.'[54] Won and Yamamoto found that the middle-income categories were significantly over-represented in their sample, as approximately 78 per cent of the apprehended shoplifters were in $5,000—$8,900 income categories, and only just over a third of the general population of Honolulu was in that category. The authors concluded, therefore, that shoplifting in supermarkets was predominantly a middle-income group activity, and not a lower-income one as might have been expected.[55]

Justice of the Peace described a study in England which was based on a sample of 2,363 shoplifters apprehended in 1966 by the security personnel of Store Detectives Ltd. Over three-quarters of the shoplifters apprehended were women, and only one person in three was referred to the police. However, this might have had something to do with the generally low value of goods stolen, averaging 14s 3d (8s 8d in grocery shops and 23s 6d in department stores).[56]

Perhaps the most comprehensive surveys of apprehended shoplifters were those conducted by Griffin in 1970 and 1971. The earlier study took its sample of 12,460 apprehended shoplifters from the records of Commercial Service Systems which operated in Southern Californian supermarkets. The sex distribution of apprehensions was almost exactly equal, 49.2 per cent of the offenders being female. Twenty-seven per cent of all apprehensions — the largest group of offenders — involved males under 18. Females under 18 were only half as likely to be apprehended. The average cost of each shoplifting incident was low at $3.80.[57]

The second study was of 7,716 apprehensions made in drug stores and 13,439 made in supermarkets (a total sample of 21,155). An almost identical sex ratio was revealed in the drug store sample as in the super-market, with males constituting 49.3 per cent of all apprehensions. The value of recovered items in the drug store was slightly higher at $5.31.[58]

A study by Fear in England provides details obtained from an analysis of 400 shoplifters apprehended in supermarkets. Fear comes up with some surprising results, particularly the fact that the 15–20 age group was least often apprehended; even the over eighties were more trouble. In fact, over a third of apprehended shoplifters were over 60. His data showed that 64.5 per cent of apprehensions were female, but the relatively low incidence of male shoplifters could perhaps partly be explained by their relatively low distribution in the over 60 population.[59]

Walsh conducted a general survey of shops in Exeter. His reasons for doing so were to examine the crime of shoplifting as an illustration of the

> cultural context within which crimes occur and to ask why some people are selected as victims rather than others, reasoning that studies so far produced have tended to focus exclusively on the shoplifting offender and his personal motivation, and for that matter his personality, rather than on the victims of shoplifting and the crime form proper, how the criminal event is occurring, not just in terms of *modus operandi,* but also in terms of the location of the criminal event in social space.[60]

Walsh believes that there are many causes of crime and many different motivations for shoplifting. He wants to move the discussion away from the individual offender and concentrate instead on the context in which the offence is occurring to provide information on the event of shoplifting. Part of Walsh's research has been alluded to earlier, this section depended upon a 10 per cent sample of shopkeepers in the Exeter area, a total of 80 shops. Walsh interviewed 61 of this sample.[61]

The high peaks of shoplifting were identified as Christmas-time and April, with the lows occurring in January and August.[62] Shopkeepers believed that the most prolific shoplifters were children: almost a quarter of shops identified them as the major offenders. Only 8 per cent of shops considered women to be the most active shoplifters, and 16 per cent believed both sexes were equally responsible. Significantly a third of the shops had no particularly strong impression on which sex offended most. Most of the shoplifters committed their offences alone, but again, group theft was most popular with 10—15-year-olds.[63]

The value of goods stolen tended again to be fairly low. A third of the shops thought that average loss was under £1, over half the shops lost an average under £5, and only 11 per cent of shops averaged thefts valued at over £10.[64]

Fifty per cent of the shops took some action to prevent shoplifting, with 9.8 per cent employing store detectives, although self-service stores were much more likely to make use of security personnel (37.7 per cent). Interestingly, only 22 per cent of the shops always called the police, and, at the other extreme, 26 per cent never referred shoplifters to the police.[65]

Walsh suggests that the main determinants of the level of shoplifting experienced by a shop are: (a) type of merchandise on offer; (b) sales policy; (c) number of staff; (d) location and layout of the shop; (e) display features; and (f) the use of security devices.[66]

Summarising the research on shoplifters apprehended in shops but not necessarily referred to the police, it appears that the male contribution varies from about a quarter to a half of all offences. Many stores identify young adolescent boys as a source of trouble (with the exception of Fear's survey), and this section usually operates in groups. Generally, the value of the goods stolen tend on average not to be high, and median values suggest that most people take articles of small value, while a few increase the average theft by taking relatively expensive items. It would seem that thefts from department stores, on average, cost more than those from supermarkets, which may have something to do with the value of goods on offer.

It is now possible to turn our attention to the literature which deals with the factors relating to the decision to refer the suspects to the police.

Reasons for referral

Before a suspected shoplifter is referred to the police, there should be a *bona fide* legal case against that person, the exact requirements of which will be discussed in later chapters. In addition, any person who does not confess to the offence, and perhaps sign a waiver admitting guilt, will have to be referred to the police. This is to preclude a suit for false arrest being brought against the shop.

Robin believes that when store detectives or shop personnel are deciding whether to call the police they consider a number of factors. If there is any evidence of professionalism on the part of the offender, or if there is suspicion of a previous criminal record, or if the value or nature of the article stolen suggests it is for resale, then the police will probably be notified. In his 1963 study, stores A and B phoned the police to check whether the suspect had a police record, and if so, that person was handed over to the police regardless of the value of the articles stolen. However, Robin believes that from the information available in his survey, adult shoplifters taking goods valued at less than $20 were usually not prosecuted, while of those stealing goods at $60 or more, 95 per cent were referred to the police. The exact relationship between value of goods and police referral was complicated in Robin's research as he was unaware of how many of the suspects had been checked with the police department for previous record, ensuring referral regardless of the cost of theft. Nevertheless, in stores A and B, only 8.7 per cent of the people taking goods valued at less than $25 were referred to the police, while 70 per cent of those taking goods above that value were subjected to police intervention. In addition, blacks were disproportionately represented in the apprehension figures for the stores.[67]

This racial bias was also discovered by Cameron, who found that the proportion of blacks among the women referred to the police was about four times the proportion found in women apprehended. Forty-two per cent of black women were prosecuted, whereas only 9 per cent of white women were similarly dealt with.[68] This apparent racial bias will be discussed below.

According to Store Detectives Ltd, age and health probably have some bearing on the referral decision, with the very young and very old, as well as the obviously mentally disturbed being less liable for police referral.[69] Merrick's survey of shops supports the view that suspects who are old, infirm or pregnant are more likely to be treated leniently.[70]

Dickens conducted a survey of shops by sending questionnaires to 250 retail groups covering over 10,000 shops in England and Wales. For those shops which maintained records of apprehensions, about 45 per cent of suspects were referred to the police. Dickens believes that the value of goods stolen was important but not decisive. Age too was an important factor, as 30 per cent of shops declared they would show leniency to children under 17 and to a lesser extent also to students. For those children under 14, however, nearly 85 per cent of shops would be sympathetic. Moreover, nearly 80 per cent of shops would not refer the elderly to the police and those who were obviously under some form of mental stress would also gain sympathy. Sixty per cent of shops replied that they would not refer visibly pregnant women to the police.[71]

The Home Office Working Party took evidence from 15 retail organisations, and received 120 questionnaires from small retailers. They concluded that there were considerable variations in the police referral policies of the stores contacted, though again, children, pregnant women and the aged were often mentioned as being treated as special cases.[72]

In a statistical study of 371 shoplifters who were apprehended in a large city department store in California, Cohen and Stark found that their results largely contradicted the labelling and conflict notion that 'deviance is in the eye of the beholder'. They concluded that 'the decision to release or prosecute the offender is largely related to what he does instead of who he is or how he is perceived'.[73] Although this appears to be an injustice to both the labelling and conflict models of deviance as they would be more likely to apply to who is apprehended, other factors may be involved in the decision to prosecute.

Cohen and Stark criticise Robin's and Cameron's earlier studies, and suggest that their data disprove the racial bias in apprehension and police referral evidenced in the earlier works (in addition to the possibility that such pre-1960 data might no longer hold). They argue that Cameron and Robin used primitive statistical analysis and did not hold constant all factors which influenced the decision on disposition.

Of the 371 persons apprehended, only three had a previous criminal record, suggesting that once a person had been apprehended for shoplifting, they were unlikely to repeat their offence. Cohen and Stark did not find a race or sex effect in the decision on case disposition, but did identify leniency towards juveniles and harshness towards the unemployed. They found the most positive effect was the value of the goods taken. Nearly three-quarters of people apprehended stealing goods valued at over $30 were referred to the police, while only about 40 per cent of those taking goods less than this value were similarly treated.

The shoplifting sample had clear racial anomalies. Whites accounted for 46 per cent of the shopping population, but only 13 per cent of apprehended shoplifters. Blacks constituted only 22 per cent of the shopping population but over half (51 per cent) of the apprehensions and Mexican-Americans were over-represented by 31 to 25 per cent. Minority members, however, were disproportionately juveniles.

When Cohen and Stark controlled for age, there appeared to be a racial bias among adults referred to the police. Among the adults, two-thirds (66 per cent) of the blacks were handed over to the police, while the percentage for Mexican-Americans and whites was just over half

(54 per cent). However, this apparent racial bias was negated when the value of the merchandise stolen was controlled. 'When the value control was introduced, there remained no racial differences among adults who took goods over the value of $30. Among juveniles, racial differences were also wiped out.'[74] Blacks, according to Cohen and Stark, were referred to the police more because they stole more valuable items than whites, and the differential in the referral rates in their study is similar to that of Robin's and Cameron's, suggesting that if they too had controlled for value then their race bias would also have been negated.[75]

Hindelang conducted a similar study to Cohen and Stark's and reinforced the latters' conclusions. He was concerned to examine the decision to call the police in terms of four factors: age, sex, race and total value of the goods stolen. A 30 per cent random sample of 1963 and 1964 shoplifting apprehensions in Southern California was collected, as well as a 40 per cent random sample of 1968 cases. He discovered that the factor most closely associated with the decision to refer the suspect was the value of the goods stolen. The variable next most associated was age, where the youngest and oldest shoplifters were leniently treated. The referral rates for non-whites to whites were almost identical (28 per cent to 25 per cent) and for males to females also (26 per cent to 25 per cent), with value of goods taken controlled.

Hindelang believes that apart from Cameron's failure to control for the value of goods stolen in her analysis, two other factors could explain the prevalence of racial bias in her study and its absence in his. First, he considers that the social and political changes which occurred between the two studies might have an effect. Secondly, Cameron's study was based on one store where store detectives operated, whereas Hindelang's was based on a number of shops where shop assistants made most of the decisions. Hindelang considers that store detectives may share official police stereotypes more than the disparate shop assistants who may be less likely to have 'official' stereotypes.

While there was no change between 1963 and 1968 in the referral rate for low-value items, there was an increase from 34 per cent to 45 per cent in the referral rate for the large-value group. As Hindelang observes, 'in terms of offences known to the police this means that even if the numbers of shoplifters apprehended had stayed the same from 1963 to 1968, a crime wave would have been generated by an apparent change in the victims' behavior.'[76]

Lundman based his research on 664 cases compiled from the records of a mid-western branch of a national department chain store, between 1973 and 1975. Using the same statistical analysis as Hindelang, Lundman's data revealed that the value of the items stolen, as well as the age and race of the suspect, all affected the referral decision. Sex did not appear to be related. Of these three factors, retail value was the most significant, followed by age, with the race of the offender only the third most important variable.[77]

The results of Hindelang's and Lundman's studies are almost identical except for the effect of race on the decision to call the police in Lundman's study. The value of the goods stolen is the significant factor in both studies, followed by the age of the suspect. Lundman advances Hindelang's hypothesis that there may be differences in the operating practices of store detectives and shop staff which could explain the race effect in Lundman's research, relying as it did on security officers — 'it may be that private police officers share stereotypes with public ones and that the managers etc., are unorganised, responding to individuals.'[78]

Summarising the evidence from these studies, it appears that the value of the items stolen is most closely related to the decision on disposal of the shoplifter. Next comes the age of the suspect, with the young and old having a greater probability of being released. In England, however, there have not been the statistical analyses such as Hindelang's, Cohen and Stark's, and Lundman's, and it would be interesting to see some comparisons on whether the age of the suspect could override the effect of the value taken. Racial effects were mentioned in the American studies, although they are not taken up in the English surveys (which does not mean to say they do not exist). Health, pregnancy and mental stability all appear to be factors in the British studies. In short, there appear to be a number of variables which can affect the decision to refer a suspect to the police, the most important of which seems to be the value of the item stolen and the age of the offender.

5 'Following exercises'

In an attempt to break away from the problems presented by dark figure research, a number of researchers, most notably Astor in the USA, have thought of the novel idea of following shoppers at random to see how many take things without paying.

Astor instructed his staff to go to a particular store and stand with their backs to the street and face the inside of the shop.

> They were then instructed to follow the first person who entered the store on their left regardless of age, sex, race, or any other characteristics, whether the person be a nun, an invalid, a hood or an average housewife. They were instructed to stay with that particular customer, selected at random, until the customer left the store. If the customer entered the fitting room, the surveillance was discontinued and the test was not counted.

If anything, our procedures should have minimised shop-lifting because (a) a shoplifter might well know that he is being followed, and (b) merchandise stolen in the fitting room was excluded from our test.[79]

Astor's research produced some significant findings. Of the 169 customers who were followed 20 took something (1 in 8.5). Three customers who were in the process of stealing noticed they were being watched and discontinued their activities. Women appeared to steal twice as frequently as men, since of 49 males followed only three stole (1 in 16), while out of 120 women, 17 stole (1 in 7). Each theft averaged approximately $8 worth of goods. There did not appear to be a race or age effect. Significantly, none of these shoplifters was spotted by a store detective. In a later study, of the 263 customers who were followed, 27 were observed stealing, giving an approximate figure of 1 in 10 people shoplifting. Again, the value of the items stolen was relatively low at $8.57.[80]

Astor conducted a further survey in four department stores in three cities; two in New York and one each in Boston and Philadelphia, respectively. The results of this study are presented in Table 2.1. On average, in this larger study 1 person in 15 stole goods valued at $5.26, and only one was spotted by a store detective.[81]

A similar study conducted in Dublin rated 1 person in 18 as thieves;[82] while a study conducted by Group 4 in England revealed only 1 person in almost 100 stealing, but this research operated using different criteria from the others as it relied on the person being arrested and convicted before they were included in the sample.[83]

In these 'following exercises', the words 'steal' and 'thieves' have been used. A central thesis of this research is that these are misnomers. What Astor's research measures is the number of people who are taking things from shops without paying; it does not, however, measure theft. As will be explained in subsequent chapters, theft requires intent. There is no dispute over the number of people taking goods in Astor's studies, but he cannot say that they are 'stealing' those articles. All of the people taking goods could be absent-minded, insane, under the influence of drugs, etc., and not know what they were doing — that is, they do not have the intention to steal, and therefore cannot be called thieves. Only the courts can decide on intent, and only they can determine who is or is not a thief. The processes by which those people taking articles (assuming they were caught by store detectives) are turned into 'thieves' are the main focus of the research. 'Following exercises' are useful to stores as they inform them how many people are taking goods, where from, and how much it is costing. There is no argument that taking goods from shops results in a loss for the shops. However, it tells us little or nothing about shoplifting — about how 'takers' are transformed into 'thieves'.

Table 2.1

Results of 'Following Studies'

Location	Numbers followed	Numbers stealing	Ratio	Average theft
New York	500	42	8.4%	$7.15
New York	361	19	5.2%	$5.36
Boston	404	18	4.4%	$3.69
Philadelphia	382	30	7.8%	$4.86
Total	1,647	109	6.6%	$5.26

6   Customer involvement in reporting and controlling shoplifting

This section discusses a number of articles where customer preparedness to report shoplifters is tested under experimental conditions. That is, shoplifting incidents are staged and varied against such factors as sex and appearance. The description of the experimental procedure is described in detail at the beginning, but for the sake of brevity it is omitted from the rest of the articles. The methods are generally the same, unless otherwise described.

Dertke *et al.* investigated customer preparedness to report a clearly observed incident of shoplifting in terms of the shoplifter's race and sex. The subjects were selected from shoppers in the paperback section of a college bookshop. The authors were not permitted to interview the subjects outside the shop. The shoppers (S) were assumed to be students, all were white, appeared to be between the ages of 18 and 30 and were alone with no other shoppers within a radius of 50 feet. The trials were carried out as follows:

> The role of the clerk was played by a white female psychology major. She wore the same type of smock and name tag worn by actual bookstore employees. She carried a clipboard and behaved as though she was taking an inventory. Thief's roles were played by black male, black female, white male, and

white female undergraduate students. All accomplices were neatly groomed and wore attire judged to be modal for the college environment.

Trials were conducted in the following manner. After an appropriate S was located, the clerk moved to within 3-4 feet of S and began her inventory. The 'thief' then approached and stood directly next to and on the other side of S, so that S was between the 'clerk' and the 'thief'. The 'thief' then reached in front of S, picked up a book, and placed the book inside his (her) shirt, stepped back and walked behind S and 'clerk' to another area of the store, out of sight and hearing of S and 'clerk'. After the 'thief' was out of sight, the clerk turned to S and asked, 'May I help you?', serving further to identify the 'clerk' as a bookstore employee and, of more importance, giving S an opportunity spontaneously to report the theft.

Responses of 30 Ss were recorded in each of the four conditions of the study. Preliminary analysis disclosed an extremely low rate of reporting (7.5%) and no differential responding as a function of the thief's characteristics. Therefore, for the remaining 120 Ss an additional question was added. If an S did not spontaneously report the theft, the 'clerk' asked, 'Did you see that guy (girl) steal that book?' The S's confirmation or non-confirmation was recorded, and the same procedure, as above, was followed before the next trial.[84]

As an extra safeguard that the S actually saw the shoplifting incident, even though it was exceptionally blatant, the accomplice posing as a thief watched the S's eyes and if no unmistakable reaction was noticed, it was considered that the incident had not been noted and the results were not counted.

The responses of the Ss were classified either as a spontaneous report in response to the clerk's 'May I help you?', or a confirmation, providing an affirmative answer to the clerk's 'Did you see that guy (girl) steal that book?'

The overall spontaneous reporting rate was low, but the confirmation rate was over 50 per cent (51.3 per cent). Blacks tended to be more often reported or confirmed than whites. A non-significant overall trend for blacks to be more often spontaneously reported than whites was found and this was carried over to the confirmation rates.[85]

Dertke *et al.* tried to account for the differences between their study and Gelfand's (discussed below). In their study there was a low spontaneous reporting rate of 6.7 per cent whereas in Gelfand's study it was higher. Dertke believes that the fact that the thief had not left the shop might influence the Ss — they might be involved as witnesses or in emotional disturbances. In addition, the campus bookshop was considered to make excessive profits and was consequently not popular with students.[86]

Gelfand *et al.*, concerned with examining who reported shoplifters, took as their sample 180 men and 156 women shoppers in two Salt Lake City chain drugstores. The median age of the subjects was 44. The majority of the 56 subjects who were later interviewed were of the Mormon faith (80 per cent). The experiment was designed to vary the location of the shoplifting event (upper-income suburban vs. lower-income central city location); also varied were the appearance of the female model (hippie vs. conventional). Despite fairly extensive procedures to ensure that the subject saw the shoplifting incident, 'only 28% of the exposed shoppers observed the staged incident despite our precision-cueing, multiple staging and attention-attracting procedures'.[87] Twenty-six of the shoppers who saw the staged shoplifting incident reported it to a shop assistant (28 per cent).

Gelfand *et al.* found that the appearance of the shoplifter was not related to customer reporting. Male customers tended to report female shoplifters more often than female customers. People raised in the country also tended to report more than those brought up in the city, though Gelfand *et al.* did not think this was due to the depersonalising effects of city life but interpreted it as resulting from social learning/ history differences.[88]

Steffensmeier and Terry also conducted a staged shoplifting experiment to test whether hippie or conventional appearance affected reporting, and whether the sex of the reporter and sex of the shoplifter were related. The shoplifting incident was staged in a similar fashion to that described by Dertke, except here there were two accomplices posing as shop assistants. Once the 'incident' was over the 'thief' moved right away to avoid any intimidation. The first store assistant stayed in the vicinity to see if the customer would report. If the subject did not report, then the accomplice left the area and the second shop assistant approached the customer and forcefully asked whether they had seen the shoplifting, and gave a second prompt.

Sixty-seven subjects were exposed to a shoplifting incident in store A, 69 in store B, and 55 in store C. The possible identities of the shoplifter were varied between hippie and conventional, and male and female. Sex of the subject shopper was also varied across the different events. Steffensmeier and Terry concluded that the relationship between appearance and willingness to report was a strong one, with hippies more readily reported. The effect of the shoplifter's sex was not significantly different, and they believed that the relationship to reporting is nonexistent. In addition, it appeared that females were no more likely to report shoplifting than males.[89]

Terry and Steffensmeier conducted a similar experimental programme to test whether customer reporting was affected by the size of the victim store. Incidents were arranged in three different-sized stores and observational data were supplemented with post-incident interviews and interviews at the shopper's home.[90] The assumption guiding the research was drawn from Smigel's[91] work suggesting that the bigger, more bureaucratic and less personal the store, the less likely customers would be to report shoplifting.

Their first hypothesis, that the smaller the size of the store the more willing customers would be to report, was not upheld in the experiment, and, in so far as a relationship between the two variables did exist, it was in the opposite direction. Secondly, they found that the impersonality or perceived bureaucracy of the store also had no effect on shoppers' preparedness to report shoplifting incidents. Similarly, they found little evidence to support their hypothesis that 'the closer the customer — clerk relationship, the higher the reporting levels'.[92]

In a further study by Steffensmeier and Steffensmeier, sex and appearance ('hippie' vs. 'straight') of the shoplifter was varied against three sizes of store. The sample comprised 191 shoppers who were exposed to the shoplifting incident, of whom 178 completed post-incident questionnaires, and 135 the home interview. The method of staging the incident was similar to that of Steffensmeier and Terry. The results of the experiment indicated that the sex of the shoplifter and the size of the store had little effect on preparedness to report shoplifting, but the tendency for 'hippie' shoplifters to be reported more often than 'straight' ones was maintained.[93]

Steffensmeier and Steffensmeier compare their findings with those of Gelfand et al. They believe that there are methodological differences between the two studies as Gelfand et al. did not ensure that the subjects actually saw the shoplifting incident, and only interviewed 56 of the 336 shoppers involved in the experiments. In addition, Gelfand et al. used only female 'shoplifters'. Steffensmeier and Steffensmeier believe that the level of reporting was higher in their study than in Gelfand et al.'s. In their study the appearance of the shoplifter had a significant effect on reporting, but had little effect in the Gelfand study, which found that male shoppers were more likely to report shoplifting: the Steffensmeiers found no difference between the sexes. Class differences in reporting were also noted, with the upper class more prepared to report in Gelfand's research, and the blue-collar worker more prepared in the Steffensmeiers'.[94]

Steffensmeier conducted another shoplifting experiment in which appearance of the shoplifter was varied. In the follow-up interviews, the subjects were tested on Trodahl and Powell's shortened dogmatism scale as well as another scale to test attitudes to hippies. Steffensmeier believes that attitudes which could be quite strongly felt would not necessarily be manifested in action when called for in emergency situations. In the research, high dogmatics showed higher social distance attitudes towards hippies, but there was no difference between high and low dogmatics in their level of reporting. Steffensmeier concluded that there was no significant relationship between dogmatism and willingness to report shoplifting, no matter whether the shoplifter was 'straight' or 'hippie'.[95]

The difference between behavioural awareness and action is the focus in a number of studies by Bickman. In his first experiment, two field studies examined the intervention of shoppers to staged shoplifting incidents, which were conducted in a university bookshop. In the first study a mass media campaign was launched to increase information and awareness about shoplifting. It was successful in achieving this and altering behavioural intentions but failed to affect intervention practice. The second field study attempted to discern whether the low reporting rate was due to a feeling of group loyalty among students. The results, however, 'indicated that although students differentially perceived a non-student shoplifter', it did not affect the rate of intervention.[96]

Bickman and Green conducted a further field experiment with two studies to examine the effects of signs instructing shoppers how to intervene in shoplifting. In the first field study, the signs had some small effect on customer attitudes towards shoplifting but no effect on report-ing shoplifting. Problems were encountered in the low response rate for reporting and consequently it was difficult to notice and interpret any differences in the reporting conditions of noticing, not noticing, agreeing, etc.

The second study was geared to overcome the low reporting rate by interposing an accomplice to ask the subject shopper whether he/she had seen the staged shoplifter (a procedure similar to that of the Steffens-meiers' research). This experimental intervention had a positive effect on the decision to report, regardless of whether the instructional signs were present. Bickman and Green concluded that signs had no effect on customer intervention but prompting by an accomplice did.[97]

Bickman undertook two more studies to ascertain whether there was a relationship between reporting shoplifting and the shopper's attitude towards authority. The subjects were 65 shoppers in a department store. The staged shoplifting events were similar to the others described above except that Bickman attempted to manipulate the pleasantness of the sales clerk. This was achieved before the shoplifting event, by having one accomplice, posing as an assistant, accidentally knock the subject and apologise profusely. A second accomplice, posing as a shopper, reinforced the 'pleasantness' condition by remarking on how nice the sales girl was. In the unpleasant situation, the conditions were reversed with the first accomplice being bombastic and the second commenting on her nastiness. The third accomplice then proceeded to fake the shoplifting event once the shopper had retired, with the pleasant/unpleasant assistant some 10 feet away.

> If the subject made no attempt to report the theft within thirty seconds after it had occurred, the clerk approached the subject and asked for the correct time. If the subject did not report at that point, he or she was given an additional sixty seconds to do so before being approached by the shopper who also acted as an interviewer. The interviewer introduced herself as a store security employee and asked the subject if he or she had seen anyone who may have been shoplifting or otherwise concealing merchandise. If the subject answered negatively, he or she was told that the store had hired a person to stage shopliftings ... the subject was asked if it was possible that he or she had seen one of those shopliftings.[98]

If the subject still denied seeing anything, the interviewer informed him/her that the person who was near her had actually staged a shoplifting and asked whether she had seen it.

Overall, 93 per cent of the subject shoppers were judged to have seen the event; 40 per cent — half spontaneously, 8 per cent when asked the time, and 39 per cent told another store employee. Bickman found, however, that the attitude towards authority was not related to the overall reporting rate.

In a laboratory setting, Bickman attempted to duplicate the experiment with only one condition of authority to report to. As expected, more reporting occurred when the subjects were cued to report any shoplifting, but again there was no significant effect of the subjects' attitude towards the authority.[99]

Finally, Bickman and Helwig conducted a field experiment to test whether monetary reward or the promise of anonymity would affect the rate of customers reporting a staged shoplifting incident. They found that neither of these variables affected customer intervention.[100]

Summarising these studies on customer reactions to staged shoplifting incidents and their preparedness to report, it appears that levels of dogmatism and attitudes towards an authority are not related. Similarly, media campaigns and the presence of signs might be effective in increasing people's awareness, but they do not affect their actions and have no effect on intervention. It appears also that the size of the store and the degree of its bureaucracy and impersonality are also unrelated. There are differences, however, between the Steffensmeiers' studies and Gelfand's. The former report that appearance has a major effect and sex does not, while the latter shows the reverse.

A number of observations can be made about these types of study. First, they are all based on fairly small samples. The Gelfand analysis with several variables depended only on 26 respondents who reported the shoplifting. Secondly, there are biasing effects, some relying solely on students, while in Gelfand a majority of shoppers were Mormons.

More generally, Skogan believes that reporting probability depends upon three factors: the attributes of the victims, the nature of the victim — offender relationship, and the seriousness of the offence.[101] This relates, of course, to victims reporting the crime and not bystander intervention, but the third factor mentioned by Skogan — the seriousness of the offence — is relevant here. One of the advantages with shoplifting is that unlike other crimes, it is relatively easy to stage. However, it is doubtful if most people would rate it as a serious crime. Moreover, in most of the above studies the value of the item stolen was relatively low, further minimising the seriousness of the offence.

Latané and Darley discuss the decision to intervene in a number of stages. First, the bystander must be aware that an incident is happening. Secondly, he must define that incident as an emergency. Thirdly, the bystander must accept some responsibility for what is occurring. Fourthly he must know how to intervene appropriately. Lastly, he must intervene.[102]

A problem throughout these studies was met at the first stage — making shoppers (who were usually busy and intent on their own purchases) notice a staged shoplifting. Terry alludes to the difficulties in his research. In personal conversation with the author he related the farcical lengths the bogus shoplifters had to go to, with extremely exaggerated and dramatic gestures. The point is, unless you are looking for it, you rarely see shoplifters. Indeed, people who are paid to observe often do not see potential shoplifters (cf. Astor).It appears, also, that many shoppers failed to intervene at the third stage mentioned by Latané and Darley; they did not see it as their responsibility.

A final point about customer intervention needs to be made. Whether a shopper observes a shoplifting incident and takes it upon himself to report it can have no immediate practical results. No store detective should arrest a shoplifter on the evidence of a customer. The customer is not trained in the laws of theft and what constitutes an arrest. The risk of making a false arrest is far too high. The store detective or shop manager may observe the 'shoplifter' to see whether they commit another offence, but if this does not happen they will not (or at least should not) apprehend the suspect. As will be discussed later, the store detective has to see the *whole* incident from beginning to end. What to the customer might be a shoplifter secreting articles in a bag may, in practice, be another ordinary shopper trying clothes for colour matches or returning goods.

Customer awareness of the problem of shoplifting and their keenness to detect suspect shoplifters may act as a general deterrent, but one of the strong findings to emerge is that customers do not see shoplifting incidents unless they are very blatant, and even if they were to report to an assistant, there is little that can be done without the suspect taking more articles.

7   Miscellaneous aspects of shoplifting

This section is not intended to survey every article written on shoplifting, merely to point out the diversity of interests in discussing shoplifting. Much of this corpus, where relevant, will be alluded to in the main body of the book. Because shoplifting attracts the attention of the public so much and is of vital interest to the retailer, the range of articles is quite large, though much of it not directly related to a criminological analysis.

To begin with there is considerable effort which focuses on improving security systems (Barbera[103]), and advising on how to make apprehensions (Oliver and Wilson,[104] Hole,[105]). In addition, ex-store detectives and security consultants often write informative autobiographies about their dealings with shoplifters (Edwards,[106] Meek,[107] Baker,[108] Taylor,[109] Francis,[110]). Moreover, shoplifting features in collections about female crime (de Rham[111]) and provides data for case histories of various sorts (Lehr[112]). Numerous people have set up committees or one-man panels to discuss what should be done with shoplifters (Adley,[113] Sohier[114]). Finally, there are those papers which discuss crusades against shoplifting (Meyer III[115], Hiew[116]).

8   Conclusion

This chapter has moved from a consideration of officially recorded offenders to attempts at dark figure research to provide more accurate data on shoplifters. All the authors have realised that those people prosecuted for shoplifting are a highly selected population, and the intensive studies of convicted offenders gave way to those of apprehended shoplifters to provide a less biased sample. As the samples increased, it became apparent that instead of being a peculiar and strange activity, shoplifting was an offence that many people engaged in at some time or another (self-report studies indicate between 50 and 70 per cent of selected populations). At the same time, there was a growing awareness that far from being an offence motivated by personal frustrations of whatever sort, it was an everyday activity. Of course, individual psychosis could explain why some people shoplifted, but with the increasing appreciation of the numbers of people involved, the search for individual motivations became less relevant. There are many reasons why people shoplift, the same as there are for fare-dodging, tax evasion, expense-account cheating, and so on, but perhaps underlying it all is greed: the desire for something for nothing.

At one end of the scale, there are studies like Gibbens and Prince's, which are based on samples of convicted shoplifters drawn from a few thousand available offenders. On the other hand, there are studies, such as Belson's, which suggest that up to 70 per cent of adolescent boys have engaged in shoplifting at least once. Interestingly, there are the exercises described by Astor which suggest that about 1 in 15 people 'take things' without paying, with the store detectives noticing only about 1 per cent of those.

This study is concerned with analysing how stores are organised to counteract the depredations of shoplifters. At the same time, a central interest is the process by which the 'takers' of Astor's studies become the 'thieves' of Gibbens and Prince's study — that is, how store detectives go about their everyday business and how they select, apprehend, inter-view and dispose of shoplifters. In Chapter 1 reference was made to the work of Douglas, Atkinson, Zimmerman and Cicourel on the use of the statistics, and, more specifically, to a large extent, this study adopts the approach to shoplifting advocated by May. [117] Although May was only concerned with adolescent shoplifting in Scotland and collected his data with a few interviews with store managers and security officers, his operating assumptions are worth consideration.

May hoped to illuminate two important points about delinquency. The first, that law enforcement is essentially a selective process, is quite straightforward and uncontentious. The second point is that in the final analysis the meaning of labels such as 'crime', 'criminal', 'delinquency', etc. only begin to take on a recognisable shape as they are applied, that is, at the stages of identification, referral and disposal. In other words, what is really involved in differential law enforcement is not so much the selection — arbitrary or otherwise — from an unknown yet theoret-ically knowable number of actual offenders, but much more the progress-ive clarification of essentially vague rules. What exactly is the rule, and to whom it applies, are questions that can only be resolved in the process of its implementation. The position which he adopts is that 'no act is inherently "criminal", "delinquent" or "law-violating". Acts will only be labelled as such as the result of some observer group, drawing attention to the behaviour, specifying its law-violating nature and then taking some action to initiate the law enforcement process.' [118] As Sudnow says, 'what death and dying are cannot be decided *a priori* but must be formulated as a problematic topic of research.' [119]

This study, then, focuses on what shoplifting is, by examining the context where it is determined, and the agents who determine it.

Notes

1. Home Office, *Shoplifting and Thefts by Shop Staff.* Report of a Working Party on Internal Shop Security (London HMSO, 1973), p. 3.
2. Institute of Grocery Distribution, *Report of a Working Party on Shrinkage* (n.d.), p. 4.
3. Cameron, M.O., *The Booster and the Snitch; Department Store Shoplifting* (Glencoe; Illinois: Free Press, 1964), p. 10.
4. Institute of Grocery Distribution, *op. cit.,* p. 5.
5. Cameron, *op. cit.,* p.11.
6. Bleakley, R., 'Stock Losses in Retail Stores', in *Studies in Shoplifting,* ed. Challinger, D. (Australian Crime Prevention Council, 1977), pp. 91−104.
7. Economist Intelligence Unit, *Store Security, Special Report No. 3,* Retail Business, 161 (July 1971), pp. 35−44.
8. Home Office, *op. cit.,* p. 10.
9. Institute of Grocery Distribution, *op. cit.,* p. 14.
10. Gibbens, T.C.N. and Prince, J., *Shoplifting* (London ISTD, 1962).
11. Gibbens, T.C.N., 'The Causes of Shoplifting', *New Society* No. 23 (7 March 1963).
12. Gibbens and Prince, *op. cit.* p. 7.
13. Ibid., pp. 7−8.
14. Ibid., pp. 11−17, 22−30.
15. Ibid., pp. 18−21.
16. Ibid., pp. 34−52.
17. Ibid., p. 78.
18. Ibid., pp. 68−89.
19. Ibid., pp. 58−67.
20. Ibid., pp. 126−31.
21. Ibid., pp. 96−125.
22. Ibid., pp. 132−45.
23. Bennett, H.M., 'Shoplifting in Midtown', *Criminal Law Review* (1968), pp. 413−25.
24. Davidson, R.N., 'The Ecology of Shoplifting', paper presented to the Institute of British Geographers (Reading: 1975).
25. Redding, R.G., 'The Social Evil', *Justice of the Peace*

(10 January 1976), pp. 17—18.

26. Walsh, D.P., *Shoplifting: Controlling a Major Crime* (London: Macmillan, 1978), pp. 75—6.

27. Murphy, D.J.I. and Iles, S.C., 'Dealing with Shoplifters', *Home Office Research Bulletin,* No. 15 (1983), pp. 25—9.

28. Harris, B., 'What is a Shoplifter?', *The Magistrate,* Vol. 35, No. 9 (September 1979), pp. 134—5.

29. Badonnel, R., 'Le Vol dans les Grands Magasins', *Chronique de Criminologie Clinique,* Vol. 92, 11 (1968), pp. 103—6.

30. Versele, S.C., 'Study of Female Shoplifters in Department Stores', *International Criminal Police Review* (March 1969), pp. 66—70.

31. Arieff, A.J. and Bowie, C.G., 'Some Psychiatric Aspects of Shoplifting', *Journal of Clinical Psychology,* Vol. 8, (January 1947), pp. 565—76.

32. Neustatter, W.L., 'The Psychology of Shoplifting', *Medico-Legal Journal,* Vol. 22 (1954), pp. 118—30.

33. Meyers, T.J., 'A Contribution to the Psychopathology of Shoplifting', *Journal of Forensic Science,* Vol. 15, Part 3 (1970), pp. 295—310.

34. Ibid.

35. Ibid.

36. Ibid.

37. Russell, D.H., 'Emotional Aspects of Shoplifting', *Psychiatric Annals,* Vol. 3 (1973), pp. 77—86.

38. Rouke, F.L., 'Shoplifting, its Symbolic Motivation', *Crime and Delinquency,* Vol. 3 (1957), pp. 54—8.

39. Arboleda-Florez, J., Durie, H. and Costello. J., 'Shoplifting — An Ordinary Crime?', *International Journal of Offender Therapy and Comparative Criminology* Vol. 21, No. 3 (1977), pp. 201—7.

40. Ibid.

41. Ordway, J.A., 'Successful Court Treatment of Shoplifters', *Journal of Criminal Law, Criminology and Police Science,* Vol. 53 (March 1962), pp. 344—7.

42. Kellam, A.P., 'Shoplifting Treated by Aversion to a Film', *Behaviour Research and Therapy,* Vol. 7 (1969), pp. 125—7.

43. Ibid.

44. Belson, W.A., *Juvenile Theft: The Causal Factors* (London: Harper & Row, 1975), p. 87.

45. El-Dirghami, A., 'Shoplifting Among Students', *Journal of Retailing,* Vol. 50, No. 3, (1974), pp. 33—42.

46. Wisher, C., 'Teenage Shoplifting: Who, Where, When, How?', *Security World,* Vol. 5, Part 10 (1968), pp. 16—20.

47. Kraut, R.E., 'Deterrent and Definitional Influence on Shop-

lifting', *Social Problems*, 23 (1976), pp. 358—68.

48. Ibid.
49. Dingle, J., 'Youth and Shoplifting', in Challinger, *op. cit.*
50. Robin, G.D., 'Patterns of Department Store Shoplifting', *Crime and Delinquency*, Vol. 9 (1963), pp. 163—72.
51. Cameron, *op. cit.*, pp. 71—2.
52. Ibid., p. 96.
53. Ibid., pp. 102—6.
54. Won, G. and Yamamoto, G., 'Social Structure and Deviant Behaviour: A Study of Shoplifting', *Sociology and Social Research*, Vol. 53, Part I (1968), pp. 44—55.
55. Ibid.
56. *Justice of the Peace and Local Government Review*, 'Shoplifting' (10 June 1967), pp. 357—8.
57. Griffin, R.K. 'Shoplifting: A Statistical Survey', *Security World*, Vol. 7, Part 10 (1970), pp. 21—5.
58. Griffin, R.K., 'Behavioural Patterns of Shoplifting', *Security World*, Vol. 8, Part 8, (1971), pp. 29—33.
59. Fear, R.W.G., 'An Analysis of Shoplifting', *Security Gazette* (July 1974), pp. 262—3.
60. Walsh, *op. cit.*, p. xv.
61. Ibid., p. 58.
62. Ibid., p. 64.
63. Ibid., pp. 67—9.
64. Ibid., p. 72.
65. Ibid., pp. 76—8.
66. Ibid., p. 84.
67. Robin, *op. cit.*
68. Cameron, *op. cit.*, p. 138.
69. *Justice of the Peace and Local Government Review, op cit.*
70. Merrick, B., 'Shoplifting. A Microcosm', *The Criminologist*, Vol. 5, No. 18 (1970), pp. 68—81.
71. Dickens, B.M., 'Shops, Shoplifting and Law Enforcement', *The Criminal Law Review* (September 1969), pp. 464—72.
72. Home Office, *op. cit.*, p. 24.
73. Cohen, L.E. and Stark, R., 'Discriminatory Labelling and the Five-Finger Discount', *Journal of Research in Crime and Delinquency* (January 1974), pp. 25—39.
74. Ibid.
75. Ibid.
76. Hindelang, M.J., 'Decisions of Shoplifting Victims to Invoke the Criminal Justice Process', *Social Problems* (21 April 1974), pp. 580—93.
77. Lundman, R.J., 'Shoplifting and Police Referral: A Re-Examin-

ation', *The Journal of Criminal Law and Criminology,* Vol.69, No. 3 (1978), pp. 395—401.

78. Ibid.
79. Astor, S.D., 'Shoplifting: Far Greater Than We Know?', *Security World,* Vol. 6, No. 11 (1969), pp. 12—13.
80. Ibid.
81. Astor, S.D., 'Shoplifting Survey', *Security World,* Vol. 8, Part 3 (1971), pp. 34—5.
82. Marks, D.A., 'Retail Store Security in Ireland', *Top Security* (September 1975), pp. 204—6.
83. Mayhew, P., 'Crime in a Man's World', *New Society,* 560 (16 June 1977).
84. Dertke, M.C., Penner, L.A. and Ulrich, K., 'Observer's Reporting of Shoplifting as a Function of Thief's Race and Sex', *The Journal of Social Psychology,* 94 (1974), pp. 213—21.
85. Ibid.
86. Ibid.
87. Gelfand, D.M. *et.al.,* 'Who Reports Shoplifters? A Field-Experimental Study', *Journal of Personality and Social Psychology,* Vol. 25, No. 2 (1973), pp. 276—85.
88. Ibid.
89. Steffensmeier, D.J. and Terry, R.M., 'Deviance and Respectability: An Obersvational Study of Reactions to Shoplifting', *Social Forces,* Vol. 51, (1973), pp. 417—26.
90. Terry, R.M. and Steffensmeier, D.J., 'The Influence of Organisational Factors of Victim Store on Willingness to Report a Shoplifting Incident: A Field Experiment', *Sociological Forces,* Vol. 6 (1973), pp. 27—45.
91. Smigel, E.O., 'Public Attitudes Towards Stealing as Related to the Size of the Victim Organisation', *American Sociological Review,* 21 (1956), pp. 320—27.
92. Terry and Steffensmeier, *op. cit.*
93. Steffensmeier, D.J. and Steffensmeier, R.H., 'Who Reports Shoplifters? Research Continuities and Further Developments', *International Journal of Criminology and Penology,* 5 (1977), pp. 79—95.
94. Ibid.
95. Steffensmeier, D.J., 'Levels of Dogmatism and Willingness to Report "Hippie" and "Straight" Shoplifters: A Field Experiment Accompanied by Home Interviews', *Sociometry,* Vol. 38, No. 2 (1975), pp. 282—90.
96. Bickman, L., 'Bystander Intervention in a Crime: The Effect of a Mass-media Campaign', *Journal of Applied Social Psychology* (5 April 1975), pp. 296—302.

97. Bickman, L. and Green, S., 'Situational Cues and Crime Reporting: Do Signs Make a Difference?', *Journal of Applied Social Psychology* (7 January 1977), pp. 1–18.

98. Bickman, L., 'Attitude Toward an Authority and the Reporting of a Crime', *Sociometry,* Vol. 39, No. 1 (1976), pp. 76–82.

99. Ibid.

100, Bickman, L. and Helwig, H., 'Bystander Reporting of a Crime', *Criminology,* Vol. 17, No. 3 (November 1979), pp. 283–300.

101. Skogan, W.G., 'Citizen Reporting of Crime', *Criminology,* Vol. 13, No. 4 (February 1976), pp. 535–49.

102. Latané, B. and Darley, J.M., 'Bystander "Apathy"', *American Scientist,* 57 (1969), pp. 244–68.

103. Barbera, V., 'Electronics Application Pioneers for Retailers: Article Surveillance Comes into its Own as a Working and Practical Deterrent', *Security World,* Vol. 11, Part 8 (1974) pp. 34–6.

104. Oliver, E. and Wilson, J., *Practical Security in Commerce and Industry* (Epping: Gower, 1978).

105. Hole, R.R., 'Shoplifting Apprehensions Can be Made to Stick', *Security World,* Vol. 9, Parts 1 & 2 (1972), pp. 26–8; 32–46.

106. Edwards, L.E., *Shoplifting and Shrinkage Protection for Stores* (Illinois: Charles C. Thomas, 1958).

107. Meek, V., *Private Enquiries* (London: Duckworth, 1967)

108. Baker, L.L., *They Always Come Back* (Bognor Regis: New Horizon, 1979).

109. Taylor, L.B., *Shoplifting* (New York: Franklin Watts, 1979).

110. Francis, D.B., *Shoplifting: The Crime Everybody Pays For.* (New York): Elsevier/Nelson, 1980.)

111. de Rham, E., *How Could She Do That? A Study of the Female Criminal* (New York: Clarkson N. Potter, 1969).

112. Lehr, K., 'Shoplifting by a Gang' (translation), *Kriminalistik,* Vol. 23 (1969), pp. 433–6.

113. Adley, R., *Take it or Leave it,* report of a study group on shoplifting (1978).

114. Sohier, J., 'Shoplifting: A Rather Ordinary Crime', *International Criminal Police Review,* 24, 229, 161 (1969).

115. Meyer, S.M., 'A Crusade Against Shoplifting', *Police Chief* (June 1974), pp. 34–6.

116. Hiew, C.C., 'Prevention of Shoplifting: A Community Action Approach', *Canadian Journal of Criminology,* Vol. 23, No. 1 (1981), pp. 57–65.

117. May, D., 'Juvenile Shoplifters and the Organisation of Store Security: A Case Study in the Social Construction of Delinquency', *International Journal of Criminology and*

Penology. 6 (1978), pp. 137—60.

118. Ibid.
119. Sudnow, D., *Passing On, The Social Organisation of Dying* (New Jersey: Prentice Hall, 1977), pp. 3—8.

3 Methodology

The methodological considerations of a fieldwork project to investigate shoplifting logically focus on the context of the offence — the shopfloor. However, as the study was intended to provide a comprehensive investigation of customer theft, it would have been incomplete without examining the role of the police and the courts. The fieldwork with the police and in magistrates' courts required a different style of participant observation from that utilised in studying store detectives, details of which will be presented in the appropriate chapters. Nevertheless, there was considerable overlap in techniques and tactics, and such features will be considered in this chapter, as well as the more general problems associated with conducting field research.

Selecting a sample

There are a variety of methods which can be employed to select a sample depending upon the purpose of the research and the exigencies of the situation. McCall and Simmons identify three types of sampling procedure. 'The first of these is some sort of quota sample, in which, for example, the observer is aware of certain formal categories of organisation members and he determines beforehand that he will interview and observe at least a few persons from each of these categories.'[1]

They categorise the second type as the 'snowball' sample. Polsky uses this form of sampling to contact criminals: 'in my experience the most feasible technique for building one's sample is "snowballing": get an introduction to one criminal who will vouch for you with others, who in turn will vouch for you with still others.'[2]

McCall and Simmons' third classification is the search for exceptions to relationships which have previously been hypothesised.[3] In addition, one can mention random samples, where respondents are contacted on a random basis.

The central focus of this study was to investigate shoplifting in its organisational context, particularly on the shopfloor. It was not possible, however, to construct a 'representative' sample of shops, as stores with similar merchandise and floor space might pursue completely different policies. Instead, it was decided to approach as many shops as possible in the time available, in order to furnish information on as many different types of practice which were operating. Consequently, use was made of a number of different sampling techniques.

In the initial phase of the research the Director of the Association for the Prevention of Theft in Shops (APTS) was approached, partly out of courtesy, partly to ask for comments, and partly in the hope of gaining access to a number of shops; this was successfully achieved in the 'snowball' fashion. However, apart from this incident and one or two others where chief security officers said, 'Have you been to see X yet? He'll help you' (or, 'He does things differently' — McCall and Simmons' third category?), most of the shops were contacted directly.

Nearly all of the major high street stores and shops were approached. Interviews were conducted at their head offices and observations of store detectives were carried out in a number of regional and metropolitan sites to test whether the practices of a particular chain varied around the country. A number of large stores that were not part of any chain were also contacted. In addition, interviews and observations were carried out in chains of smaller retailers. Finally, 100 short interviews were conducted with small shops which did not belong to a larger organisation. Of all the shops and stores which were approached only one refused permission to observe their store detectives, but even here an interview was given. Hundreds of interviews were completed and a total of six months was spent in the company of store detectives. The time spent in each shop varied from a week in the larger stores to perhaps half a day in a small grocers with a peripatetic store detective. The regions covered ranged from London to Newcastle, Plymouth to Liverpool, Hertfordshire to Cheshire. The research sample does not claim to represent every type of retail outlet, but it is hoped that the size of the sample is sufficient to ensure that a wide variety of practices are covered.

Gaining entrée

Johnson believes that gaining entry into the research site is important for two reasons. 'First, the achievement of successful entrée is a pre-condition for doing the research.'[4] Second, it is important as it may affect the relationship between the initial entrée to the setting and the validity of the data subsequently collected. He continues that the methods of gaining entrée should vary with the organisation to be studied and the purpose of the research. Furthermore, the researcher has to provide a plausible explanation of the projected study, in terms understandable to the hosts, and grounds to ensure their cooperation. As McCall and Simmons say,

> one of the most important bonds in any sort of social relationship is the rewards that each party receives from it; if a relationship is not profitable to the participants in some sense, it will tend to be terminated. It is quite clear what the observer will gain from such relationships, but the implicit problem is what the research subjects will get out of their relationship with the observer.[5]

Schatzman and Strauss advise the researcher to promise some sort of feedback or perhaps to give some useful observations.[6]

In presenting the research project to the host organisations two factors were involved in acceptance. First, it was promised that the researcher would not obstruct the work of the security personnel and that any results would be anonymous and confidential. Secondly, it was posited that some results might emerge which would illuminate the whole question and which might eventually influence policy. In other words, it was made apparent that the research could not do any harm, and there was a possibility (however faint) that it might do some good.

The BSA principles of practice state:

> The sociologist should subscribe to the doctrine of 'informed consent' on the part of the subjects and accordingly take pains to explain fully the objects and implications of his research to individual subjects. The sociologist has a duty to explain as fully as possible and in terms meaningful to the subjects what his research is about, who is undertaking and financing it and why it is being undertaken.[7]

Johnson realises, however, that there is a paradox inherent in such statements for, with many field studies, the topics to be investigated will not become apparent until the project is well under way. In effect, it becomes difficult to present a cogent précis of the proposed research when the researcher does not yet know the focus to be adopted. 'The key to resolving the paradox', according to Johnson, 'is the cover story, the claims made by the investigator in his research proposals and letters of introduction by which he legitimates his request for access to the setting.'[8] Johnson believes that such strategies are necessary in order to gain entrée to the research field at the same time as reducing the chances of outright rejection. The cover story, for Johnson, helps to 'defocus' the project and make it more general.

In presenting this research it was not necessary to provide a cover story to defocus its aims. Instead, the project was described as an information study designed to complement studies based on official statistics, in order to provide a more comprehensive picture of what shoplifting really looked like on the shopfloor, and its inherent problems. Obviously, some shops were more reluctant to cooperate initially than others, but most agreed readily. Indeed, anticipating a degree of reservation, the researcher went prepared with many arguments for the study only to be pre-empted by such questions as, 'OK, when do you want to start?'

In discussing how to establish field relations, Dean *et al.* say that, 'Generally field contacts should move from persons in the highest status and authority positions down to the actual participants in the field situation one wants to study.'[9] The usual procedure in this research was to contact the chief security officer (CSO) at the appropriate store or head office. Normally, this person could give permission for the research to proceed. Where his[10] authority was insufficient, he could arrange for senior directors to be present at the first interview.

Two points can be made about this level of approach. First, the CSO was a critical contact who often had the authority to approve the research, but nearly always had the power to veto it. If he thought the research would disrupt the smooth running of his department then other store personnel would be unlikely to force the issue. Consequently, it was not just courtesy which prompted this initial contact, but it was seen as tactically advantageous. Secondly, the CSO would know his own organisation better than an outsider. If he were able to give permission for the research to proceed then time would be saved, and, if further authority were required, the CSO would know whom to contact. The chief security officer was seen, and was seeable, as the obvious point of reference in approaching the stores.

According to Schatzman and Strauss, 'the researcher adopts tactics which are comfortable for him: some researchers use the phone easily; some prefer writing first, and then following up with a visit'.[11] The usual procedure in this project was to write first to ask for a meeting at which the research could be discussed. Johnson refers to the 'rhetoric of science' used to persuade officials to give permission for the research, and talks about the use of letterhead stationery and academic titles to further academic respectability.[12] The letters addressed to the shops and stores for this project requested an interview and covered a brief description of the research. Once one or two prestigious retailers had agreed to cooperate their names were mentioned. Importantly, the letter was typed on Home Office stationery. The research, therefore, was shown to be academically respectable and had the support of a number of leading retailers. In addition, it was also seen as conveying the authority and, perhaps more critically, the discretion of a government department. There was also an implicit promise of influencing policy, however remote.

Method of study

McCall and Simmons believe that:

> It is probably misleading to regard participant observation as a single method. Rather, in common parlance, it refers to a characteristic blend or combination of methods and techniques that is employed in studying certain types of subject matter .... We shall view participant observation not as a single method but as a type of research enterprise, a style of combining several methods towards a particular end. That end is an analytic description of a complex social organisation. By an analytic description we mean something much more than a journalistic description: an analytic description (1) employs the concepts, propositions and empirical generalisations of a body of scientific theory as the basic guides in analysis and reporting, (2) employs thorough and systematic collection, classification and reporting of facts, and (3) generates new empirical generalisations (and perhaps concepts and propositions as well) based on these data.[13]

Schatzman and Strauss put the position more succinctly, 'the field researcher is depicted as a "strategist"; for without linear-specific design — for the most part precluded by the natural properties of his field — the researcher must develop procedure as he goes.'[14] Although participant observation can be characterised as a blend of methods, several authors have attempted to classify various types of field research.

Schwartz and Schwartz make a distinction between 'active' and 'passive' researchers. The passive participant observer is keen to react as little as possible with the subjects. He is concerned with observing the participants and any contact with them is deemed as jeopardising the objectivity of the research. As an ideal type, the passive researcher is similar to the scientist observing the behaviour of subjects behind a two-way mirror. On the other hand,

> the 'active' participant observer maximises his participation with the observed in order to gather data and attempts to integrate his role with other roles in the social situation. His activity is accepted, both by himself and by the observed, as part of his role. His intention is to experience the life of the observed so that he can better observe and understand it.[15]

Gold has a more sophisticated typology of four different roles for the field researcher, ranging on a continuum from the complete participant, through the participant-as-observer and observer-as-participant, to the complete observer. The participant-as-observer is closer to the complete participant and the observer-as-participant is nearer to the complete observer.[16] Gold identifies two problems with the role of complete participant and considers that one or the other has to be faced in this type of research. First, the researcher may be unable to carry out the expectations of his assumed role because he is dubious about revealing his true identity. Secondly, and more familiarly, the researcher may so adopt the goals and attitudes of his fellow participants that he 'goes native' and incorporates or replaces their value system for his own.

The participant-as-observer is similar to the complete participant except for the fact that both the participants and the researcher know his true identity and know that theirs is a field relationship. Consequently, problems with role-playing are reduced, but there are still risks of accepting the belief system of the subjects without question.

> The observer-as-participant role is used in studies involving one-visit interviews. It calls for relatively more formal observation than either informal observation or participation of any kind. It also entails less risk of 'going native' than either the complete participant role or the participant-as-observer role. However, because the observer-as-participant's contact with an informant is so brief, and perhaps superficial, he is more likely than the other two to misunderstand the informant, and to be misunderstood by him .... These frust-ratingly brief encounters with informants also contribute to mistaken perceptions which set up communication barriers the field worker may not even be aware of until too late.[17]

The ramifications of this mode of field research will be discussed more fully below as it is, in many respects, closest to the role adopted in this study. It will be demonstrated, however, that the disadvantages of this role were overcome.

Finally, there is the complete observer who does not interact with the participants but merely observes them (a role not unlike that of the 'passive' researcher depicted by Schwartz and Schwartz). Gold argues that the more participation involved, the greater the risks of 'going native'. Reciprocally, the more observation there is, the greater the risk of 'ethnocentrism', or seeing other people's cultures through the researcher's own experiences.

In a further refinement of typology, Schatzman and Strauss isolate six different aspects of the method, which range along a continuum according to the degree of participation by the researcher.[18] First comes the laboratory-type setting where the researcher remains outside the field context and observes. Secondly, the fieldworker is physically present in the situation, but does not interact and observes passively. These two types correspond in some measure to Gold's complete observer and the 'passive' observer of Schwartz and Schwartz. The third type identified by Schatzman and Strauss is that of limited interaction, where

> the researcher engages in minimal, clarifying interaction. In this type of situation, the observer does not set himself apart from the participants. His interventions in the flow of interaction are confined mainly to seeking clarification and the meaning of ongoing events. He does not attempt to direct interaction into channels of his own choosing. This type of activity has two distinct advantages: it gets at meaning, and meets the expectations of the hosts insofar as the researcher is not only an observer, but is revealed as personable and interested; through his comments or questions his apparent agenda is indicated. The agenda is understandable and appears appropriate; therefore, the observer can be thought of as at least 'kind of' a member of the group. This allows them quickly to minimize, even temporarily forget his presence, and thus return the situation nearly to 'normal'. The option is especially useful when the researcher is wary of intruding his person too obviously, when people are just too busy or where there is a danger to someone in his intruding.[19]

This quotation is interesting for two reasons. First it depicts a similar mode of research to that of Gold's 'observer-as-participant', and secondly, it corresponds to the predominant method used in this research, of which more below.

The fourth mode of participant observation characterised by Schatzman and Strauss is that of active control, where the fieldworker controls the interaction along predetermined lines in order to gain certain sets of data. Typically, active control occurs in the formal interview. The fifth and sixth modes of research role are both of the complete participant type — the only distinction between the two being that in one the researcher is covert and in the other he interacts with the participants' full knowledge of his identity.

Earlier, reference was made to the variety of methods inherent in the phrase 'participant observation', some of which have been discussed. During a long and intensive period of fieldwork a number of these roles were adopted for different situations. For example, during the course of initial interviews, the researcher corresponded to the active control mode. On the other hand, when watching suspects being interrogated, the appropriate role was that of the passive participant observer, or complete observer.[20] However, for much of the time, the role adopted was that of the 'observer-as-participant', or of 'limited interaction'. Schatzman and Strauss point out the advantages of this role, while Gold is more aware of its limitations. In the present research the advantages were enjoyed whilst the disadvantages were avoided.

One advantage of the role is that it avoids the problem of 'going native', while getting at meaning and understanding of the respondent's world. However, Gold is of the opinion that because contact with informants is usually brief, the interaction may be superficial and the researcher may fail to get at the respondent's meaning. This difficulty was avoided in the research, partly because the first observations tended to be for the longest periods (up to a week), and partly because subsequent visits were repetitions. That is, although some visits were relatively short, their content did not differ markedly from visits to other stores. Although practices varied from store to store the basic background and problem of shoplifting remained constant. In this way, the problem of superficiality and lack of understanding was avoided. Consequently, the research enjoyed the benefits of these two similar methods — that is, getting at meaning without the risk of 'going native' — while avoiding the problem of superficiality.

It is now possible to discuss in more detail the field tactics utilised in the research.

It was mentioned earlier that the chief security officers were contacted and invited to give an interview. The interviews, which lasted from 1½–2½ hours, were informal and loosely structured, but certain relevant points were always covered. The main topics included general security, estimation of losses, prosecution policy, staff training, and arrest and interview procedures. At the interviews, dates were arranged to visit particular stores and to accompany store detectives. In some cases the researcher was introduced to the store detectives at the initial interview, which facilitated relationships at subsequent meetings. Some authors have argued that store detectives are wary of researchers and may be hostile to them. No such attitudes were encountered in this project; on the contrary, most of the security personnel were extremely cooperative and encouraging.

As they walked round the shopfloor, the store detectives were asked why they became suspicious of particular people, why they followed some and not others, why they stopped some people, and why they ceased following others. Unlike Ditton's experiences with 'Bronco' paper, [21] it was possible to take abbreviated notes whilst walking with the store detective, and these were later expanded. When the action occurred too quickly — for example, during an arrest, or when note-taking might have alerted a suspect — notes were taken after the incident.

In quieter times (and there were many occasions when staff out-numbered customers,) the researcher would pose hypothetical questions to the store detective: 'What would you do in this situation?'; 'Official policy says this. How do you react?', etc. The detectives' knowledge of the laws of arrest, how to make apprehensions, what notes they took, and how they made particular decisions, were also noted. Strauss *et al.* identify a number of different types of question, all of which were used in this phase of the research in addition to the interviews: 'in the later stages of research, we increasingly adopted a "posing" type of question, which involved putting a case to the respondent.' [22] These posing questions included the 'challenge', the 'hypothetical question' and the 'ideal' which either the researcher or the respondent could describe. The challenging or devil's advocate question involves some rhetorical heat and it was not used directly in the research, and certainly not until interaction between the researcher and informant was well-establish-ed. On occasions, the researcher would challenge the informant but would diffuse the situation by allocating controversial opinions to specific others, or more usually to the general population (e.g. 'Some people say ...').

Considerable use was made of the hypothetical question throughout the research and, as Strauss *et al.* confirm, it is a valuable device for rounding out the respondent's thought structure and, of course, unlike the challenging question, it does not arouse emotions.

Strauss *et al.* identify two variations on the technique of posing the ideal. 'First, the respondent can be asked to describe the ideal situation .... Second, while the fieldworker can still pretend to be somewhat naive, he can assert an ideal to see what response is elicited.' [23] Both of these techniques were used in the research, in addition to which, information elicited from the chief security officer could be contrasted with that from the store detective, and vice versa.

Issues of participant observation

Before discussing the advantages and disadvantages of reinforcing interviews and surveys with observation, it will be constructive first to demonstrate the deficiencies of relying solely on observation. McCall and Simmons believe that there are three important factors mitigating against the use of observation alone.

> (1) the organisation is typically being manifested in several locales simultaneously, (2) the organisation has typically been in existence for some time before the scientist undertook his study, and (3) many of its features or determinants (such as the motives, intentions, interests and perceptions of its members) are only imperfectly inferable by direct observation.[24]

To repair these deficiencies, the researcher relies upon data provided by records, files, informants and respondents.

The importance of observation in field research, however, needs emphasising. Schatzman and Strauss believe that two difficulties flow from exclusive reliance on interviews, surveys and questionnaires.

> First, any given person may be no more able to describe and explain his own actions than anyone else's: his vocabulary may be poverty-stricken or his perspective too difficult to comprehend by listening or reading alone (also, he may lie or 'put on' the interviewer). Second, interview or questionnaire procedures constitute situations in their own right; therefore, what persons report in either case often better reflects those situations than the referential ones which the techniques were designed to ascertain. Referential situations are too quickly and readily coverted by any given respondent into relatively idealized models when he is talking with researchers outside the 'real' situation.[25]

Becker and Geer also advocate the use of observation to complement interviews. They consider that participant observation fieldwork is similar to the anthropological model except they realise, 'as Icheiser has put it, we often do not understand that we do not understand and are thus likely to make errors in interpreting what is said to us.'[26] For the anthropologist everything is unfamiliar — the customs, the rituals, and critically, the language. For the field researcher, in his own society, language provides a commonality with the subjects. There is an inherent danger that the fieldworker will take it for granted that his understanding of a concept corresponds to that of the respondent and critical cultural differences will go unexamined; indeed, they will go unrealised.

Becker and Geer believe that

> participant observation provides a situation in which the
> meanings of words can be learned with great precision
> through study of their use in context, exploration through
> continuous interviewing of their implications and nuances
> and the use of them oneself under the scrutiny of capable
> speakers of the language. Beyond simply clarifying matters
> so that the researcher may understand better what people
> say to each other and to him, such a linguistic exercise
> may provide research hypotheses of great usefulness.[27]

In our research, much use of the term 'professional' was made by
store detectives during the fieldwork. The researcher's concept of
'professional' gleaned from general criminological studies and previous
shoplifting research suggested such aspects to be included in the term
as full-time occupation, theft for resale, criminal contacts, etc. Initially,
the researcher took security staff's use of the word to correspond with
his own. However, it appeared that the concept was being used considerably more than research by previous writers (cf. Chapter 2) who perhaps
were underestimating the extent of professionalism in shoplifting,
would suggest. On the contrary, during the course of the extensive
observation of shoplifting incidents, it transpired that the store detectives
had a completely different notion of 'professionalism'.

For store detectives, a professional did not necessarily have to rely
on crime as a full-time occupation, nor were the goods necessarily
stolen for resale. Moreover, such 'professionals' need not have criminal
contacts, belong to a deviant sub-group, or have a criminal record. It
emerged that the typical phrase, 'They were real professionals' referred
not to the usual considerations but were more a reference to the skill
of the suspects. Thus any shopper who stole without appearing nervous,
who did not break down when apprehended, who stole the goods
quickly and efficiently, and who appeared calm throughout would be
described as 'a real professional'. Such an ideal type was used to contrast
with the archetypal 'little old lady' who did not know what she was
doing, appeared confused, stole in a conspicuous fashion, and was
emotionally disturbed when apprehended. Thus the term 'professional',
for store detectives, carried different connotations than in general use.
It related to the fact that store detectives rarely dealt with what the
police would term 'professionals' and consequently the concept referred
to skill and calmness. At the same time, security staff would sometimes
refer to shoplifters as 'professionals' when the term corresponded to
general use. It was only through observation that this fine distinction
could be determined. As Becker and Geer say, 'In short, participant
observation makes it possible to check description against fact and,

noting discrepancies, become aware of systematic distortions made by the person under study; such distortions are less likely to be discovered by interviewing alone.'[28] For example, in one department store, the CSO declared that all apprehended persons were referred to the police. In practice, however, his store detectives used their initiative on the shopfloor. They were unwilling to refer children (especially those under 10) to the police, and consequently tended to deal with them on the shopfloor.

McCall investigated the problems of quality control of participant observation, and isolated a number of effects which are the principal concerns regarding observational data.[29] Two of these — the problems of ethnocentrism and of 'going native' — have been discussed above, more significant here are the reactive effects and limitations on observation. Limitations on observation were counteracted by the size of the sample and the extent of the observations conducted. These were supplemented with interviews and such hypothetical questions as, 'Have things always been like this?', 'Is this a problem only for this area?', etc. Thus it was possible to ascertain whether policy varied nationally, and whether it had changed over time.

Bias may occur in the research through the reactive effects of the 'observer's presence or behaviour on the phenomenon under observation, with the result that the observer does not have the opportunity to observe the very thing that he may have hoped to observe and that he may in fact believe he is observing.'[30] McCall believes that the best check against this form of bias is a comparison of observed events with an informant's description of similar events at which the researcher was not present. During the fieldwork, interviews were checked against observations for each individual store and observations were compared with the hypothetical situations mentioned earlier. In addition, data from one particular shop or chain was used to check data from different stores, often using the devil's advocate-type question. The effects of bias were thus minimised.

On a detailed level, Dean and Whyte examine ways of assessing whether an informant is telling the truth, and isolate a number of relevant factors.

> (1) Are there any ulterior motives which the informant has that might modify his reporting of the situation? .... (2) Are there any bars to spontaneity which might inhibit free expression? (3) Does the informant have the desire to please the interviewers so that his opinions will be well thought of? (4) Are there any idiosyncratic factors that may cause the informant to express only one facet of his reactions to a subject?[31]

The threat of idiosyncratic factors was countered by the large number of respondents: if there were any peculiarities among some of the respondents it is likely that they would have cancelled each other out. In addition, as Dean and Whyte advocate, questions were asked in different ways and summaries of the researcher's understanding of answers were provided to prevent misunderstandings. Bars to spontaneity were countered with assurances that interviews and observations were completely confidential, no names would be used, and no reports would be given back to management. Because of these factors and probably also the fact that there was little to be secretive about, respondents tended to be very open, often criticising chief security officers and contradicting their beliefs — 'This is what it's really like'; 'This is what we really do', etc. Interestingly, store detectives on the shopfloor would often pursue more tolerant policies if their superiors were strict, and more strict ones if they were lenient.

The informant's desire to please the researcher did not appear to be a large problem as it was made clear that opinions would not be forwarded to management and the researcher was peripheral to the store detective's working life.

The authors believe that sometimes the threat posed by ulterior motives can be counteracted by pointing out that the researcher is in no position to influence the situation. This was successfully done, but it does not counteract all of the problem. In extreme cases (for example, interviewing criminals), although the researcher may prove his inability to influence events the respondent may still be wary of revealing the full facts as they might portray him in a bad light, or even leave him open to criminal investigation. Store detectives do not present the same problems as criminals — they are, after all, acting legally. Nevertheless, the researcher was aware of two problems concerning ulterior motives. First, some store detectives were aware of their isolated position and felt some public hostility, somewhat akin to being a traffic warden, only more so. This may have been a bar between store detectives and researchers from universities, but as this field-worker was employed by the Home Office, it became apparent that he was seen, in some ways, as being 'on their side'. Indeed, evidence of this was forthcoming when store detectives talked about their isolation and how they rarely described the exact nature of their job, but replied with vague answers, saying, 'I work for store X'. During these conversations, it emerged that the security personnel would only reveal their true status to fellow detectives, the police, magistrates and 'people like you'. In the 'them and us' situation, the researcher was included in 'us'.

The second difficulty with this effect of ulterior motives was underpinned by not having anything to hide or be secretive about. Store detectives act lawfully and are allowed to use 'reasonable force' in apprehending suspects. The fieldworker was aware of the possibilities of store personnel exceeding their legal authority by using too much force or by pressurising suspects during interviews. Store detectives, then, might use more force when not accompanied by the researcher. However, to a large extent, this did not appear to be a problem. When arresting a suspect, the store detectives generally forgot the presence of the researcher in the heat of the moment, and acted in what appeared to be a routine manner. In addition, most of the apprehended persons returned to the shop quite peacefully and there was no need for any force whatsoever by the security personnel. Store detectives are trained to manage apprehensions peacefully and they generally do this so effectively that force is redundant (see later chapters for how this is achieved). Obviously, on occasions, inexperienced or unsuitable store detectives will exceed their authority and there will be some incidents of violence However, during the research, the most noticeable feature to emerge was the very routine nature of the apprehensions; the use of force was usually irrelevant and where on the limited occasions that it occurred, it was usually on the part of the suspect.

In evaluating the validity of the data provided by field research, Dean and Whyte believe that 'the major way in which we detect distortion, and correct for it, is by comparing an informant's account with the accounts given by other informants',[32] and, as has been demonstrated, this procedure was followed throughout the research.

Viditch and Shapiro believe that there are two ways of assessing field research, and also survey data. The first is the test of 'internal consistency'.

> The careful anthropologist, for example, will cross-check the reports of one informant against those of another, and will pay careful attention to discrepancies between avowals in one context and facts which are allowed to 'slip out' in another. These are 'internal' consistency checks because they compare, within the confines of the same method, one observation with another.[33]

They argue, however, that the external validity of the survey or participant observer method could be enhanced by checking each against the other. In this way, they hope to demonstrate that the consistent picture proved by the chosen method corresponds to reality. Although in this research a survey, in the traditional sense, was not carried out, it is arguable that the data provided by interviews partly corresponded to this method. Further, although the research focus was different, results do not contradict the earlier survey conducted by the Home Office Working Party.[34] In short, the current research was consistent and corresponded to reality.

Ethical considerations

There were no problems with interviewing or observing store detectives, who were all individually informed about the nature and purpose of the research. Wax alerts us to the presence of power relationships in organisations: senior management gives permission for the research to proceed, while junior personnel are not consulted but are constrained to co-operate.[35] This was not a difficulty with the research, as many of the store detectives were used to being accompanied and observed, and it was made clear that the researcher would not interfere or hinder their work and would not report back to management. When there were quieter periods, a researcher expressing interest in the store detective's job helped while away the hours. When there were busy periods the store detectives seemed genuinely keen to show the researcher 'what it was really like'. On no occasion was any real violence by store detectives witnessed. Occasionally a firm grip might be utilised, but incidents requiring more force were not observed. Store detectives often expressed reluctance to become involved in such situations because they feared for their own safety and in logistical as well as humanitarian terms it made good commercial sense to have store detectives on the shopfloor rather than in hospital.

Only on one occasion was there a disquieting and potentially violent incident, which involved a teenager who attempted to escape apprehension. Two store detectives held his arms tightly and marched him to the interview room. He protested that they were hurting him and they argued that they would loosen their grip if he stopped struggling. Before this could be resolved, the interview room had been reached and the situation calmed down.

To avoid upsetting suspected shoplifters, the researcher did everything to maintain a low profile. No notes were taken in front of suspects during interviews, instead the researcher often stood outside of the room where he was out of view and took notes. When the researcher was in the presence of the suspect, he did nothing to counter the impression that he was just another assistant or store detective. The only people to question the researcher's presence were the arresting police officers, but they were soon put in the picture, away from the suspects. In short, the suspects were not aware of the research project and the presence of a researcher did nothing to affect the situation.

Only on one occasion was the researcher's identity threatened, and this, ironically, was for a case of employee theft. During this incident, a part-time pensioner was caught 'fiddling' the till and was taken to the interview room. As will be shown later, such cases are more difficult to prove than shoplifting and present security staff with more problems. Initially, the researcher was in the interview room with the suspect, the arresting store detective and the chief security officer. However, both store personnel left the room to discuss their next moves, leaving the researcher alone with the suspect. The old man was obviously frightened and suffering some considerable anxiety and enlisted the researcher's support. Part of his defence was that the £5 note in question was not stolen but came from his wage packet and consequently had a staple mark in it. The suspect asked the researcher if he could see where the staple had marked the note, which he was able to do and subsequently pointed out to the security officers on their return. This did not affect the outcome of the case as anybody with decent eyesight could have seen the staple marks. What was more disquietening, however, was the man's request of 'What should I do?'. Apart from the fact that the researcher did not know what he should do, it was difficult to give a reasonable response without disclosing the research status. The researcher resorted to sophistry ('I'm new here' — which was true, as he had only been there a week) and maintained the erroneous impression of store detective status. There was a strong temptation to leave the room, but for legal and medical reasons, this was not a viable option. The researcher should not have been placed in such a position and ensured that it did not happen again.

A problem which might have occurred was where the researcher spotted a suspected shoplifting — should he inform the store detective or ignore it? It was decided before commencing the observation that any such incident would be ignored, partly because the researcher was reluctant to influence events to such an extent, and partly through a reluctance to accept responsibility for the prosecution of a shoplifter, whether guilty or not. In the event, this problem never arose. Because the researcher was concentrating on the store detectives and the people they were watching there was little opportunity for independent action and the researcher never discovered a suspicious person before the store detective did.

In one case, which will be reported more fully subsequently, outside information could have been used to influence events. A store detective had arrested a young, black teenage girl who was reluctant to give her name. Finally, she confessed to being 'Angela Davis'. This appeared a little implausible to the researcher (although obviously not impossible), who had some difficulty in keeping a straight face, particularly when the store detective proceeded to call the girl Angela. This was not a particularly controversial example: the researcher did not want to interfere and suggest the girl was lying, which would certainly have influenced the situation, and in any case, she could have been telling the truth, it just seemed unlikely (in fact it was). All such considerations were quickly forgotten, however, when the girl hit the store detective and made an attempt to escape.

In summary, store detectives and other personnel were aware of the aims of the research, while the researcher maintained a confidential, non-involved profile. While suspects were unaware of the research being conducted and did not know of the researcher's true identity, *nothing* was done which would exacerbate their anxiety. This was critical, as for many shoplifters, apprehension and police referral was an exceptionally traumatic experience and the knowledge that they were being researched, however anonymously, would only have served to increase their alarm. *No suspect, guilty or not, was even slightly hurt by the research.*

Focus of the research

The methodology of the research and its focus have been heavily informed by the work of Sudnow on death and dying. The following quote is worth repeating as it succinctly states the assumptions of much of the present research merely by substituting 'shoplifting' and 'stores' by 'death' and 'hospitals'.

> In the role of 'non-participant observer', I have sought to get close to occasions of 'dying' and 'death', record what transpires in the behaviour of staff members of the institutions on such occasions, and analyse some of the general features of that behaviour. My central effort has been to locate 'death' and 'dying' as organisationally relevant events, conceive of their handling as governed by the practically organised work considerations of hospital personnel and ward social organisation, and sketch out certain themes which appear to bring together a set of observed facts about social practices relating to 'dying' and 'death'....
>
> A central theoretical and methodological perspective guides much of the study. ... That perspective says that the categories of hospital life, e.g., 'life', 'illness', 'patient', 'dying', or 'death' or whatever are to be seen as constituted by the practices of hospital personnel as they engage in their daily routinised interactions within an organisational milieu....
>
> Rather than entering the hospital to investigate 'death' and 'dying' as I conceived them, I sought to develop 'definitions' of such phenomena based on actions involved in their recognition, treatment and consequences. 'Death' and 'dying' are, from this perspective, the set of practices enforced when staff employ those terms in the course of their work day on

the hospital ward .... My emphasis is on the 'production
of dying and death'.[36]

Similarly, the emphasis of this research project is on the 'production of
shoplifting and shoplifters'.

Notes

1. McCall, G.J. and Simmons, J.L., *Issues in Participant Observation*
   (Reading, Mass.: Addison-Wesley, 1969), p. 64.
2. Polsky, N., *Hustlers, Beats and Others* (Harmondsworth;
   Penguin Books, 1967), p. 129.
3. McCall and Simmons, *op. cit.,* p. 65.
4. Johnson, J.M., *Doing Field Research* (New York: Free Press,
   1975), p. 50.
5. McCall and Simmons, *op. cit.,* p. 43.
6. Schatzman, L. and Strauss, A.L., *Field Research: Strategies
   for a Natural Sociology* (New Jersey: Prentice-Hall, 1973)
   pp. 28—32.
7. Homan, R., cited in 'The Ethics of Covert Methods',
   British Journal of Sociology, Vol. 31, No. 1 (March 1980),
   pp. 46—59.
8. Johnson, *op. cit.,* p. 60. The choice of the phrase 'cover story'
   by Johnson is perhaps unfortunate as it implies some form of
   deception. Nevertheless, the point is a valid one. Most field
   researchers are not aware of precisely what they want to study
   until they have been in the field for some time. In order to
   gain access, however, they must present some account of the
   purpose of the research. In this project, a general picture of the
   study's aims was presented and once this was accepted it was
   possible to develop more specific topics in the field. This is
   not necessarily a problem of ethics but can more readily be
   seen as a problem with explaining much field research to the
   public.
9. Dean, J.P., Eichhorn, R.L. and Dean, L.R., 'Establishing
   Field Relations', in McCall and Simmons, *op. cit.,*
   pp. 68—70.
10. Most CSOs were male, most (but by no means all), store
    detectives were female.
11. Schatzman and Strauss, *op. cit.,* p. 20.
12. Johnson, *op. cit.,* p. 64.

13. McCall and Simmons, *op. cit.,* pp. 1–3.
14. Schatzman and Strauss, *op. cit.,* p. vii.
15. Schwartz, M.S. and Schwartz, C.G., 'Problems in Participant Observation', in McCall, and Simmons, *op. cit.,* pp. 89–104.
16. Gold, R.L., 'Roles in Sociological Field Observations', in McCall, and Simmons, *op. cit.,* pp. 30–8.
17. Ibid.
18. Schatzman, and Strauss, *op. cit.,* pp. 59–63.
19. Ibid., p. 60.
20. While the role in the interrogation situation was that of complete observer, this did not prevent the researcher asking questions about the interview at a later date when he was acting more as an observer-as-participant. As the data suggest, the roles of participant observation are flexible and the researcher must be prepared to change quickly from one to another and back again.
21. Ditton, J., *Part-Time Crime. An Ethnography of Fiddling and Pilferage* (London: Macmillan, 1977), p. 5.
22. Strauss, A. *et al.,* 'Field Tactics', in McCall and Simmons, *op. cit.,* pp. 70–2.
23. Ibid.
24. McCall and Simmons, *op. cit.,* p. 4.
25. Schatzman and Strauss, *op. cit.,* p. 6.
26. Becker, H.S. and Geer, B., 'Participant Observation and Interviewing', in McCall and Simmons, *op. cit.,* pp. 322–31.
27. Ibid.
28. Ibid.
29. McCall, G.J., 'Data Quality Control in Participant Observation', in McCall and Simmons *op. cit.,* pp. 128–41.
30. Ibid.
31. Dean, J.P. and Whyte, W.F., 'How Do You Know if the Informant is Telling the Truth?', in McCall and Simmons *op. cit.,* pp.105–14.
32. Ibid.
33. Viditch, A.J. and Shapiro, G., 'A Comparison of Participant Observation and Survey Data', in McCall and Simmons, *op. cit.,* pp. 295–302.
34. Home Office, *Shoplifting and Thefts by Shop Staff. Report of a Working Party on Internal Shop Security* (London HMSO, 1973).
35. Wax, R.H., 'Reciprocity as a Field Technique', *Human Organization,* II (3) (1952), pp. 34–7.
36. Sudnow, D., *Passing On. The Social Organisation of Dying.* (New Jersey: Prentice-Hall, 1967), pp. 3–8.

4 Shoplifting: its historical and legal context

The history of shoplifting

> Then, without any transition, the policeman told them how
> that very morning he had arrested a fine, strapping young
> woman who had just been shoplifting in a pork butchers.
> When they had stripped her at the station they found ten
> sausages on her, suspended round her body, front and rear.[1]

Despite the recent concern about shoplifting, it is not a new word or
activity. Reference to 'The Lifting Law' was made in 1597,[2] and the
modern usage of the term, specifying theft from shops, dates from
the seventeenth century when shoplifting became an established
feature of everyday life. According to Walsh the word, 'shoplifting' was
first heard of in England in 1673:[3] 'Of the Shoplift − she is commonly
well clad', and 'The tenth is a shoplift that carries a Bob,/when he
ranges the City the Shops for to rob.'[4] In 1692, Scarronides mentions,
'how Grecian Shop-lifts Brake open honest Trojan doors',[5] but whether
this usage corresponds to the modern idiom is a moot point. In 1680,
for example, Kirkman states that 'Towards night these Houses are
throng'd with people of all sorts ... Shoplifters, Foilers, Bulkers.'[6]

The offence was officially recognised in the preamble to the 1698
Act 10 of Parliament, William III, c. 12: 'The Crime of stealing goods
privately out of Shops and Warehouses commonly called shoplifting..'[7]
Under the Act, shoplifting was a capital offence, and it was not until
1820 that Sir James Mackintosh succeeded in abolishing the death

penalty for the offence of 'stealing five shillings from a shop'. Edwards describes how two women shoplifters were dealt with: 'Nan Harris — a Shoplift ... she was called down to her former judgement and hanged in the 20th year of her age, at Tyburn, on Friday, July 13, 1705.'[8] A few years earlier there was the case of Moll Jones, 'A Shoplift ... but her Graceless Grace being sent to Newgate and condemned for her life at the Old Bailey, she was hanged at Tyburn in the 25th year of her age, on Friday, December 18, 1691.'[9] He also records that,

> In the Summer of the year 1726, shoplifters became so common and so detrimental to the shopkeepers, that they made application to the Government for assistance in apprehending the offenders; and in order thereto, offered a reward and a pardon for any who would discover their associates in such practice.[10]

This amnesty to informers led to the downfall of the notorious Jonathan Wild who had built up an empire of 'fencing', partly on the proceeds of shoplifters. His career merits a short digression.

Until his death, Wild operated an ingenious system by which he controlled much of London's underworld; acting as an agent through whom victims of crime could recover their stolen property, which Wild had bought from the thieves, at a price. For example, if a gold watch were stolen from a prosperous gentleman, Wild would let it be known, either directly to the victim or through advertising, that the watch could be recovered for a fee; and the arrangement was duly completed. This system was so economically superior to that operated by other fences that thieves willingly approached him and, unlike his predecessors, Wild did not usually have to resort to the provisions of the Highwayman's Act to coerce his thieves into cooperation.

> In order to sustain the balance upon which his system depended [says Klockars], Wild had to counter the claim that he was nothing but a fence. He did so by emphasizing that integral part of fencing which most strongly contradicts the charge of being too intimate with thieves. He proclaimed himself to be 'Thief-Taker General of Great Britain and Ireland', and proceeded to earn that puffed-up title.[11]

Any thieves who did not cooperate with Wild, or otherwise earned his displeasure, were duly arrested and dispatched.

Three women shoplifters — Holmes, Burton and Robinson — were to be Wild's downfall. They shoplifted some lace and 'fenced' it through him, but Burton informed on her colleagues and on Jonathan Wild as well. The warrant for Wild's arrest included the charge that 'for many years past he had been a confederate with a great number of highway-

men, pick-pockets, house-breakers, shop-lifters and other thieves'.[12]
There were two indictments against him: the first accused him of stealing the lace with the three women. This charge was dismissed because,
although Wild had planned the theft, he argued that as he had not
entered the shop, he could not have stolen the goods. The second
indictment came under 4 George I, C ll, s. 4, which had been passed
in 1718 as a section of the Transportation Act.

> It was so obviously directed at Wild [says Klockars] that it
> acquired the nickname 'Jonathan Wild's Act'. Under this Act,
> Wild was now charged with receiving ten guineas from the
> blind shop woman for the return of her property without
> discovering, apprehending or causing to be apprehended the
> felon who had stolen the lace.[13]

Wild was found guilty of this charge and was duly hanged.

Shoplifting, then, is not a new activity: it was just as common in
England in the early eighteenth century as it is today. This is not to
suggest that the act of stealing from merchants dates only from William
III's time; there is every reason to believe that theft from stalls is as old
as the practice of buying and selling. It is not until more recent times,
however, that information has become available about amateur shoplifters who, arguably, are the most significant thieves.

Walsh considers that the modern shop has its origins in the medieval
fairs which travelled from town to town, and were a source of entertainment as well as of commerce. The medieval market stallholder who
neglected the threat posed by thieves would soon have been put out of
business:

> Gradually, over the years, as street markets became more
> permanent and more organised, there developed a specialised
> method of buying and selling; a ritual in fact, which among
> other things was specifically constructed to reduce the prob-
> ability of successful theft occurring.[14]

For example, the use of a board or counter upon which the trader
placed his goods became customary, with the seller on one side, the
customer on the other and strict conventions about transgressions.
Gradually, fairs became more specialised and developed into markets
associated with particular locations. As the fairs became more permanent,
so too did the merchants' stalls, being made more substantial and
weatherproof. The earliest shops had no glass windows to protect them
from theft and the use of plate glass was not widespread until the late
nineteenth and early twentieth centuries. Windows were made either
by using small panes of clear glass set in lead frames, or by larger but

opaque, sheets set in timber. These windows created a special technology for theft as will be seen below.

The form of theft reflected the organisation of merchandising. Chesney describes the ways in which goods were purloined from the marketplace.

> In poor districts one often found narrow streets almost like oriental bazaars, lined with shops that were little more than open-fronted caves, their stock festooned about the entry or laid on trestles. These conditions naturally encouraged street prowlers. Urchins, naturally, were a particular bane to food sellers, who commonly thrashed out of hand those they caught. On foggy, twilit London evenings, gangs of youths would work their way through a poor shopping district, marking suitable plunder; then one lad would whip away a chosen object and disappear into the murk while others in the gang, idling in the road, acted as 'stalls' to obstruct and misdirect any pursuit.[15]

And Edwards describes the methods used by an early shoplifting gang, tactics which are not unfamiliar today.[16] The gang comprises three people: the 'lift', the 'marker' and the 'santar'. The lift, dressed as a gentleman, is accompanied by the marker and asks to see some merchandise. Eventually he asks for something which entails the shopkeeper turning his back, whereupon he gives some gear to the marker. The marker then signals to the santar who happens to be strolling past the shop front and, on the pretext of discussing some business, the marker hands the stolen goods to him. The santar then effects his escape with the booty without having once entered the shop. In this way, the goods are selected by one, secreted by another, and disposed of by a third. The elegance of this operation is that the shopkeeper is unlikely to know where the goods are, whether they have been stolen or misplaced, and there is nothing to connect them with the lift.

Women enjoyed several advantages when shoplifting. In Victorian times, women wore full length dresses with layers of petticoats and puff sleeves, this made them good 'screens' because of their size and gave them a number of places to secrete goods. There was usually a slit pocket in one side of the dress and the enterprising shoplifter could sew a large pouch under her dress with access through the pocket. Sometimes, the more daring women shoplifters would attach two hooks under their dress and were then able to secrete heavy rolls of material.[17] The woman would be caught *in flagrante* if apprehended, but this was tempered by Victorian morality which required policemen to take the women to the station to be searched by a matron. A policeman had to be sure of his facts when arresting a woman as he was liable for any expenses travelling to the police station if the woman proved to be innocent (or at least, without any goods on her).

Chesney discusses the activities of three 'palmers' which are similar to those mentioned by Edwards.

> The classic procedure was for one palmer to play the
> exacting customer, demanding to see a range of goods,
> determined to match this with that, till the counter was
> piled and jumbled. While she kept the shopman busy,
> hopping up his steps to bring down more samples from
> the shelves behind, her companion idly looked over the
> heap of stuff and at the right moment snaffled some
> expensive, compact item. Meantime the third thief,
> keeping an eye on the rest of the shop, tried to post
> herself so as to shield the first two. After a pull or two
> the principal shopper would become dissatisfied with the
> assistant's efforts, and, leaving the poor man to put his
> stock back in order, walk out of the shop with her friend.
> By this time, the stolen goods might well have been removed
> by the third of the trio.[18]

Gangs of urchins could not pretend to be *bona fide* customers in elegant shops and consequently had recourse to the practice known as 'star-glazing'. A group of boys would peer through the lead pane windows and one would attempt to shatter a small pane without dislodging it. He would then apply a large brown sticking plaster to the broken pane and pull it away with the small piece of glass attached. The thief then reached through the hole and stole some small article which was handed to one of his confederates and all the boys scattered into the crowd. If the shopkeeper were aware of the theft he would not know which boy to pursue.[19]

McIntosh describes four types of criminal organisation – the 'picaresque', 'project', 'business' and 'craft'.[20] The activities of many of the skilled shoplifting gangs of previous centuries exhibit a remarkable correspondence with the 'craft' model.

> The craft organisation, typical of people performing skilled
> but small-scale thefts and confidence tricks, is a small, fairly
> permanent team, usually of two or three men, each of whom
> has a specific role to play in the routinised thefts in which
> the team specialises.[21]

It is arguable that this model persists today. Indeed, as we shall see later, many of the techniques perfected by shoplifting gangs have barely changed over the centuries.

In the last quarter of the nineteenth century, department stores developed to cater for all the needs of a mainly bourgeois clientele under one roof. Walsh believes that the most revolutionary changes in merchandising were the introduction from America of 'voluntary wholesale chains and retail buying groups, and new merchandising techniques, especially important being self-service and self-selection'.[22] For example, in 1950 in England there were fewer than 500 self-service grocery shops, but ten years later this figure had multiplied to 6,500. Customer preference was important in this dramatic development, but the most significant factor was its low cost. Traditional shops relied heavily on a large complement of staff to serve the customer. This was practicable when wages were low, but became uneconomic with the steadily rising cost of labour. Self-service permitted management to reduce the number of staff employed on the shopfloor and increase the size of their premises to make them more cost-effective, the benefits of which could be passed on to the customer. Other shops followed the trend to self-service in order to remain competitive.

The legal context

Until the Theft Act 1968, shoplifting and other related offences were regulated by the Larceny Act 1916, which was a confusing amalgamation of previous legislation. Smith defines a simple larceny as occurring where D by a 'trespass took possession of goods which were in the possession or custody of P without P's consent'.[23] This provided the basis of the common law. Under the 1916 Act, the concept of 'taking' was expanded and consolidated.

Section I(I) of the Theft Act 1968 states that 'A person is guilty of theft if he dishonestly appropriates property belonging to another with the intention of permanently depriving the other of it; and "thief" and "steal" shall be construed accordingly.'[24] An offence of theft, then, comprises four elements which need to be established for a satisfactory prosecution: (a) dishonesty, (b) appropriation, (c) property belonging to another, and (d) the intention of permanently depriving. These can be divided into the *actus reus* and the *mens rea* of theft. Appropriation of property belonging to somebody else constitutes the *actus reus*, or the physical act of the offence, and the *mens rea*, or intention behind the act, consists of the 'dishonest' intention permanently to deprive. Naturally, much fine legal knowledge is expended on these four categories (see, for example, Smith[25] and Griew[26]) defining the exact nature of property, appropriation, etc. It is not necessary to delve too deeply into the legal ramifications here: a simple explanation will be sufficient.

According to Smith the 'most obvious examples of appropriation are the typical thefts where D takes possession of P's property',[27] where property includes money and all other property, real or personal. Section 3 (1) of the 1968 Act states:

> Any assumption by a person of the rights of an owner amounts to an appropriation, and this includes, where he has come by the property (innocently or not) without stealing it, any later assumption of a right to it by keeping or dealing with it as owner.[28]

Where a property is transferred to a person, even though there are questions about the rights of transfer, provided that the person acted in good faith, he is not guilty of theft. Griew warns that

> In an analysis of the basic definition of theft it is inevitable that attention should be given separately to the element of appropriation and to the required intention. But a separation that is convenient for purposes of exposition will be misleading if it suggests a total divorce in reality. Appropriation and intention are inextricably bound together.[29]

The intent aspect is discussed in Section 6 (1) of the Act:

> A person appropriating property belonging to another without meaning the other permanently to lose the thing itself is nevertheless to be regarded as having the intention of permanently depriving the other of it if his intention is to treat the thing as his own to dispose of regardless of the other's rights; and a borrowing or lending of it may amount to so treating it if, but only if, the borrowing or lending is for a period and in circumstances making it equivalent to an outright taking or disposal.[30]

Section 7 sets the maximum penalty (on indictment) for theft to be a period not exceeding ten years' imprisonment.[31]

The significance of these four aspects of theft and their consequences for the organisation of store security will be discussed at some length in the ensuing chapters. It is sufficient here to note that in practice the *mens rea* aspects of theft are as crucial in the day-to-day operations of store detectives as the *actus reus*.

While store personnel are governed in the same way as the police by the provisions of the Theft Act 1968, their powers of arrest are different. Security personnel in England and Wales have no special powers under the law and possess no special legal privileges.[32]

> It follows that security officers in a public place have no powers to stop and arrest any person except those powers enjoyed by any private individual, and store detectives have no power of arrest beyond that enjoyed by any private

individual.[33]

According to Oliver and Wilson, 'an arrest is the taking or restraint of a person from his liberty in order that he shall be forthcoming to answer an alleged crime or offence. It is not necessary to touch or lay hands on a person to arrest him.'[34] Where a suspect is arrested without a warrant he must be informed of the charge and the basis of the arrest, unless it is obvious to all why he is being stopped. For all practical, legal purposes, there is little difference between 'detained' and 'arrested', but the former reminds private citizens of their obligation to hand the detainee to the police at the first opportunity. Once arrested, suspects should not be left alone in case they try to dispose of the stolen goods or harm themselves.

Draper points out that even the police have no general powers to arrest a person on a criminal charge; they are normally obliged to apply for a warrant. A police officer may detain a person without the authority of a warrant if he suspects that a person has committed an arrestable offence, (even if no offence has actually occurred) provided the officer has reasonable grounds for so believing.

> The difference between the powers of the constable and those of the private citizen is, therefore, that in order for the latter to make a lawful arrest on suspicion of guilt, an arrestable offence must actually have been committed — no defence of reasonable belief in its having taken place exists.[35]

However, if the store detective is acting in good faith and without malice, then courts are likely to be sympathetic.

Under the Criminal Law Act 1967, s.3(1): 'Any person may use such force as is reasonable in the circumstances in the *prevention* of crime or in effecting or assisting in the lawful arrest of offenders or suspected offenders or of persons at large.'[36] There appear, however, to be no legal guidelines to what constitutes 'reasonable force', and a common-sense view is generally taken.

If store detectives' powers of arrest are different from those of the police, they are both governed by the Judges' Rules. The first of the Judges' Rules were devised by the King's Bench Division in 1912, revised in 1918 and are now to be found in Appendix A, subsection E of the *Judges' Rules and Administrative Directions to the Police* (1978). These Rules were formulated principally to govern the way the police interview suspects, but under Rule 6 they are extended to private citizens: 'Persons other than police officers charged with the duty of investigating offences or charging offenders shall, as far as may be practicable, comply with these Rules.' The basis of the Rules is contained in the following paragraph.

That it is a fundamental condition of the admissibility
in evidence against any person, equally of any oral
answer given by that person to a question put by a
police officer and of any statement made by that person,
that it shall have been voluntary, in the sense that it has
not been obtained from him by fear of prejudice or hope
of advantage, exercised or held out by a person in authority,
or by oppression .... Non-conformity with these Rules may
render answers and statements liable to be excluded from
evidence in subsequent criminal proceedings.[38]

In questioning suspects then, police and security officers may not use
threats or promises, should allow the suspects to explain their actions
and use language which is clearly understood. Once a police officer has
reasonable grounds to suspect an offence has been committed, he must
caution the suspect and record what is said and at what time. The exact
format of the caution, as described under Rule 2 will be elaborated in
later chapters dealing with arrest and police referral.

The statistical context

In 1982, shoplifting accounted for nearly 14 per cent of offences of
'theft and handling stolen goods', and this offence category accounted
for over half of notifiable offences recorded by the police.[39] In other
words, shoplifting accounts for about 7 per cent of all notifiable offences.
The number of shoplifting offences has been steadily rising, but because
of new counting procedures introduced in 1980 to improve the consistency of police recording of multiple offences, figures from this year
onwards are not directly comparable to previous years. Moreover, since
the Theft Act 1968 offence classes, particularly for theft, are not generally comparable. However, the relationship of shoplifting to indictable/
notifiable offences can be approximated (see Table 4.1).

Table 4.1 shows the number of shoplifting offences recorded by the
police since 1950. It is apparent that a dramatic increase began in the
late 1950s which could be related to the introduction and growth of
self-service shops. Since 1960 the number of offences has more than
doubled every ten years. It is also clear from the table that the total
number of all indictable/notifiable offences has risen dramatically in
the last 30 years. What is apparent, however, is that the number of
shoplifting offences as a percentage of total indictable offences has
increased at a faster rate. In the 1950s shoplifting represented between
4 and 5 per cent of total indictable offences, rising to 6 per cent by the

Table 4.1: Offences of Shoplifting as a Percentage of Indictable/Notifiable Offences [40]

Year	Shoplifting [a] offences	Indictable/notifiable offences (000s)	Percentages
1950	23,013	479.4	4.8
1951	24,652	549.7	4.5
1952	24,128	536.2	4.5
1953	21,736	495.3	4.4
1954	21,941	456.1	4.8
1955	23,308	462.3	5.0
1956	25,756	508.1	5.1
1957	29,690	578.7	5.1
1958	34,194	668.8	5.1
1959	35,123	722.5	4.9
1960	41,535	800.3	5.2
1961	48,466	870.9	5.6
1962	52,954	965.7	5.5
1963	55,906	1,060.1	5.3
1964	60,139	1,171.2	5.1
1965	66,427	1,243.5	5.3
1966	68,288	1,315.7	5.2
1967	70,971	1,316.8	5.4
1968	78,490	1,407.8	5.6
1969	91,169	1,498.7	6.1
1970	101,822	1,568.4	6.5
1971	119,281	1,665.7	7.2
1972	126,844	1,690.2	7.5
1973	130,161	1,657.7	7.9
1974	164,063	1,963.4	8.4
1975	175,552	2,105.6	8.3
1976	180,993	2,135.7	8.5
1977	217,276	2,463.0 [b]	8.8
1978	203,643	2,395.8	8.5
1979	203,122	2,376.7	8.5
1980 [c]	206,175	2,520.6	8.2
1981	225,342	2,794.2	8.1
1982	242,304	3,088.3	7.8

Notes:
a. Until 1968, known as larceny from shops and stalls.
b. From 1977, excluding all offences of criminal damage less than £20.
c. Figures for 1980 onwards are not directly comparable because of different counting rules.

end of the 1960s. During the 1970s and into the 1980s, however, the percentage rose to about 8 per cent, and on occasions, almost to 9 per cent. What is clear is that shoplifting is a significant offence, which has been rising steadily over the decades. Furthermore, its importance among total indictable offences is also increasing.

Because of different counting procedures and changing categories of offences, it is difficult to compare the importance of shoplifting to the 'theft and taking/handling' category. Taking the figures from 1971 onwards, however, it appears that shoplifting is becoming increasingly represented in the offence category of theft and handling. In 1971, it represented 11.9 per cent of all such offences, but by 1976 it had risen to 14 per cent, a position it has maintained since, give or take a few percentage points.[41]

The clear-up rate for shoplifting is very high, as almost by definition, a suspect will have been apprehended for the offence to have been discovered.

> An offence recorded by the police is said to be cleared
> up if a person has been charged, summoned or cautioned
> for the offence, if it is discovered that the offence was
> committed by a child under the age of criminal responsibility,
> if the offence is taken into consideration by the court in
> sentencing an offender, or if a person known or thought to be
> guilty of the offence cannot be prosecuted or cautioned.[42]

In 1982, 88 per cent of offences were cleared up, the other 12 per cent being accounted for by attempts and offences where the suspect escaped.[43] For those police forces conscious of their figures for solving crime, shoplifting offences are very welcome, as they increase the overall clear-up rate for indictable crime dramatically.

Table 4.2 shows the value of the property stolen in 1982. 'Nil' value thefts include attempts where the offender was stopped before leaving the store, and incidents involving articles of unknown value. Some shoplifters, for example, steal plastic carrier bags which can be used at a later date to secrete stolen articles from the same chain of retailers, and it is likely that such items would be registered under 'nil' value. The average theft from shops in 1982 was £32, but this average is increased by the thefts of those few shoplifters who steal extraordinary amounts. Significantly, almost half the offences involved £5 or less and 82 per cent of offences involved the theft of items valued at less than £25. It is apparent then, that the majority of shoplifters are involved with relatively trivial thefts, while a few steal considerable amounts.

Having examined the historical development of shoplifting, its statistical position, and placed it in its legal context, it is now possible to proceed to a discussion of interviews with chief security officers.

Table 4.2: Offences of Shoplifting Recorded by the Police and Value of Property Stolen, 1982 [44]

Value of goods taken	Nil [1]	under £5	£5 & under £25	£25 & under £100	£100 & under £500	£500 & under £1,000	£1,000 & under £5,000	£5,000 & under £10,000	£10,000 & under £50,000	£50,000 & over	Value Stolen
Number of offences	5,439	111,751	81,702	30,267	10,737	1,802	554	34	13	5	Offences

Total = 242,304

1 Most of these offences will be attempts, but some offences of unknown value may be included.

Notes

1. Zola, E. *L'Assomoir* (Harmondsworth: Penguin Books, 1974; First published 1876), p. 296 .
2. Edwards, L.E., *Shoplifting and Shrinkage Protection for Stores* (Illinois: Charles C. Thomas, 1958), p. 4.
3. Walsh, D.P., *Shoplifting. Controlling a Major Crime* (London: Macmillan, 1978), p. 23.
4. *Oxford English Dictionary* (Oxford University Press, 1971; compact edition).
5. Ibid.
6. Walsh, *op. cit.*, p. 23.
7. Ibid. p. 23.
8. Edwards, *op. cit.*,
9. Ibid., p. 8.
10. Ibid., p. 5.
11. Klockars, C.B., *The Professional Fence* (London: Tavistock, 1974), pp. 16–17.
12. Ibid., p. 23.
13. Ibid., p. 26.
14. Walsh, *op. cit.*, p. 1.
15. Chesney, K., *The Victorian Underworld* (Harmondsworth: Pelican Books, 1970); p. 155.
16. Edwards, *op. cit.*, p. 4.
17. Cf. ibid., p. 7, and Chesney, *op. cit.*, p. 154.
18. Chesney, *op. cit.*, p. 157.
19. Ibid., p. 156.
20. McIntosh, M., *The Organisation of Crime* (London: Macmillan, 1975), p. 28.
21. Ibid., p. 28.
22. Walsh, *op. cit.*, p. 6.
23. Smith, J.C., *The Law of Theft* (London: Butterworth, 1979; 4th edn), p. 5.
24. Home Office, *Theft Act* (London: HMSO, 1968), p. 1.
25. Smith, *op. cit.*,
26. Griew, E., *The Theft Acts 1968 and 1978* (London: Sweet & Maxwell, 1978; 3rd edn).
27. Smith, *op. cit.*, p. 23.
28. Home Office, *op. cit.*, p. 2.
29. Griew, *op. cit.*, p. 27.
30. Home Office, *op. cit.*, p. 4.
31. Ibid., p. 4.
32. The exception is section 19 of the Protection of Aircraft Act 1973, by which the Trade Secretary can confer special powers

on airport managers and others by virtue of a direction under section 10. As yet, however, this power has not been used.

33. Home Office, *The Private Security Industry. A Discussion Paper* (London: HMSO, 1979) p. 8.
34. Oliver, E. and Wilson, J., *Practical Security in Commerce and Industry* (Epping: Gower Press, 1978; 3rd edn), p. 93.
35. Draper, H., *Private Police* (Harmondsworth: Penguin Books, 1978), p. 85.
36. Oliver and Wilson, *op. cit.*, p. 96.
37. Home Office, *Judges' Rules and Administrative Directions to the Police.* H.O. Circular No. 89 (London: HMSO, 1978), p. 8.
38. Ibid., p. 6.
39. Home Office, *Criminal Statistics (England and Wales)* (London HMSO, 1982; presented in 1983).
40. Ibid., and preceding issues of *Criminal Statistics.*
41. The percentage of shoplifting to 'theft and handling' offences for the years 1971 to 1982 is as follows:

1971	–	11.9%	1977 – 14.6%	
1972	–	12.6%	1978 – 14.1%	
1973	–	13.0%	1979 – 14.3%	
1974	–	13.8%	1980 – 14.0%	
1975	–	13.8%	1981 – 14.0%	
1976	–	14.0%	1982 – 13.8%	

Source: see note 39.

42. Ibid., p. 38.
43. Ibid.
44. Ibid.

5 Interviews with chief security officers

> Many stores display big signs reading 'Shoplifters Will Be
> Prosecuted'. This has its drawbacks, though. The bookstore
> at Texas Technology College, Lubbock, Tex., put up a
> dozen such signs only to have five stolen within 24 hours.[1]

Chapter 3 described how the chief security officers and their managers
were approached and interviewed. This chapter details the results of
those interviews. In total, interviews were completed with the representatives of 25 major retailers. Fifteen of these were chain stores, ranging
from supermarkets and clothes shops to department stores. The other
ten retailers were either single department stores or stores which, though
part of a chain, made their own security arrangements. The latter tended
to be the large metropolitan branches. The interviews were generally
conducted with CSOs, or with a director or manager responsible for
overall security. Occasionally, a representative from the management
side gave a joint interview with the CSO.

The majority of chain stores were centrally administered from a head
office, where there was a CSO with overall responsibility for security.
A number of the stores were organised regionally, however, and were
administered by a CSO assisted by regional security officers. Often,
the CSO was also responsible for a region, with his own team of store
detectives. Occasionally, the CSO was not directly involved with everyday security activities and concentrated instead on managerial policy
and decision-making. A random sample of 100 small local shops were

also contacted and interviewed briefly. These shops were usually run by one or two people and could be classified as family businesses. From the interviews, it emerged that small shopkeepers considered shoplifting to be a problem and that the main culprits were believed to be children. Because of the obvious problems involved in apprehending and detaining a suspect when only one person was working in the shop, the police were rarely called. The small shopkeeper controlled shoplifting by such informal methods as threats, warnings and the occasional 'smack round the ear'. Very few official shoplifters were generated by the activities of small shopkeepers and police involvement tended to be *ad hoc* and largely fortuitous. Small shopkeepers could not afford the services of store detectives, but in common with the larger retailers, they were able to purchase some of the variety of security devices available to the trade. Before discussing the role of store detectives in larger retailers (the data provided from the main sample of interviews), it will be apposite to analyse the part security hardware plays for all retailers in controlling shoplifting, and shrinkage in general.

Security devices

The range of security devices available to retailers to combat theft is extensive. Some devices concentrate specifically on deterring or apprehending the shoplifter; others are more useful for preventing staff or delivery thefts. Many can be used in either situation and are effective in reducing shrinkage generally. A very few of the retailers abnegated the use of conspicuous security devices in the belief that customers might find them offensive. This, however, was a minority view. Nearly all of the retailers, whether large department stores, or one-man businesses used security mirrors, often in conjunction with signs warning that shoplifting was theft and that thieves would be prosecuted. In the larger retailers, signs warned of the presence of patrolling store detectives. Increasingly, the euphemism of 'shoplifting' is being replaced by the harsher term of 'theft' in these notices. Thorsen writes that 'the convex detection mirror is often a first line of defence against shoplifting and pilferage'.[2] The Home Office Working Party also puts the case for security mirrors:

> The use of mirrors as part of the shop's decor, or convex
> mirrors which facilitate the surveillance of blind corners
> are all devices which make it plain to the customer that he
> may be watched. They can also be used to keep entrances
> to stock rooms, receiving bays and fitting rooms under
> observation. They may have a deterrent effect particularly
> if seen to be used by staff. It should be remembered, however,

that mirrors could also be used by the experienced shoplifter who could know when he is not under observation. They are relatively cheap and even in a small shop assist staff to keep every area of the shop under observation. In supermarkets and self-service stores with a number of gangways between display units, they can be valuable in eliminating blind spots. But they can be effective only if staff are available to use them and are trained in the drill they should follow when they observe suspicious behaviour. [3]

A few CSOs reinforced the view that there were dangers with mirrors as thieves could use them too, but the general consensus was that 'They can't do any harm and they might do some good.'

Thorsen describes another security device, which, because of its cost, is restricted to the larger stores: the closed circuit television camera, or CCTV. This can be of the 'sputnik' design, with a number of lenses radiating from a single housing or, more frequently, simple television cameras positioned to provide the greatest viewing area. Television cameras permit concealed observers to see extensive parts of their stores quickly. They can also be linked with video-recorders to provide tapes of specific incidents. There are difficulties in their operation, however. As Thorsen says, some form of communication between the person watching the display unit of the camera and the store detective on the shopfloor is necessary. [4] Once again, the Home Office Working Party is informative on this issue:

Surveillance devices are an effective deterrent only where they are seen by the customer to be responsible for detection. On their own they can take no action against the thief and even as aids to arrest they need to be used with caution. If a theft is observed through the use of surveillance equipment, and this is particularly true of CCTV, it is usually necessary for the observer to remove his attention from the equipment whilst he physically approaches the suspect. This leaves an interval during which the suspect is not under surveillance and in which he may dispose of the goods seen to be taken, perhaps by depositing them in another part of the shop or by passing them to an accomplice. This puts the shop at risk of being the subject of an action for wrongful arrest. [5]

The person watching the television screen may have the means of communicating a description of a suspect to a store detective without leaving the monitoring screen. But this too has its difficulties, as the

Home Office Report points out:

> The use of CCTV in a large crowded store also presents the difficulty of identifying, in the shopping area itself, the person whose behaviour has been observed on the monitor screen. In the interval between being observed on the monitor screen and being approached in the shop the suspect may well have moved from one part of the shop to another .... To sum up, the detection value of conventional CCTV is negligible but it may be of value as a deterrent. Its deterrent effect may also be greater on certain age groups such as the old or very young.[6]

The use of CCTV was a controversial issue among the stores surveyed. Its disadvantages were highlighted: it was expensive to install; it required a number of people to monitor the screens in rotation; and there were difficulties in communication between the person monitoring and the store detective. As yet, video-recordings have not been widely used as evidence.

Video-recordings have been used to persuade suspects to plead guilty, as in a case reported in *The Guardian*,

> A video-recording was yesterday the instrument of shop-lifting convictions in a London court. It was stated at Knightsbridge Crown Court that a S's store detective, Mr. B.L., saw Brian K, aged 41, and his wife, Margaret, packing ladies silk suits into a carrier-bag on his security monitor. He recorded their actions, but the couple vanished with nearly £600 worth of goods before he could stop them. A week later he spotted the couple in the store again. This time he confronted them and when told of the film they confessed ....
>
> After the hearing a S's spokesman said: 'This is the first time a video-recording has been used to convict shoplifters in a London court.'[7]

However, several years earlier video-recordings had been used as evidence at Liverpool juvenile court:

> Three youths entered the small electrical department in the basement of L's — Liverpool on Saturday, 3 January 1976. Their actions aroused the suspicions of the Chief Security Officer and he video-recorded subsequent activity on Photo-Scan equipment. The recording showed that the youths had removed two hair dryers from behind a counter and placed them on top. They then went away and changed clothing with each other (this was apparently because they

were aware that Photo-Scan cameras were in use and reckoned that the change would confuse any watcher into believing that they were new arrivals in the store!). They then returned to the counter and slipped the hair dryers under their clothing. They left the sales area before the security staff could apprehend them. There was no corroborative evidence from the sales staff and the exact nature of the items stolen was not known. On the following Monday they were recognised when they returned to the store. They were detained and the police were called. They denied committing any shop theft and even when shown the recording of them still stuck to their story. The police searched their homes, but did not recover the stolen goods. The court proceedings on 24 July 1976 were adjourned because Counsel's advice was wanted before the defence would allow the video-recording to be admitted in evidence. At a summary trial at Liverpool Juvenile Court on 10 September 1976, the youths pleaded 'not guilty'. The video-recording was submitted and accepted as evidence. The proceedings lasted two hours and all three were found guilty. This was the first occasion that a video-recording had been accepted at a court in Liverpool, and to the best of our knowledge, the first time that it had even been accepted in this country as evidence of shop theft.[8]

About a quarter of the retailers in the sample used CCTVs in their larger outlets. Significantly, three of the retailers had at one stage used CCTVs but had had them removed in the belief that they were 'useless'. Another retailer said that he would discontinue using cameras but felt that it would be seen as an invitation for shoplifters to return. This store only turned on the television monitors when interviewing suspects to promote the store's reputation for vigilance. At other times the monitors were left off. If the general deterrent effect of CCTVs caused some controversy, it was agreed that they could be useful for targeting specific problem areas, such as high-value gondolas, delivery ramps, vaults and suspected staff.

Another recent innovation in store security has been the introduction of electronic tagging of merchandise. Thorsen describes how this system operates:

The basic principle is that store property may be 'tagged' with a substance, or circuitry, that elicits a response from a matching sensor when the two get within specified range of each other ... any individual departing such an area with store property in his or her possession will set off an alarm. When the merchandise is paid for, and is no longer the property of the store, the electronic device identifying the item by means of the alarm response is removed or deactivated.[9]

Barbara advocates the use of this system, and believes it was responsible for a 25 per cent reduction in shrinkage in his store, and that, additionally, twice as many dishonest staff were arrested as the previous year.[10] Although tagging individual items is time-consuming, the advantage of the system is that the number of store detectives can be reduced dramatically. The Home Office Working Party points out the advantages and disadvantages of this method of shrinkage control.

> It should be remembered that activation of the device may not, of itself, constitute evidence of theft. It is therefore important to ensure that, at the time goods are paid for, they are wrapped and a receipt is given. In using this system care must be taken not to accuse the suspect until confirmation has been received by asking him to retrace his steps, passing again through the detector field.[11]

One of the disadvantages mentioned in the report is the failure by staff to remove or desensitise the tag once the item has been sold. This would, at best, result in embarrassing confrontations with honest customers, or, at worst, suits for false arrest. In addition, if a shop concentrates its security resources at the exit, suspicious activities in the shop itself may be missed. Experienced thieves will take advantage of this and remove the tags in the knowledge that they can then leave with the articles secreted without triggering the alarm. Retailers guard against this by making it difficult to remove the tagging devices without destroying the article or arousing suspicion.

In the stores surveyed, two department stores used tagging devices in discrete areas, but did not rely on them exclusively; and three shops employed no store detectives, relying on tagging devices as their only protection against theft. These three shops were all boutiques with only one or two exits. It appears that tagging devices are particularly suitable for this type of shop. Similar security arrangements have been noted in record shops where magnetic tags are placed inside the record cover and sealed with plastic film, to be removed at the cashpoint/exit.

It appears that the magnetic sensitising system has a number of advantages over traditional security methods, but there are also disadvantages. At the moment, it is relatively easy and cost-effective to tag expensive items such as clothes and records, but more difficult and expensive to sensitise low-cost items such as groceries. A more serious problem rests in the size and layout of department stores. Such shops are intended to attract large numbers of customers and necessarily need a number of wide entrances to facilitate the flow of shoppers (and to satisfy safety and fire regulations). Tagging systems are not as effective where there are many customers bustling through a wide entrance. It is difficult to identify the culprit who has triggered the alarm in such situations, and the dangers of stopping the wrong person are obvious. It seems that, for the moment, tagging devices are best suited to smaller retailers with only a few access points. As one respondent phrased it, 'We tried 'X' (brand name for tagging devices, but it was expensive and best for small shops with one door.'

Another recent innovation has been the introduction of Early Warning Systems. Neighbouring shops in a particular street or precinct warn each other when troubled by known or suspected shoplifters, particularly professionals. This scheme is relatively quick, needing only one or two calls by phone or two-way radio to adjacent shops. Provided it is not overloaded with a surfeit of information, it is a useful tactic against the depredations of experienced thieves. Many of the retailers in the sample already participated in Early Warning Systems and found them useful. Others were planning to join.

The variety of security devices available to retailers is extensive. Apart from the more visible devices discussed above, many stores also used loop-alarm systems, which thread through such items as fur coats and radios; two-way mirrors; multiple cables; security displays; and pressure pads. Although these devices are important in securing valuable items, they are not used to protect the bulk of merchandise available and, consequently, they do not figure much in the day-to-day control of shoplifting.

The increasing use of technological devices to combat theft in shops has come to official notice. A discussion paper on *The Private Security Industry* suggested that, 'The use of mirrors, cameras and plain-clothes staff can, however, arouse concern amongst the innocent as well as amongst those who would prefer their criminal activities not to be observed.'[12] The paper noted that the *Younger Committee on Privacy* (para. 511) was aware of concern over the use of surveillance devices, but considered that, 'While there is room for the development of good practice in the use of equipment for crime prevention it is difficult to see how formal control over surveillance devices could be confined to their use for that purpose.'[13] In their evidence to the Home Office Working Party, the Consumer's Association suggested that few complaints arose out of the use of security devices.[14] Under the guidance of the author, Hastings conducted a simple survey to gauge attitudes to security devices in stores.[15] In the survey, 240 respondents were asked whether they were aware of security devices and whether they found them 'off-putting'. The results are presented in Table 5.1.

It is apparent from the table that customers are highly aware of CCTV

Table 5.1: Awareness of and Reactions to Security Devices

| Question: | 1. | Have you ever noticed any anti-shoplifting devices? |
| | 2. | Do you find these off-putting? |

	Ever noticed	Find off-putting
Cameras/CCTV	89%	15%
Notices	90%	5%
Tagging devices	59%	4%
Mirrors	68%	9%
Detectives	42%	7%
Others	8%	1%

and signs, and to a lesser extent, mirrors and tagging devices. There seems to be little general opposition to most forms of security device. The only security device which could be said to arouse any concern was CCTV, perhaps because it reminds people they are under observation and therefore potential suspects. For the rest, it appears that public anxiety (as opposed to the milder 'find off-putting') is low.

Store detectives

Two of the chains of retailers in the sample employed store detectives from private security organisations and consequently did not have a corresponding security structure for security personnel. Four other retail groups did not use store detectives, three relying on magnetic tagging devices and one relying on store assistants and managers as protection. Security responsibilities for these six retailers were thus either devolved to an outside organisation with its own bureaucratic structure, or were subsumed under other managerial functions. All other retail chains employed their own store detectives who were treated in the same way as other personnel. This section examines the organisation and training of those store detectives.

All the CSOs who were interviewed were male and only a few of their deputies were females. Similarly, nearly all of the regional security officers were male. By contrast, the majority of store detectives were female; indeed many stores employed only female store detectives; while none employed men only. The predominance of women store detectives partly reflected the opinions of management that women were considered to make better store detectives, — an assumption based on stereotypical notions about the inherent curiosity of women. The number of female store detectives was also explained in part by the nature of the retailer's business and the general pattern of shopping in Britain. It was believed that there were few places where women shoppers would be noticeable, whereas the variety of mechandise that men could purchase was restricted by social *mores.* Where the customers were predominantly female, the store detectives were almost exclusively women. Where the customers were both male and female there was more likelihood of male store detectives. Underlying the preference for female store detectives was the generally low wage structure prevalent in the retailing industry which might have resulted in a self-fulfilling selection bias.

Many of the stores preferred to employ ex-police officers as store detectives as they were believed to be responsible, self-reliant, with a firm knowledge of the law and good contacts with the police force. On the other hand, many stores were equally determined not to employ ex-police officers as it was felt that the experience of police authority made them unsuitable for store detective work, the danger being that ex-police officers might rely on powers they had previously exercised but were not now applicable. Many stores had no firm preferences for their store detectives' background however, and a large number of security personnel were sales assistants 'who had worked their way up'.

Store detectives could be 'in house' (permanently stationed in one shop), peripatetic, or a combination of the two. In the larger stores there was always a permanent store detective presence, which ranged from a sole operative to as many as 20–25 personnel. At the other extreme were the peripatetic store detectives who were often employed by chains of small shops. To maximise cost-effectiveness, store detectives would travel from shop to shop, spending as little as one or two hours, and up to one or two days, in each shop. In between these two types of store detectives were the mobile store detectives, often under the supervision of a regional security officer, who would act as an élite 'task-force', concentrating on specific problem stores for a short while before moving on to the next.

Many of the retailers employed uniformed security staff, who were almost without exception male. The duties of such staff included a large anti-shoplifting aspect, but complemented the work of store detectives rather than competed with it. For example, male uniformed personnel were often used to support the store detective during an arrest, to reduce the risk of physical violence. Uniformed security officers were often positioned at the main entrances of the stores where they could prevent such 'undesirable elements' as drunks, vagrants and rowdy gangs from entering. They were also used for a variety of other tasks, including escorting cash, guarding suspects and watching deliveries; and where a security presence was felt advantageous but did not merit the full-time attention of store detectives, or indeed, where the latter might be inappropriate.

Store detectives, whose main responsibility was the control of shop-lifting and, to a lesser extent, employee theft, were all in plain clothes. The Home Office report writes about the ethics of using plain clothes detectives:

> We have considered the suggestion that the deterrent
> effect of store detectives would be increased if they all
> wore an identifiable uniform. We are agreed that the
> presence of uniformed detectives, or indeed of any identi-
> fiable shop staff, deter the opportunist shoplifter or the
> absentminded, but we are of the opinion that their use
> can be of assistance to the professional thief. In order to
> detect offenders, as well as deter them, it is essential to
> use plain clothes detectives, either alone or with uniform-
> ed staff at the same time. We see nothing unethical about
> the use of plain clothes detectives. Their use by the police
> has long been accepted by the public, and the detection of
> crime would be seriously hampered without them.[16]

The use of plain clothes store detectives was also considered to have a strong deterrent effect, particularly in conjunction with signs warning of their presence. With uniformed security guards, potential shoplifters might wait until they were unobserved before stealing; with plain clothes detectives, however, they could never be sure that they were unobserved. By wearing plain clothes, the store detective becomes anonymous: she could be any shopper, and correspondingly, any shopper could be a store detective — a daunting prospect for many potential shoplifters. Ironically, in many small shops where signs warn of store detective activity, security staff may operate for as little as one hour per week, but engender insecurity in the casual shoplifter and provide a constant deterrent effect. No uniformed guard could foster such unease.

The laws concerning theft and the Judges' Rules, controlling powers of arrest and interrogation were discussed in Chapter 4. From this, it was apparent that there was a need for detailed training before store detectives operated by themselves and arrested suspects. As with any good police work, the skills of the efficient store detective cannot be learned solely in the classroom but must come from experience on the shopfloor. Store detectives' training, then, can be divided into the formal instruction during which they learn the laws relating to theft, arrest, etc., and the informal education where they learn how best to make themselves inconspicuous, how to make problem-free arrests, and how to conduct interviews. In addition, they will have to learn how to present evidence in court, how to take notes for evidence, and how to minimise the risks of false arrest. Obviously, practical experience will modify and elaborate abstract regulations, the one informing the other. Becoming a 'good' store detective, able to apprehend suspects and secure prosecutions with a minimum of embarrassment to the store, is not a straightforward process, therefore, not surprisingly, the extent of training for store detectives and sales personnel varied from retailer to retailer, often but not solely depending on the size of the organisation. The attitude and general ideology of the chain also appeared to be significant in the emphasis it placed on security education. At one extreme was the chain of shops where instructions on how to manage shoplifters were almost non-existent. Then there were those retailers who relied solely on electronic tagging devices where assistants had a short period of training before watching exits and waiting for the alarm to sound. The training here was often the responsibility of the individual manager or manageress of the shop. Agency detectives had a common core instruction programme, which usually consisted of one week's theoretical lessons followed by three weeks' practical training on the shopfloor under the supervision of an experienced store detective. Several stores sent their trainee detectives to courses run by the International Professional Security Association (IPSA), and then placed them under the tutelage of a senior store detective for a number of weeks. The large retail chain stores were able to organise their own in-house training programmes. The best of these consisted of a three-week formal course, followed by 3—6 months on the shopfloor under the supervision of an experienced store detective. The average time for this type of training varied from 1 to 3 weeks of formal instruction, supplemented with films, demonstrations and seminars, after which came 1—3 months' experience on the shopfloor under supervision. In one large department store the training for store detectives consisted solely of reading an instruction manual and accompanying experienced personnel; and in a chain of small shops, training was mostly effected on the shopfloor, augmented with two or three days under the tutelage of the assistant chief security officer.

The extent of store detectives' training, then, varied considerably from retailer to retailer. In some shops it could be as little as a couple of days' informal practice on the shopfloor, in others, informal and formal instruction could last up to three months. The instruction did appear to be more extensive than that reported by May, however.[17]

The training given to sales staff and managers was also discussed at the interviews. During their induction to the store, assistants were usually given a brief outline of security problems covering the legal position and how to spot suspect persons. The first line of defence advocated was to ask the customer if they needed assistance as this was seen as good commercial policy, and made potential shoplifters aware that they were under observation. If sales staff believed a person to be shoplifting they were generally instructed to inform the store detective if available, otherwise to contact the manager or person delegated to deal with shoplifters. Most stores were reluctant to allow sales assistants to become involved in arresting shoplifters: it was generally considered that assistants did not have the training to arrest shoplifters, and there was therefore a high risk of false arrest or violence. The reluctance to involve sales assistants in controlling shoplifters other than as sentinels for suspicious behaviour is confirmed by May,[18] and also by Bennett: 'Generally, the assistants were not trained to prevent shoplifting, under-staffing and overwork made this even more difficult.'[19]

The lack of training for some store detectives has occasionally caused public disquiet, as has the infrequent incident of corruption. The need for licensing or registering store detectives is periodically mooted. It is difficult, however, to look at store detectives in isolation from the rest of the security industry. The need for more rigorous control of all aspects of the industry has often been recognised and particularly disquietening is the perceived threat of people with criminal convictions in positions of trust. The various ramifications of licensing and registration of the security industry as a whole are weighed in a Home Office Discussion Paper,[20] but it appears that no immediate action is countenanced. It is even more unlikely that measures will be introduced for the control of store detectives alone. Nevertheless, the disparities evident in the training of store detectives give cause for some concern. For most retailers, the training of their security staff is sufficient and competent; for some, it is excellent. There are a number of store detectives, however, who are operating with little instruction and with these in mind, it would be gratifying to know that there was a standard, minimum period of training necessary before practising as a store detective.

Chief security officers were asked about the rules they laid down for apprehending shoplifters and the records kept on the number of apprehensions made during the previous year. While they tended to be remarkably consistent on the former, the variation in detail for the latter was immediately apparent, although again, the vagueness in replies does not appear to be as marked as in May's research.

The first requirement mentioned by the security officers was that the whole incident had to be seen before the suspect was apprehended. This meant that the store detective had to watch the suspect approach the counter (or gondola), take an article and secrete it. It was stressed that the customer now had to be observed continuously and uninterruptedly until leaving the shop. The suspect was usually allowed to take one or two steps outside the shop to prevent claiming that they still intended to pay. The store detective next identified herself, sometimes with the assistance of an identity card.

Differences in company policies began to emerge at this stage. Some store detectives were instructed not to touch the suspect, although most were allowed to touch the arm with their fingers or hold the suspect's elbow with their hand. Regulations on what to do if the suspect struggled varied considerably. Some store detectives were allowed to make the apprehension, 'using reasonable force'. Others were restrained from becoming involved in public altercations. Violence in the street, it was believed, would be bad publicity for the store and might result in the store detective becoming injured and inactive for several weeks. When store detectives were told not to become involved in fights they were often advised to inform the suspect that they would follow them until a police officer could perform the arrest. This threat was sometimes sufficient to persuade aggressive suspects to return to the shop.

The wording advocated by the retailers in making the accusation against the suspects again varied. Few stores advised a direct accusation of theft as this could force the suspect into a confrontation and exacerbate the consequences of false arrest. Often, a fairly bland statement, such as, 'I have reason to believe you have X on your person for which you have not paid. Would you come back to the manager's office where we can sort it out?', was advised. Even more circumspect was the gentle, 'There seems to be a problem with some of your goods. Would you come back to check it?' All CSOs believed that an experienced store detective would succeed in persuading a suspect to return peacefully in 95 per cent of cases. However, most were also of the opinion that the use of force to resist arrest was increasing.

All the CSOs were aware of the problems that could result from false arrests and communicated these fears to their staff. They considered that if the detectives followed instructions exactly then such cases were unlikely. In addition, the CSOs believed that if the store detective acted politely and reasonably throughout the incident then it was sometimes possible to extricate themselves without too much embarrassment. A small number of retailers admitted to having been sued in the courts 'sometime in the past' (and usually before the CSO took up his post), and a few had settled out of court. Although there was a tendency for retailers to minimise the number of actions taken against them for false arrest, the number of actual cases appears to be very small, and it is doubtful if there are people in the UK who deliberately act suspiciously in order to sue the retailer for false arrest, as is suspected in the USA.

Arresting shoplifters is not the only way of dealing with them, however, and the CSOs were questioned on alternatives to apprehension. In his study, May argued that children were viewed as disruptive threats to sound business, and were consequently dealt with differently from other potential shoplifters: 'Children and teenagers use shops other than as retailers, e.g., as meeting places or amusement centres. Not only are they disruptive to store assistants, security personnel, etc., but they may put off other more serious shoppers.'[21] Children can be excluded from the shop but, as May points out,

> a policy of exclusion, however, runs so clearly counter to some of the fundamental principles of modern retailing. Stores are anxious in the first place to get as many people as possible on the premises, not to erect obstacles in their way. So even with juveniles it is a policy likely to be pursued only fitfully and with discretion.[22]

The chief security officers were reluctant to operate a whole-hearted policy of banning individuals from their stores. Apprehended shoplifters were often warned never to return, but security personnel did not have the resources to enforce the ban. However, store detectives believed that they could remember 'faces', and this may have been a sufficient threat to restrict banned people from their stores. Many of the CSOs reinforced May's point about children. As one of them put it, 'children are a damned nuisance'. Gangs of children and teenagers were seen as especially troublesome. Some shops banned children during school hours, others excluded children from particular schools. On other occasions groups of children were told to be quiet and/or escorted from the shop. As mentioned above, uniformed security guards have a part to play here. Because children are a low status group, store detectives and uniformed personnel were able to control them without recourse to arrest. Indeed, the point was made several times that children and teenagers were problems not because they were potential shoplifters, but because they disrupted the orderly processes of modern marketing. Likewise, drunks and vagrants were frequently cited as the type of person who would be watched and escorted from the shop.

From the data provided in the interviews, it became apparent that security personnel controlled shoplifting largely by a policy of apprehension, with certain categories being treated as exceptions. The next chapter demonstrates that store detectives in practice have a variety of methods for controlling shoplifting that fall short of apprehension. The number of people apprehended for the previous year was also elicited and the results, where available, are produced below. Only one store declined to provide statistics, the others were either unable to do so, or declared that they could only give rough estimates.

Table 5.2:   Number of Suspects Apprehended Annually

	Type of shop	Numbers apprehended
1.	Large national chain of clothes shops	1,591
2.	National chain of medium/small shops	Unknown
3.	National chain of medium shops	400–500
4.	National chain of newsagents	1,300 approx.
5.	Individual department store	1,200 "
6.	Individual department store	500 "
7.	Individual department store	323
8.	National chain of department stores	6,100 "
9.	Individual department store	700–1,000
10.	National chain of supermarkets	13,500 "
11.	National chain of supermarkets	7,000 "
12.	Individual department store	250 "
13.	National chain general merchandise department store	1,000 "
14.	One chain of medium shops	Unknown

It is apparent that only a few of the retailers kept precise records on the number of apprehensions that were made. Most of the totals were approximations, and were rounded up. These figures will be repeated in the next section together with the percentage referred to the police. Before discussing these figures, however, it is necessary to examine the regulations covering the interview of suspects and the factors considered when calling the police.

Interview and disposal

May believes that store detectives have a dual accountability, — first to the manager of the particular store in which they work and, secondly, to their CSO located at head office.[23] The relationship between store detective and manager divided many of the stores surveyed. With some retailers, the store detective had a large degree of autonomy in determining the disposal of shoplifters. Indeed, for some retailers, management had no involvement whatsoever in the apprehension, interview and disposal process, the store detective making all the decisions. On the other hand, in many stores, the store detective's authority was more formally circumscribed and she was often responsible to the manager. As one chief security officer declared, 'It's good P.R. to make the store detective responsible to the manager.' For these retailers, the manager or deputised person was closely involved in the interview process and perhaps even in the apprehension process.

Before the interview began, however, all the chief security officers emphasised the need to take the suspect to a private place. In the larger stores, there were often specially designated security rooms, usually next to the security staff's office. In the smaller shops, the interview might be conducted in the manager's office or just a small corner of the storeroom. The stress on privacy for the interview resulted from a desire to avoid public confrontations, to protect the customer, and to increase control over the situation.

The usual procedure once in the interview room was for the manager or senior store detective to identify themselves and inform the detainee that they were suspected of theft. Often, the store detective would have already familiarised the manager with the details of the case. The suspect was then asked to listen to what the store detective had to say, and the details of the suspected theft were read out. The suspect was then given an opportunity to reply. Provided that the grounds for arrest were satisfactory, and unless the situation fell into the discretionary categories discussed below, the manager or store detective informed the suspect that the police would be called. The dialogue during these interviews, which is discussed in Chapter 6, was often far more elaborate than the brief rules produced by the CSOs, but it was stressed that if the police were not to be called, the suspect would be warned and often asked to sign some form of disclaimer.

The boundaries for discretion reported in the interviews varied in application from retailer to retailer, but there were a number of common categories. As the Home Office Working Party declares:

> From the evidence supplied by retailers, it is apparent
> that there are considerable variations in their policies
> with regard to the prosecution of detected offenders ....
> Among those retailers who claim to prosecute in every
> case many admit to making exceptions on cases where
> they feel the circumstances call for compassionate
> treatment. In particular, children, pregnant women and
> the aged are mentioned as being treated as special cases.
> All are agreed on one factor necessary for prosecution —
> the existence of satisfactory evidence.[24]

The report goes on to recommend that all detected offences, including those by staff, should be referred to the police as it was felt that the police were in the best position to decide whether or not to prosecute. However, as is demonstrated in Table 5.3, many stores still operated with discretionary policies, and for some retailers it is apparent that the majority of apprehended shoplifters are treated leniently and not referred to the police.

The basis for the lenient treatment of shoplifters varied between the stores. At one extreme, there was one department store which followed the advice of the Working Party and referred all apprehended persons to the police. At the other there were those retailers who followed such vague guidelines as 'We use our common sense', or 'Every case is treated on its individual merits'. Most stores, however, were favourably disposed to the familiar categories of children, pregnant women, pensioners and the mentally or physically disturbed (see Chapter 2). A few retailers operated with cash limits — for example, they would not call the police for sums involving less than £1. In addition, referral guidelines were said to be waived when the security personnel were under pressure as, for example, at sale times and during the pre-Christmas rush. One retailer reported that during the previous summer they were obliged to release anybody stealing less than £25 as their resources were so stretched.

During the time spent observing store detectives it became obvious that the formal rules for apprehension and police referral were flexible guidelines, and that the store detectives used many tactics to control shoplifting. In subsequent chapters, therefore, the police referral rates reported in the interviews will be interpreted in light of data revealed

Table 5.3: Apprehensions and Referral Rates for Suspects

	Type of shop/chain	Numbers apprehended	Percentage referred to police
1.	Large national chain of clothes shops	1,591	100%
2.	National chain of medium shops	Unknown	100%
3.	National chain of medium shops	400–500	100%
4.	National chain of newsagents	1,300 approx.	100%
5.	Individual department store	1,200 approx.	almost 100%
6.	Individual department store	500 approx.	98%
7.	Individual department store	323	83%
8.	National chain of department stores	6,100 approx.	80%
9.	Individual department store	700–1,000	75%
10.	National chain of supermarkets	13,500 approx.	60%–66%
11.	National chain of supermarkets	7,000 approx.	40%
12.	Individual department store	250 approx.	33%–50%
13.	National chain of general merchandise stores	1,000 approx.	25%–50%
14.	One chain of medium shops	Unknown	33%

by the everyday operations of store detectives. Before examining this information, however, it will be informative to discuss the part of the interview which dealt with employee theft and its contribution to shrinkage.

Distinction between losses

Once all the significant topics concerning shoplifting had been discussed and rapport had been established, the focus of the interview turned to employee theft. This controversial topic was deliberately raised towards the end of the interview to ensure that (a) all the data on the relatively non-controversial subject of shoplifting had been elicited without being placed in jeopardy, and (b) the respondent would be more likely to be forthcoming after rapport had been established with the interviewer. Chapter 2 discussed whether it was possible to distinguish between theft by customer and theft by employee, and concluded that unless the culprit was caught in the act, it was almost impossible to do so. The interviewees were probed on this question to see if they were at variance with other reported sources.

The majority of the retailers in the survey believed that it was not possible to distinguish precisely and rigorously between losses due to shoplifting and losses due to employee theft. But opinions were freely expressed. Although many more shoplifters were caught, it was generally believed that employees stole more. Some chief security officers considered that shoplifting's contribution to losses by theft was as low as 20–30 per cent, while others believed it was as high as 80 per cent. Estimates varied with the size of the store, the type of merchandise sold, the wages paid, the reputation of the store, and the calibre of staff it attracted. The majority of security officers were of the opinion that shoplifting and employee theft were approximately equal with small variations either way.

All security officers confirmed that it was much more difficult to catch employees stealing than shoplifters. It was pointed out that staff had a greater opportunity to steal. Customers were inside shops for only brief periods, were unfamiliar with shop routines, and did not know the identities of the store detectives. By contrast, staff were constantly in the shops, knew the procedures, and were often familiar with the store detectives. Critically, as Dickenson emphasises,

> However attractive the merchandise in the shop may be,
> the cash, portable, negotiable and unidentifiable, is the
> most attractive item around the premises and such is the
> nature of the retail trade that this cash (which includes
> the profit) comes pouring in to be received by usually,
> the lowest paid members of the retailer's staff.[25]

Customers have little or no opportunity to steal cash.

Staff have greater opportunities to steal goods and cash and know when best to steal and how best to conceal the act. In addition, they are authorised to handle goods and cash, and unless they are particularly blatant, will not be noticed when doing so. In short, it is very difficult to catch employee thieves.

A few retailers in the sample relied upon the police to apprehend dishonest staff, while others placed their faith in the agency store detectives they had employed. (A somewhat forlorn hope in the event, as agency detectives never left the shopfloor to investigate delivery points or stock-rooms.) In practice, the main agents for apprehending staff were store detectives, often prompted by a suspicious management. A few of the retailers placed their faith in 'test purchases' whereby a store detective or other security personnel from a different shop made specimen purchases to check whether the assistant was under-ringing the till. In general, however, test purchases were not believed to be cost-effective, although they were often used to trap an assistant who was already suspected of theft.

Although most store detectives had responsibility for employee thieves, they tended to concentrate almost exclusively on shoplifters. Chief security officers admitted this, but realised that a store detective who concentrated on staff alone could go months without apprehending anybody, in addition to which they would probably cause resentment and bad feeling among the staff. Although security officers appreciated the depredations caused by their own staff, they concentrated on their customers as they believed that this was the most cost-effective use of their personnel.

Once an employee had been apprehended the decision on whether to refer the case to the police became more complicated than for a shoplifter. Decisions on apprehended staff were usually made at a higher organisational level than for shoplifters, often as high as the board of directors, and frequently by reference to head office. Part of the reason for this is that it was believed to be bad for morale when employees were prosecuted. It was also often difficult to prove that an employee had stolen and the case might be time-consuming. Management had another option, however, and this was to dismiss the employee. Often on joining, staff agreed to a set of company rules for the handling of cash and till procedures. It was then possible to dismiss the suspect for a breach of regulations without recourse to the police. Generally if the employee were prosecuted, they would also be dismissed, but the reverse was not necessarily true.

The chief security officers believed that where there was a *prima facie* case of theft, the assistant would be prosecuted and dismissed. Where there was an area of doubt, the employee might be dismissed, asked to resign, or given a disciplinary warning. In dealing with staff thieves, management had a greater number of options available and consequently were able to exercise more discretion. The threat of unemployment was a powerful weapon for retailers to wield, but usually when dealing with staff, management was circumspect, as the following quotes reveal.

Store A: If there is a *prima facie* case then I report it
             to the police, but first I have to check with

head office. We do dismiss rather than
prosecute.

Store B: I do not have the authority to deal with staff,
they have to go to the managing director.

Store C: They are instantly dismissed. Two to three out
of five are prosecuted, depending on the
personnel manager and a director. (The chief
security officer did not approve of this as he
followed a strict apprehension-police referral
policy for shoplifters and wanted to do the
same for staff.)

Store D: They are usually given a warning, disciplined or
dismissed.

Store E: We do prosecute our own staff but we dislike the
publicity. We are also troubled with accusations
of unfair dismissal.

Store F: We prosecute as long as the case is clear. If the
case is grey we get them to resign. Prosecution
depends upon the blatancy and the amount
taken.

Employee thieves, then, create far more problems for security
personnel, and once they have been apprehended are treated with more
discretion. Nevertheless, some staff thieves find themselves in the unfortunate position of being prosecuted by the police, dismissed from their
job, and unable to find another position without references. It is doubtful if shoplifters are punished as severely.

In the closing brief part of the interviews, chief security officers were
asked about their ideologies in controlling shoplifting and whether they
had any criticisms of the criminal justice system. Generally, security
officers praised the work of the police, although there were a few minor
criticisms about the inexperience of young officers and the time it took
them to respond to calls. Many retailers were distressed by the policy of
the Metropolitan Police District (MPD), however, under which the stores
had to prepare, conduct and pay for their own prosecutions. This was
considered to be inequitable and some security personnel thought their
stores were out of pocket by prosecuting shoplifters in London. Other
CSOs, however, were sympathetic to the MPD; they did not approve of
the policy but understood that the MPD had special difficulties.

Criticisms of the courts tended to be less pointed. There was some disapproval about the level of fines varying from area to area, and a general approval for the severer fine. In some areas, store detectives were not required to attend court if the suspect pleaded guilty, and many security officers favoured this practice. Some security staff were not bothered with the courts — as far as they were concerned, their responsibility ended when the police were informed. A few others viewed shoplifting as symptomatic of a general social malaise and were keen to see the return of corporal punishment and hanging (though it was not made clear if this was for shoplifting).

When questioned about their ideology for controlling shoplifting, most respondents expressed a preference for prevention — 'prevention is the best way' — but 'prevention' meant two things. For a minority of retailers, prevention entailed accepting responsibility for petty pilfering — 'Petty shoplifting must be faced up to by retailers,they can't put the responsibility on anyone else' — and doing everything possible to deter the customer from becoming a shoplifter. Under this ideology, apprehension was the final resort.

For most security officers, however, the preference for prevention was nothing more than a general belief that it was easier to control crime by deterring criminals than by attempting to catch them. Critically, for these security officers, prevention of the general problem could, and usually did, go hand in hand with a policy of detection and apprehension. It was believed that by arresting and prosecuting individual shoplifters, others would be deterred. It appears, however, that the strongest deterrent is the risk of apprehension and not the unpleasantness of prosecution and severity of the sentence. People will be deterred from shoplifting if there is a strong chance of their being apprehended, but evidence from 'following exercises' and self-report surveys suggest that this is not the case. Many people have shoplifted and relatively few have been caught.

How these two opposing ideologies worked in practice will be explored in the next chapter.

Notes

1. Mapes, G., 'Campus Shoplifting', *Security World* (May 1968), pp. 29—32.
2. Thorsen, J.E., 'The War on Shoplifting', *Security World* (November 1975), pp. 22—34.
3. Home Office, *Shoplifting, and Thefts by Shop Staff*, Report of a Working Party on Internal Shop Security (London: HMSO, 1973),

pp. 39—40.

4. Thorsen, *op. cit.*

5. Home Office, *op.cit.*, p. 40.

6. Ibid.

7. *The Guardian,* 21 October 1980.

8. *Retail Review,* 'Video Recordings as Evidence', *The Newsletter of the Industrial Police and Security Association* (January 1977), p. 9.

9. Thorsen, *op. cit.*

10. Barbara, V., 'Electronics Application Pioneers for Retailing', *Security World,* 11 (1974), pp. 34—6.

11. Home Office, *op. cit.*, p. 42.

12. Home Office, *The Private Security Industry: A Discussion Paper.* (London: HMSO, 1979), p. 16.

13. Ibid.

14. Home Office, *op. cit.* (1973), p. 28.

15. Hastings, G.B., 'Customer Attitudes Towards Security Devices in shops and Preparedness to Report Shoplifting', *Abstracts on Criminology and Penology* (1980), pp. 639–42.

16. Home Office, *op. cit.* (1973)., p. 19.

17. May, D., 'Juvenile Shoplifters and the Organisation of Store Security: A Case Study in the Social Construction of Delinquency', *International Journal of Criminology and Penology,* 6 (1978), pp. 137—60.

18. Ibid.

19. Bennett, H.M., 'Shoplifting in Midtown', *Criminal Law Review* (1968), pp. 413—25.

20. Home Office, *op. cit.* (1979).

21. May, *op. cit.*

22. Ibid.

23. Ibid.

24. Home Office, *op. cit.* (1973), p. 24.

25. Dickenson, S., 'Theft and the Retailer', *Security World* (April 1970), pp. 171–4.

6 The world of store detectives

THOU SHALT NOT SHOPLIFT. People who break the eighth Commandment are causing a headache ... at a Cathedral. So steps are being taken to remind visitors to Chelmsford Cathedral's Bookstall that thou shalt not shoplift. Now volunteers will man the bookstall, which used to be left unattended.[1]

Julie is thirteen years old. She had eleven items — all stolen — in her bag, total value over £15. 'It's the change of life. I know that because my friend told me that when her mum was caught it was her change of life.'[2]

Introduction

This chapter is divided into two parts. Part one will focus on how shoplifting is treated in the media and how shoplifters are classified, and will also examine the methods used by professional shoplifters and employee thieves. Part two will look at how store detectives operate on the shopfloor; what makes them suspicious; how they make apprehensions, conduct interviews and decide on disposal; alternative methods of controlling the shoplifting population will also be discussed. Finally, a model for viewing the organisation of store detectives' work will be proposed.

PART ONE

The media and shoplifting

Cohen argues that, 'Societies appear to be subject, every now and then, to periods of moral panic. A condition, episode, person or group of persons emerges to become defined as a threat to societal values and interests.'[3] He further maintains with Young that the main agents for these panics are the mass media.[4] Cohen continues,

> the media play on the normative concerns of the public and by thrusting certain moral directives into the universe of discourse, can create social problems suddenly and dramatically. This potential is consciously exploited by those whom Becker calls 'moral entrepreneurs' to aid them in their attempt to win public support.[5]

During the latter part of the 1970s a 'moral panic' about shoplifting arose. This was fuelled by the media distorting events, as Cohen says, by exaggerating their seriousness and presenting them in sensational and melodramatic language. Shoplifting was typically discussed using a military metaphor, complete with battles, invasions, wars and storm troops. Some of these distortions are evidenced in the following extracts.

It's War on Shoplifters

A national crime-fighting force went into battle today ... to stamp out Britain's £550 million a year shoplifting spree. The new force — The Association for the Prevention of Theft from Stores — will co-ordinate anti-crime measures in every major town and city.

It will spearhead a drive for stiffer penalties for shoplifters and urge foreign embassies to deter thefts.[6]

It is interesting to note the implication that 'foreigners' were responsible for the increase in shoplifting. The notion of a battle against shoplifters was reiterated in other newspapers, for example: *'Campaign to Beat £550 m. Shop Thefts'*[7] and *'Shops In Theft War'.*[8] By 1977, the campaign had become an all-out war:

War on the Shop Thieves

An all-out war on shoplifters who cost the country an estimated £625 million each year was promised today with a call for stiffer penalties and new security measures in London shops.[9]

Now the preparations of store detectives were described as: ' *"Storm Troops" get ready for War with Shoplifters.'*[10]

Although it was possible to create a moral panic about shoplifting, it was more difficult to categorise shoplifters as 'folk devils'. Mods and rockers, the archetypal folk devils, committed their 'offences' in full view of the general public. By contrast, shoplifters go to considerable lengths to avoid public scrutiny. Moreover, unlike mods and rockers, there is no readily recognisable subculture of shoplifters. The vast majority are ordinary people who have only their offence in common: they do not share a distinctive style of clothes or enjoy a common life-style. However, attempts were made to 'scapegoat' (cf. Chapman[11]) foreign shoplifters, particularly those from the Middle East, and the Arab shoplifter became the closest equivalent to a folk devil.

Foreign shoplifters, particularly those from Iran and other Middle East countries were widely reported in the press. Attention was often drawn to how much cash the shoplifters carried at the time of their arrest. Magistrates were incensed that foreigners should steal from 'our' stores, when they obviously had more than enough money to pay for the goods. Others were aroused by what they saw as the conspicuous wealth of the Arabs, and decried their depredations. In the West End courts, foreigners were subject to severe fines.

Newspapers took their role as moral entrepreneurs seriously. For example, the Daily Mail described foreigners as *'They come, they see ... they shoplift';* and described their background thus: 'almost all the West End's shoplifters are people of substance in their own country — if they weren't they could never have afforded to come here in the first place.'[12]

Warnings were given by magistrates: 'Mr. H., Marlborough Street magistrate, said yesterday the people who shoplift although they have ample means to pay will meet exemplary punishment in his court.'[13] The same magistrate was true to his word:

> A woman who went shoplifting with £9000 in her purse said she was sorry when she was caught, a court was told yesterday. The magistrate commented: 'I'll make her even sorrier in a few minutes' — and fined her £4000.[14]

Somewhat inconsistently, later the same day, Mr H.

> gave a conditional discharge to a Polish woman who admitted stealing a £1.10 pair of socks from a London store .... Mr. H. said, 'She was confronted by a display of goods the likes of which she probably does not see at home. If it should come to the notice of the Polish authorities, I should say that I regard this as a very trivial matter.'[15]

The *Sunday Express* succinctly summarised the burgeoning xenophobia: 'When an Iraqi woman tourist was fined £3000 for shoplifting, there must have been relief that at last, foreign predators were getting their come-uppance.'[16]

A report on one particular magistrate is worth citing at length:

Sir I, and the 'Thieving Iranians'

Sir I., former Chief Justice of Hong Kong and Brunei, confessed yesterday that the kind of justice he now dispenses will not stop London's shoplifting tourists. As magistrate at Marylebone Court, he has seen hundreds of well-to-do thieves pass through the dock. And the worst offenders, he said yesterday, are Iranians. Under the Ayatollah's regime in Iran, a thief can lose a hand. Here Sir I. fines them as much as £500 — and invariably they pay there and then from a huge wad of notes. For a man who sent killers to the gallows in the Far East, the lack of a real deterrent sentence is galling. This week, a 24 year-old Iranian secretary was brought before him with a flimsy excuse for taking a bra, a tape cassette and four other items from F.'s [name of store]. 'Of all the foreign nationals who visit this country, the Iranians are the biggest thieves of the lot,' he told her. 'You plunder our shops.' The outburst probably had more effect than the fine of £120 and £40 costs....

He looks kindly on the suggestion that offenders should have their passports stamped with details of the conviction so that they could not return to Britain.[17]

The call for stamping passports was earlier mooted by Baroness Phillips:

New efforts are being made to curb London's foreign shop-lifters with a direct approach to their embassies. Baroness Phillips, Director of the recently formed Association for the Prevention of Theft in Shops, has been contacting embassies to try to get them to persuade their nationals to pay.[18]

The idea of warning foreign embassies was also adopted by Scotland Yard.[19]

More recently, the moral panic over shoplifting has tended to die down, even though there are currently more offences reported than there were during the peak 'panic' year of 1977: in 1982, for example, there were 242,304 offences.[20] It is unlikely, however, that media interest in shoplifting is over, but merely lies dormant awaiting another resurgence in 'the war'.

What kind of shoplifting incidents are reported by the media? Roshier isolates four factors relevant for the depiction of all crimes: the seriousness of the offence; 'whimsical' circumstances; sentimental or dramatic circumstances; and the involvement of famous personalities, either as victims or offenders.[21] All four are applicable to shoplifting.

Although each individual offence of shoplifting generally involves a small sum, estimates of its total cost (abstracted from undisclosed sources and presented out of the context of total shrinkage) often make it a very serious matter. Occasionally, 'super-shoplifters' are discovered and their illicit gains are so large as to be newsworthy in themselves. Often, shoplifting incidents are presented as strange, ironic or humorous; frequently, sympathy is invoked for the impoverished, absent-minded pensioner who steals a tin of food for a family pet. The involvement of high-status persons in shoplifting is often reported and, occasionally, several of these factors are combined, as with Lady Isobel Barnett, a well-known person who became involved in shoplifting with tragic repercussions. Examples of these four categories are provided below.

Perhaps the most famous individual shoplifter to come to the attention of the media was the so-called 'super-shoplifter', whose depredations were so serious as to merit comparisons with any bank robber:

Super Shoplifter Had £90,000 Haul In His Flat

A shoplifter's flat was a cross between a department store and an art gallery — it contained 1100 works of art and luxury goods worth £90,000, a court was told yesterday.[22]

More recently, another alleged 'super-shoplifter' has been discovered:

Bra Trick Theft from L.

Five rings worth £100,000 were sneaked out of L's attached to a woman's bra, prosecution alleged at the Old Bailey. J.H., 54, of Wembley, denied theft.[23]

Often the boundaries between the whimsical cases and the sentimental and dramatic ones are blurred, as the following examples demonstrate:

P.C. Makes a Fine Mess of Shoplifting

Policeman A.B. wasnt't much cop as a shoplifter. He was spotted by a store detective as he tried to steal from a Birmingham supermarket. Then he ran off straight into a car and injured his knees. Finally, the limping lawman tried to escape again, but was caught by the police after a brief chase. A.B., a 34-year-old father of two, of Strichley, Birmingham, was fined £40 for theft yesterday by the city's magistrates. He will now lose his job and home.[24]

Feuding Sisters Started a Contest in Shoplifting

Two sisters who fell out with another woman launched
an astonishing shoplifting contest in an attempt to out-
steal her, a court heard. The trial of theft snowballed out
of all proportion and in 15 months, 19-year-old E. and T., 23
stole goods worth hundreds of pounds. They included
furnishings, food, do-it-yourself materials, toys, clothing,
52 items from one visit to M., a set of door chimes and
16 pairs of men's briefs. The two married sisters were
allegedly introduced to shoplifting when they agreed to
help a third woman who bragged how easy it was not to
get caught. But when they fell out with her they went
stealing in opposition.[25]

Shoplift Customs Man fined £1000

S.S., 31, staying at Nottingham Place, Marylebone, admitted
stealing 81 items of clothing worth £193.34 from three
Oxford Street stores 'in a moment of weakness'.[26]

Ring Thief has to Swallow Jail

A tourist who swallowed a £630 diamond ring after swop-
ping it for a paste one in a West End Store was jailed for six
months yesterday. When T. was stopped outside the store
the ring had disappeared ... but eventually it turned up,
Marlborough Street Court was told.[27]

Perhaps the most famous of all whimsical shoplifting incidents is
the one involving the 'frozen chicken', which was mentioned throughout the research and is cited in various newspaper reports. Usually the
shoplifter was reported to be a man who fainted whilst waiting for the
arrival of the police, not because of the excitement but because the
frozen chicken he had hidden underneath his hat had been pressed
against his bald head, interrupting cerebral bloodflow. In the *Daily
Mirror* the sex of the shoplifter had changed:

A woman, escorted to the manager's office for putting
other goods in her straw-basket, was waiting for the police
to be called. Then store staff noticed water trickling from
under her hat and down her face as the bird began to thaw.[28]

Two years later, the position of the frozen chicken had changed:

He remembers one girl who was questioned for 90 minutes.
Then she couldn't stand it any longer. She pulled a frozen

chicken from between her legs! 'It's known in the business as crotching,' Mr. B. says, 'In her case it must have been very uncomfortable.'[29]

Discussing shoplifters generally, Baroness Phillips again relates the story 'of the very old lady collapsing that very cold winter when poor old ladies were dying of hypothermia, and they found a frozen chicken under her coat.'[30] Baroness Phillips, however, appreciated that the 'classic case' was almost certainly apocryphal. It is apparent that much mythology has grown up around the offence of shoplifting. This is perhaps only to be expected for a 'folk crime' which is enforced by such a heterogeneous group as store detectives.

Examples of famous people arrested for shoplifting are legion, as the following extracts exemplify.

Job 'took toll' on M.P. who shoplifted

J.D., the MP, and a former Under-Secretary, was yesterday found guilty of two shoplifting charges by a jury at the Inner London Crown Court.[31]

Senior Civil Servant Admits Theft

A 'mad day' in the life of a senior civil servant cost him a £240 fine at Hastings yesterday and may lose him his £11,500 a year job.
Mr. A.D. (38), a chief information officer ... pleaded guilty to three charges involving thefts from antique shops and asked for seven similar offences to be taken into consideration.[32]

Shoplifting GPs are on the Increase [33]

Police Chief's Wife Stole

P., 50, whose £10,000 a year husband, H., is an Assistant Chief Constable ... pleaded guilty to stealing a £1.49 packet of frozen prawns.[34]

Football Girls go Shoplifting

The wife of Hungary's World Cup captain and the fiancée of another star player have been caught shoplifting.[35]

Shoplifting Fine of Judge's Wife

A Lebanese judge's wife on holiday in England was fined £300 with £25 costs at Marlborough Street yesterday for stealing a cardigan and a jumper worth £57.50 fromY.'s in Oxford Street.[36]

Thefts by Wives of Diplomats [37]

The Shoplift Shame of a Princess

A princess's chauffeur waited outside a city's store while she shopped lavishly. In her handbag, fitted with a combination lock, she carried more than £8,000 in cash and travellers' cheques. But Princess X. 'forgot to pay' for a £5.95 handbag. And yesterday she was fined the maximum £1000 for shoplifting. [38]

Bishop Accused of Shoplifting. [39]

Finally, the sad case of Lady Isobel Barnett illustrates how newsworthy categories can be combined to produce incidents which involve the famous, are sentimental, then tragically dramatic, and which have serious implications for the criminal justice system as a whole (this case will be discussed more fully later). The classifications of shoplifters used in the literature differ from those used by the media, and the next section analyses these other categories.

The classification of shoplifters

This section examines the classification of shoplifters made by other researchers and security officers. Particular attention is paid to professional shoplifters and the so-called 'Fagin' shoplifters, as these are seldom discovered in field research. The ultimate section will look at employee thieves, as these too are infrequently caught and, although a significant part of shop shrinkage, do not feature much in the literature.

The simplest and most pithy classification of shoplifters was provided by one chief security officer, who averred that there were only three types of shoplifter — 'the needy, the greedy and the seedy'. He believed that the needy were rare, the seedy (drunks and vagrants) were infrequent, and that the largest category were the greedy — the people who wanted something for nothing.

On the other hand, Verill divides shoplifters into juveniles, housewives, drunkards, drug addicts and professionals. [40] Post has a similar classification but considers shoplifters to come from all backgrounds, and believes that they fall into two broad categories: ordinary customers and professionals who steal for a living. [41] This dichotomy is reflected by Cameron, who classifies shoplifters on the basis of the use they make of stolen merchandise. The commercial shoplifters or 'boosters' are those who steal goods for resale; the pilferers or 'snitches' steal goods for their own use. [42]

Sutherland defines a professional thief as one who steals professionally. Stealing professionally is a regular, full-time occupation which involves detailed planning and the exercise of special skills. Often the professional thief moves around the country and has, in common with other professional criminals, a distinctive life-style and subculture.[43] Edwards defines the professional thief as one who makes a living from crime.[44] Cameron distinguishes between 'heels' and 'boosters'. Heels concentrate on shoplifting, while boosters are often involved in other forms of criminal activity as well.[45] Gibbens and Prince emphasise resale to prepared outlets in defining professionals but believe that these may not easily be differentiated from those who steal to provide for their families.[46] Walsh further reminds us that the concept of professionalism has to be distinguished from planned and artful raids by determined amateurs.[47] This distinction had important ramifications for the field-work.

When talking to store detectives during fieldwork observations about particular problems in shoplifting the researcher was struck by the frequency with which the term 'professional' was used. For example, individuals were often described as 'real professionals' and references were frequently made to gangs of professionals they had encountered in the past (cf. Chapter 3). This was confusing, as all the literature had suggested that professionals accounted for only a small part of shoplifting, and although their depredations were serious, they were rarely encountered. And yet the picture which emerged from store detectives was that professional thieves were regularly discovered. At first, it seemed that store detectives might be trying to glamorise their jobs and make them more exciting by discussing the 'real' criminals. Alternatively, it might be that although not frequently encountered, the threat of professionals loomed large in their everyday work routines. Both of these elements may have been present, but it was not until a considerable period of observation had been completed that a more likely answer was provided. Store detectives were not necessarily exaggerating or dramatising their work, instead, they were confounding the notions of professional and professionalism. When they talked of professionals they were referring to anybody who acted in a calculating and deliberate manner (cf. the distinction made by Walsh). It transpired from further questioning and amplification that professionals in Sutherland's sense were rare occurrences, but amateurs who were calculating, cool and determined were more regularly spotted. However, the distinction between opportunist/amateur theives and professional was rarely emphasised. Store detectives, committed to the symbolic role of 'thief-taker', tended to minimise the significance of spontaneous stealing and saw most theft as deliberate, whether conducted by a professional or not.

Apart from the earlier case of the 'super shoplifter', a number of other professionals have been reported in the press.

Thieves Trick Shops

A gang of up to 40 thieves, described by the police as 'highly professional' has stolen tens of thousands of pounds over the past six months from shops in the North of England and Midlands by the simple trick of distracting the attention of assistants. The gang, thought to be based at Liverpool, works in teams of two to five men. They steal from shops with one or two assistants, and move in when the staff is cashing up at the end of the day.[48]

Drug Addict Gang Plundered Shops of £130,000 in Goods

Heavy prison sentences were imposed yesterday on a shoplifting gang who plundered 150 shops of goods valued at £130,000. Some of the thieves needed £100 daily to satisfy their craving for drugs. The main targets were LP records and cameras from shops across England and Wales.[49]

Christmas Box Trapped Shoplifter

A Greek tourist who armed himself with a mock Christmas parcel fitted with a trapdoor to go shoplifting was sentenced yesterday to a month's imprisonment suspended for two years and fined £120 with £60 costs, at Marlborough Street. A., 22, a student, on a European tour, admitted stealing a £4.68 bottle of perfume from a West End Store and having the empty parcel for use in thefts. Mr. D.H., the magistrate, examined the parcel, a wooden box wrapped in Christmas paper and bearing messages of seasonal goodwill in three languages.

Mr T.L., prosecuting, said the perfume 'disappeared' from T.'s knee when he placed the box over it and closed the trapdoor with an attached piece of string 'so that it continued to look like a Christmas parcel'. A sharp-eyed store detective spotted him. He told police he bought it from a man in Edinburgh who had three similar boxes to sell. Mr R.G., defending, said T. was persuaded by a fast-talking Scotsman to part with Deutschmarks 50 (about £13.50) for the box.[50]

The obvious disadvantage of using such 'booster boxes' and the other equipment specially designed for shoplifting, is that if caught it is difficult to plead absent-mindedness or inadvertance. The presence of a booster box leaves little doubt about the intent of the owner.

Despite the availability of specialised shoplifting equipment, the basic methods of shoplifting have not changed over the centuries. The following extracts of twentieth-century shoplifters should be compared to those at the beginning of Chapter 4.

> A middle-aged man and two female companions paused outside a ladies ready-to-wear shop in a busy suburban mall. They peered at the window display as any casual shopper might. 'Are you ready?', Mr. G. asked. 'Hazel? Sylvia?' The women nodded and went on studying the window display. Mr. G. entered the shop and approached the clerk at the notions counter. 'I'd like to see some scarves,' he said. 'Something that will go with my wife's wine-coloured suit. She likes abstract designs.' The clerk brought out a selection of scarves and spread them on the counter. 'Perhaps she'd like one of these?' Mr. G. pretended to study fabrics and price tags. After a few minutes Hazel and Sylvia entered the store. Hazel carried a small handbag, Sylvia a shopping bag. While Sylvia strolled among the garment racks with her shopping bags, Hazel approached the only other clerk in the shop. 'I'd like to see a white blouse with a stand-up collar in size thirty-six,' she said. The clerk led her to the blouse racks and pulled out a few selections. 'Are any of these what you have in mind?' Hazel browsed, considering, rejecting. 'Perhaps something like this one,' she said finally. 'Do you have something like this in silk?'
>
> While both the clerks were busy with Mr G. and with Hazel, Sylvia approached a rack of expensive dresses. Choosing the highest-priced garment on the rack, she removed it from its hanger, dropped it into her shopping bag, and left the store. Moments later, the clerk helping Mr G. at the scarf counter saw the empty hanger on the dress rack. Excusing herself, she hurried into the mall corridor, looking for the customer who had been in the shop a moment before. But in the throng of people she was unable to spot her. Returning to her station, she called the mall security office. While she was making the call, Mr G. and Hazel quietly left the store, heading in opposite directions. They met a short time later in the parking lot. Their shoplifting act had been so well planned and had been carried out so smoothly that the clerk they had hoodwinked was unaware that she had been the victim of professional shoplifters.[51]

Lehr describes a similar operation in Germany:

The members, the oldest 32, the youngest 24, travelled
with their own cars mainly in Southern Germany and
Switzerland. Mostly in town centres they searched out
likely looking clothing shops and boutiques where few
sales assistants were to be seen. They entered the shops
in twos or larger groups. Whilst one of them looked for
an opportunity to take some goods, the other(s) diverted
the sales assistants present.[52]

Baker describes a more complicated operation which involved the
use of receipts. Two or more of the gang enter the shop; one of them
does the stealing while the others watch to see if the shoplifter is
followed out of the store. If she is, then the accomplices immediately
purchase an item similar to the one stolen, replace the article but keep
the receipt and claim that the stolen article had actually been purchased,
but the partners had been separated. This is a very difficult tactic to
counter and the store detective has little option but to let them go.[53]

Professionals as discussed above pose serious problems for store
detectives. The most critical is actually seeing them stealing, as professionals are usually so adept that store detectives rarely ever see them,
unless by accident. Even if they are aware that professional gangs are
operating, store detectives are wary of making arrests because they will
not know if the suspect has passed on the goods to an accomplice.
Consequently store detectives attempt to deter professionals, as discussed in the previous chapter, by 'breathing down their necks'. Not surprisingly, no professionals were observed during the fieldwork, but a
number of incidents were seen where professionalism was exhibited.
In the first case, an Israeli woman stole a cashmere sweater, and it was
only by chance that the store detective noticed her. The store detective
described the woman as a 'beautiful shoplifter' as she did not look
round to see if she were being watched, but went straight to the counter
and took the sweater, placing it in her bag. If the store detective had not
happened to be standing next to the woman she would not have been
suspicious, for, as will be shown later, nervous glances are one of the
first things store detectives look for. As with the 'super-shoplifter'
described earlier, the direct approach is the hallmark of the professional
and is difficult to spot.

On two separate occasions, in two different cities, so-called 'crotch-
workers' were observed. In the first, a girl was seen to enter the shop,
select a goat-skin rug and conceal it under her skirt between her legs.
The store detective attempted to stop the girl outside the shop, but the
girl ran and, despite the burden of the rug, managed to outpace and
then elude the store detective. On the second occasion, two girls selected a number of LP records and secreted them between their legs. The
store detective pursued them outside the shop and the records were

dropped and recovered, but the girls escaped.

The 'Fagin syndrome'

Another category of shoplifters, rarely caught, but forming part of the folklore of shoplifting are the children/adult gangs. The 'Fagin syndrome', named after Dickens' character, involves adults who train children, often below the age of criminal responsibility, to steal, or who use a child as an accomplice. It has been described in the literature, for example de Rham discusses one such gang:

> Every few days, some of the children would be gathered together and driven into the centre of town by one parent or the other in a moribund family jalopy. Each one had a list, compiled jointly by the parents, of things he or she was to steal from the store at which he would be deposited. Anyone who failed received a beating upon his return home; success, on the other hand, brought smiles to Mother's face and even elicited an occasional kiss or rare word of kindness or praise ....
> Ma Riley — for that was what they called her after Ma Baker of Chicago — was clearly not an ordinary woman. A professional and very accomplished thief, she instructed all her children in the refinements of shoplifting until they were old enough to know what they were doing and understand that they must never be caught.[54]

Similar cases have been reported in the British press.

> A mother trained her two young children to help her on shoplifting sprees, a court heard yesterday. While her eleven-year-old son kept look out, her little girl, aged seven, pushed stolen goods into the mother's bag, Marlborough Street magistrates court was told. The shoplifting career of the mother, Iraqi tourist Mrs N.I., was on a massive scale, the court heard. When arrested Mrs I. had £650 on her, said J.B., prosecuting. Mrs I, 38, admitted stealing fifty-seven items of clothing from London West End shops. She was fined £600 with £60 costs. The children were not charged because they were acting on their mother's instructions.[55]

> A Persian tourist who played 'touch shoplifting' with her 13-year-old son, at a West End store was fined £400 with £20 costs yesterday. Mrs S.B., 37, would touch selected 'souvenirs' and her son would whisk them into their bags

as they browsed around S.'s, said Mr J.B., prosecuting at Marlborough Street court. When they were stopped, the mother tried to blame the boy and started beating him, he said. The boy sobbed as he and his mother staying at Tooting, admitted stealing 15 items of jewellery, tights and aftershave lotion together worth £32.85. The boy was conditionally discharged for a year.[56]

Son, 13, Taken Shoplifting[57]

Family from Egypt went Shoplifting[58]

Girl, 7, used in Shoplifting[59]

An inspector from Scotland Yard talked about the methods used in this type of theft.

Whole families are going out on Saturday afternoon shoplifting expeditions, a Scotland Yard woman police inspector said yesterday. 'Children often aged only eight or nine — too young to be prosecuted — are used because if they are caught retailers are often likely to give them a smack on their bottom and send them home. Mother and father do the 'shopping' ... and the children wheel the trolley innocently past the check-out to a car where the grandparents are waiting. Before the staff have time to do anything they are long gone.'[60]

Only one case of adults stealing with their children was observed during the fieldwork. On this occasion a man and a woman were shoplifting with their two children. The man was selecting items, taking them and passing them to the accompanying children. The children would then take the items to their mother waiting outside the store. The situation presented difficulties for the store detective as she was aware that the parents could deny responsibility by blaming the children. The problem resolved itself, however, for while the store detective sought assistance to deal with the mother and children while she concentrated on the man, the father became lost in the crowd and could not be found again.

The next section concentrates on the problems posed by employee thieves in shops. In any period of field research, there are not likely to be many cases of employees being caught stealing, and so much of the data for this section relies on the media and other literature, augmented by some records and one case abstracted from field notes.

Employee Thieves

Employee thieves, like professional shoplifters, are not frequently discovered, and when they are, management often has an equivocal attitude to their treatment, as the following extract illustrates.

Trouble in Big Store

Thirty names came to light when police investigated alleged thefts by staff at a big London store. Then ... the investigation ground to a halt. As the CID were preparing to bring charges the management of B. in Kensington told them they would prefer to deal with the affair 'as an internal matter'. At first, five suspected staff members were interviewed at Kensington police station. Then detectives were given the names of another twenty-five who were alleged to be involved. A senior detective told me: 'We could charge some of these people right now, but we would have to rely on B,'s to provide evidence. They now say that they don't want charges brought at the moment.'[61]

This incident demonstrates two points. First, as Smigel and Ross[62] and Robin[63] say, bureaucracies, including large department stores, are often more concerned with maintaining their public image than in prosecuting staff. The concept of a law enforcement system with a personal victim often does not correspond to the best interests of a company. Companies are often unwilling to admit that they have erred in selecting dishonest employees. Retrieval of stolen goods and preservation of their good name are frequently more significant than prosecution. Prosecution is viewed as a last resort, but companies have other punishments available to them, as will be shown.

The second aspect of the incident is, as Martin argues, that the disposal of dishonest employees is largely determined by management's preference.[64] The seriousness of the offence(s) and the repercussions which might affect the company are also considerations. For employee thieves, the role of management is critical as, without their evidence, the police can rarely substantiate a prosecution. It is unlikely that the police will discover employee thieves in shops by themselves and are dependent upon management furnishing the evidence; if management decide to withdraw their charges, there is little the police can do.

The attitude of the press is also sometimes equivocal. The depredations of staff thieves are often newsworthy, but are seldom reported in the same bombastic fashion.

Staff Take Twice as Much as Shoplifters

At a conference in London, Mr K, of the Group 4 Total
Security Organisation, said: 'A cashier can "earn" an
extra £10 to £15 a shift by ringing up false amounts for
items.'
In some stores, he claimed, shop assistants ran highly
organised departmental bartering rings. Girls on, say,
a cosmetic counter swopped items for tights, skirts and
other articles — all of which were illegally taken from the
store.[65]

The frequently endemic nature of employee theft is illustrated in the
following extract:

Shoe Thieves Foot the Bill

There was an 'atmosphere of corruption' in a shoe shop
where the entire junior sales staff turned to theft. Five
girls — all now sacked — stole stock worth a total of
£830, London's Marlborough Street court heard yesterday, One of them walked out of the shop, L's of Bond
Street, with an expensive pair of boots, and went straight
across to G's store to sell them to an employee for £20.
Her defence counsel said: 'When she first worked at the
shop, theft was already rife, and she was corrupted by
what she saw.'[66]

Moreover, this extract demonstrates that some employee thieves may
be prosecuted and also lose their jobs. Many cases are not so straightforward as this, however. There is often a conspiracy prevalent which
encourages and controls the amount of pilfering, as the following case
shows.

The Front-Line Fiddlers

Low wages and a nod-and-a-wink from his (R.'s) bosses put
him on a course for a corrupt career. It's not just confined
to the managers.
   I reckon about seventy-five per cent of supermarket staff
— cashiers, assistants, stockroom workers and food preparers
— are into some fiddle or another. Many of the middlemen
between the food manufacturers and the retailers — van
drivers, dispatchers and checkers are also crooked. In my
last manager's job, I earned £4,500 a year honestly. I made
another £50 a week dishonestly. The business is really bent.
It starts because you have to cheat the shoppers — and that's

usually the housewives — on behalf of the company. The
truth is, most supermarkets refuse to accept even the
normal level of shrinkage. If you cheat for the company,
it's a short step to stick some on for yourself. At the wages
they pay, you've got to.[67]

A similar situation is described by Ditton: 'The W. salesmen are trapped
in an organisational dilemma. Whilst they have no realistic alternative
but to make money on the side, doing so is sometimes punishable by
the very people [the management] who demand the practice in the first
place.'[68] He reiterated in *Controlology*,

'There's a certain amount they're prepared to close their
eyes to. To be blunt, the management close both eyes to
fiddling (where the customers lose) and one eye to dealing
and pilfering. The one eye that remains open in the latter
case is firmly transfixed upon the inside men.'[69]

The equivocality displayed by management in the treatment accorded
to dishonest employees is well illustrated in the following cases taken
from the records of one chain of shops which was alert to the dangers
of staff thieves.

Case 1: An assistant was interviewed by security and admitted
consuming goods valued at £1.08 without paying.
Cautioned.

Case 2: A checkout operator failed to record a test purchase
of £1.03 made by security. Her till was found to be
only 41p over. It was also found that she had previously
operated her till in an irregular manner. Cautioned.

Case 3: The manager failed to record a test purchase of 94p
made by security. The till was found to be £4.10p
over and there was no audit roll in the cash register.
An undated cheque issued by the manager was found
in the safe. The safe was £3.80 short. A week later
the safe was found to be £20.50 short but when
checked again the following day by the area manager
was found to be correct. The manager could not
satisfactorily explain why he had not recorded the
purchase of 94p. Cautioned.

Case 4: A customer reported seeing a checkout operator
putting a £1 note in her sock. She was questioned
by the manager who found 3 £1 notes in her sock.
This was an obvious case of theft but it could not
be proved. She was dismissed for a breach of company

rules.

Case 5: Security detected a male assistant stealing a bottle of milk. Dismissed.

Case 6: Following adverse stock results from the meat department a detailed investigation was conducted by the meat supervisor and security, resulting in the butchery manager being interviewed. No firm conclusion was reached concerning the discrepancies and there was no direct evidence concerning any criminal activity of the butchery staff. However, at the conclusion of the interview the butchery manager tendered his resignation, which was accepted.

Case 7: The provision hand was interviewed by security after the depot manager discovered roast pork was missing from an order. The provision hand admitted stealing and disposing of the meat and was dismissed. Police were informed and he was charged with the offence.

A number of features emerge from these cases. The first is the use of test purchases by security staff, which seems fairly common for this chain. However, it was pointed out that test purchases were seldom used randomly but nearly always to check staff who were already under suspicion. The second point to notice is that management has a number of ways of dealing with staff suspected of stealing: They may caution them for a breach of staff rules (cases 1, 2 and 3); they may dismiss them for either theft or a serious breach of staff rules (cases 4 and 5); and finally, management may decide to dismiss the individual(s) involved and refer the case to the police for prosecution (case 7). Discretion would appear to be exercised according to the seriousness of the case and the ease with which theft can be proved. Nevertheless, there still remain anomalies in the punishments imposed. For example, in case 1, the assistant admitted stealing and consuming goods valued over £1, but was only cautioned, whereas the assistant in case 5 was dismissed for theft of a bottle of milk.

Case 4 is illuminative because it exemplifies the archetypal method of stealing cash in stores — 'short-ringing'. Dickenson describes the varieties of ways this is achieved: 'Some assistants take a £1 from the till early in the day and then ring 5s. short four times during the day.' That is, for a purchase of a £1, they will take a £1 from the customer but only ring 75p (15s.) up on the till.[70] Dickenson continues,

> In some cases, the money is not put into the till at all, particularly if the whole amount is being stolen. Assistants

who pocket the full amount of the sale hope that if questioned on the day it happens they can produce the money from their pocket [or sock?] and plead forgetfulness.[71]

In many stores discrimination appeared to be made between the treatment of staff and management theft; as one security officer put it, 'When management nicks things nobody wants to know, security just keep making reports.' Moreover, some managers, particularly those who realised they were relatively indispensable to the company, often engaged in the practice of 'borrowing' from the tills, sometimes leaving IOUs, but often not. As Keeton observes, even if the manager intended to pay back the money the next day, it makes no difference to the offence, it is still theft.[72] It appears that some managers are reluctant to apprehend staff if it causes bad feeling.

During the field research only one incident of staff theft was observed, and this was largely fortuitous. A pensioner who was employed as a part-time cashier was spotted acting suspiciously by the store detective. The cashier had rung up the till after the customer had left and the store detective observed that although the article was valued at £3 — the sum the cashier had taken from the customer — only £1.99 was rung up. The store detective enlisted a colleague to make a test purchase, whereupon the cashier registered the correct amount but did not tender a receipt. A number of receipts were noticed lying next to the till. After a period of observation, the cashier was seen to leave the till open and when he served the next customer he took money out of the till and kept it in his fist. Apparently, the cashier had been engaging in under-ringing, taking the excess out later and keeping receipts back to substantiate future transactions. The cashier was then accused by the store detective but denied that he had any money in his hand. After a while, he admitted having money in his hand but declared that he had previously placed some change of his own in the till and was only taking back what was owed to him. A manager was called and the till was checked. The cashier was then taken up to the security office where he was further questioned, but maintained his story. In practice, he could have been dismissed for breach of company rules over till procedure (e.g. never leave the till open; always give receipts; never use your own money for change, etc.) The CID were called, as was usual practice for employees suspected of theft, and the interview was left to them, and he finally admitted that he had been stealing. Although, everybody felt a little sorry for him, he was dismissed and appeared in court the next day charged with theft. As he was of previously good character, the magistrates were lenient and gave him a conditional discharge.

This part of the chapter has examined the ways in which store thieves (including employees) are classified in the literature and has discussed those thieves one would not expect to feature in any field study. Part two, investigates the ways in which store detectives identify, control and process the great majority of shoplifters, and provides a model to explicate their decision-making.

PART TWO

Introduction

This part concentrates on how store detectives organise their work so as best to combat shoplifters. First we examine the screening procedures adopted by store detectives and discuss the reasons for selecting certain individuals or groups as targets for investigation. Then we look at the ways store detectives attempt to control the shoplifting population. Tactics such as 'banning' and 'exclusion' will be covered, as well as the more prevalent 'informal methods' which are available. In this section, also, the law-enforcement model of apprehension, interview and police referral will be discussed. Finally a model is proposed for analysing the activities of store detectives.

Selection procedures — what store detectives look for and what makes them suspicious

The 'following exercises' discussed in Chapter 2, suggest that many people shoplift without being discovered. A reasonable proposition, therefore, would be that if store detectives followed random customers they would inevitably catch some taking goods, as did the researchers. However, nothing reported in the literature suggests that this occurs, and certainly no store detective observed during the fieldwork operated in this fashion. Instead, it became obvious that security personnel operated selection procedures for differentiating potential shoplifters from honest customers, and that they acted upon these distinctions in the belief that they were maximising their efficiency. What, then, makes a store detective suspicious of a customer?

May believes that 'identifying shoplifters, is, in the first place, an essentially intuitive process which requires an ability to sense the "wrongness" of people or behaviour.'[73] And certainly during the field study, many store detectives referred to their 'sixth sense' for spotting shoplifters; responses such as, 'I don't know how really, I just know', and, 'It's something I just feel', were typical. However, after extensive fieldwork, it transpired that what was originally conceived of as intuition and was presented as a quasi-mysterious 'sixth sense', was deeply-rooted in the rational world. How was this so?

May argues that the process of screening shoplifters is accomplished in two stages. First is the typification of people; second, the typification of behaviour. Critically, he points out that, 'Essentially, the identification of shoplifting proceeds from a stereotype of the "genuine shopper". It is not so much a question of this or that person acting like a shoplifter but this or that person *not acting* like a typical shopper.'[74] The classification of customers and their behaviour, then, as that of potential shoplifters can only be comprehended by reference to the 'normal' shopper. In short, it is not so much what the *shoplifter does* as what the typical *customer does not do.* Although the following examples are couched in terms of how shoplifters operate, they become noticeable to store detectives because they are not the way *bona fide* customers behave. Far from being an intuitive process, these classifications are the result of logical analyses of what the ordinary customer does. Such analyses may be automatic and massively detailed but they are nevertheless the products of rational minds.

Cameron, for instance, believes that 'the typical shopper looks at merchandise and ignores other people in the store; the shoplifter constantly watches people in order to know whether or not he is being observed or followed.'[75] Edwards cites the examples of the woman who was apprehended because of the way she took off her coat: 'Ordinarily, a coat is casually thrown over an arm when it is removed. This woman removed her coat and folded it in a "fussy" way, so that it formed a pocket. She then stole a suit and concealed it in the pocket formed in the folds of the coat.'[76]

Journalists who have accompanied store detectives on the shopfloor report similar suspicious actions.

> 'A bloke with an empty plastic bag, especially if it is
> crumpled [a 'bad bag'], is always suspicious. Women
> go out shopping with an empty bag, but men don't;
> they expect to be given a bag when they buy something.'
> C.F. reckons he spots potential shoplifters instinctively,
> 'there is something about the way they pick goods up
> without really looking at them, and turn round to see if
> anyone is watching.'[77]

> 'She was the kind of woman you would not notice in a
> crowd. But the store detectives at D. in London's
> Oxford Street noticed her immediately. 'Wowee, watch
> those eyes,' a detective whispered. The woman was at
> the purse counter. But her eyes weren't on the goodies
> in front of her. I missed the moment when she slipped
> a brown purse into one of the bulging carrier bags she

142

was carrying. But the detective spotted it.[72]

We watch their eyes. You can see if they're interested in the goods, or if they're looking around them. Most of all we watch their hands.[79]

Shoplifters tend to look about them a lot — it's called the owl-head syndrome — to see if they're being observed. They might move in a strange, jerky way as they slip things into their pockets or bags. They might be wearing heavy, bulky clothing in warm weather; they might faint or drop items as a diversion.[80]

By contrast, Baker describes a case where ordinarily the shoplifter would have escaped attention.

I saw David come into my store at about 3 o'clock one afternoon. He went straight to the grocery section and I saw him take two tins of meat and a packet of tea. He took a rolled up plastic carrier bag from his pocket, put the items inside and made for the door. No technique, no hesitation. He relied on speed and avoiding any suspicious movements. This incidentally is the most successful method of lifting. Had he not been known to me by sight I would not have given him a second glance. There were no guilty looks, no wandering around various counters, no unnecessary handling of goods.[81]

This direct approach is comparable to the method used by the 'super-shoplifter' discussed earlier, and it is significant to note that it is so hard to detect precisely because the thieves are acting like normal shoppers and not making themselves suspicious.

As a slight digression, two further cases that store detectives might be aware of can be mentioned. Meek describes the way in which apparently broken arms in slings may be used as a storage place for secreted articles and a cover for a real arm which discreetly does the stealing.[82] An even more comical example is provided by Edwards, who talks about men who use false buttons attached to elastic in their fly openings to conceal small articles, in the knowledge that their furtive actions would be interpreted as those of an embarrassed man who has just discovered his predicament.[83]

Fieldwork observations provided the opportunity to question store detectives on what made them suspicious. By accompanying store detectives as they patrolled the shopfloor it was possible to examine each decision they made: why certain people were suspicious; why others were not; and why they stopped following certain people and when. It was thus possible to extend and amplify the screening procedures discussed in the literature to incorporate a detailed and complex analysis of customers and their behaviour.

Many of the store detectives accompanied in the field study reacted to the signals traditionally assumed to be given by potential shoplifters (i.e. non-typical customers). For example, in one store the detective spotted a man with a large flight bag that was open and being held awkwardly. This was sufficient to make the detective suspicious and follow the man until he left the shop. In another store, the detective spent some time observing a girl who was handling jewellery with one hand, while concealing necklaces with the other until she eventually left without taking anything. In the same store, a man with a rolled-up carrier bag was seen to carry a sweater from the men's wear department, where he would normally be expected to pay for it, into the cosmetics department, and consequently, was followed until he returned the sweater. In addition, many people were observed and followed because of the awkward way they carried bags or coats, or because they were constantly looking around furtively. Few of these incidents developed into shoplifting cases.

Confronted with an undifferentiated mass of potential suspects, small inconsistencies are often sufficient to warrant further attention, particularly when the store is not busy and there is nothing more urgent demanding the store detective's attention. Of necessity, much of the store detective's time will be spent following perfectly innocent shoppers who just happen to be holding their bags awkwardly or who are inappropriately dressed. On occasions, potential shoplifting situations may be averted, and on others, people may be apprehended. Moreover, the person with the old carrier bag may be soon ignored if another more suspicious individual is sighted, or if the store detective is required to assist in another, definite apprehension.

Thus far, the fieldwork observations exemplified the traditional suspicious activities, but further research revealed the complicated analyses store detectives undertook in classifying shoppers. Not only did they operate with a typification of the ordinary customer, but this categorisation was subdivided in terms of the person's age, sex and appearance, as well as the type of goods being purchased, as the following cases demonstrate.

Store detectives classified people and their behaviour in terms of assumed sexual characteristics. For example, it has been observed that people who look furtively around them are considered suspicious because they are not acting like genuine shoppers. On several occasions, men who appeared to be looking around were cursorily dismissed by the store detective. The reason for this was that they were accompanied by women. Men by themselves who were looking around were suspicious, but if they were with women, their actions were interpreted as those of a (typical) bored husband or boyfriend, not interested in shopping, and whose actions were therefore not those of a potential shoplifter. As long as the woman was behaving like a genuine customer, the man was not suspicious.

A subtle ramification of this sexual classification was noticed in another department store, where a solitary man was observed in the lingerie department. To the researcher, the man appeared nervous and suspicious, but the store detective explained that men typically behaved like that in the lingerie department, and that he could have been looking around for someone the same size as his girl-friend to help him in his choice. However, the man then went into the trousers department and continued to act furtively, He now became suspicious to the store detective, who watched him closely until he left. The same actions, then, can be that of a normal shopper in one context (a man in a lingerie department), but are immediately suspicious when transferred to another department.

Shoppers can also be classified in terms of the goods they are purchasing or are interested in. For example, a store detective in a large supermarket became suspicious of a man and woman loading goods into their shopping trolley. To the researcher, this seemed to be exactly what everybody else was doing, but the store detective explained the different patterns of grocery shopping. Some people shopped for a few items that they had run out of; others shopped for a specific event, such as a party or picnic. More generally, people did their weekly shopping in the supermarket, where, it was explained, they purchased everyday, mundane items such as bread, toothpaste, vegetables and soap. The trolley being used by this man and woman had none of these cheap but essential commodities, and was filled instead with expensive joints of meat, and tins of ham and salmon. Because the couple had no inexpensive but necessary items the store detective became suspicious of them and anticipated that they would attempt to wheel the trolley out of a side door without paying for anything. Whether the pair were affected by nerves or became aware of the store detective's attentions, they soon abandoned their trolley of meats and left the supermarket without buying anything.

One of the reasons that children and adolescents make security personnel alert is that they are often considered not to have sufficient means to make expensive purchases. Their presence in such typically young people's departments as toys, cosmetics, boutiques and records is, in itself, unremarkable. When they wander into the more expensive clothes, jewellery, camera and hi-fi departments they are more worthy of attention. The appearance of adults may also be taken into consideration. Although store detectives are well aware that scruffy, old people may be eccentric millionaires, their presence in the expensive furs salon will be more suspicious than their expensively attired counterparts.

Customer behaviour, then, can be minutely classified in terms of age, appearance, sex and what they are buying. Included in these categoris- ations are conceptions of eccentric but 'normal' shopping behaviour, or, as it was often described, 'too obvious' behaviour. For example, the researcher noticed a group of children playing with some model cars and asked the store detective if this were not suspicious. The detective replied that the children were too engrossed with the toys — if they had intended to steal them they would have done so already and would not have become involved in playing. On another occasion, the researcher observed a teenage girl in the jewellery department with five rings in her hand, but again the store detective dismissed this as being 'too obvious'. Finally, a whole family was observed seated at the top of an escalator, piling mounds of new clothes into new suitcases, but this incident was interpreted as a family organising their purchases in order to carry them more conveniently — it was far too obvious and eccentric to be con- strued as a potential shoplifting situation.

Thus far, it has been argued that store detectives classify people and behaviour in terms of what ordinary customers do. For all the talk of intuition, the identification of potential shoplifters relied on a rational analysis of customer activity; on a sense of what a typical customer would *not* do. However, a number of store detectives were seen to oper- ate with typical *shoplifter* stereotypes, and disturbingly these stereo- types were almost always of a racist nature. Many references were made to 'spooks', 'nig-nogs', 'wogs', and 'sooties'. This racism was often trans- lated into action, so that any 'black'[84] people were viewed as suspicious and were followed, and this was particularly noticeable for anybody who was of Rastafarian appearance. Some store detectives were equally prejudiced against Asians ('They give me the creeps'), but most hostility was reserved for young blacks. One store detective considered that 'negroes' had a chip on their shoulder and had a tendency to be violent. On occasions, in anticipation of violence, more force than was custom- ary was expended to restrain black youths, who, in turn, reacted more aggressively, perpetuating a vicious circle. Apart from their 'blackness' there was often little reason to follow many black youths, and yet they were described as suspicious types. Further questioning only elucidated the response that they were suspicious because they were 'black'; and 'blacks' had proved to be shoplifters and generally trouble in the past. As discussed below, this can become a self-fulfilling prophecy.

An ironical aspect of this discrimination was demonstrated in two similar department stores, located next to each other. In one, black women were generally believed to be shoplifters and were routinely followed, while the men were largely ignored unless they became suspicious in their own right. In the adjoining store, the reverse obtained: black men were viewed with suspicion, while the women were generally ignored.

One store detective always followed women who had bleached their hair peroxide blonde, in the belief that if they had the cheek to do that, they would do anything. Apparently she made a considerable number of arrests of peroxide blondes. Given that far more people take things from shops than are ever caught, it is likely that targeting on one specific group, however selected, is likely to prove 'successful', and a self-fulfilling prophecy is established. 'Blacks' are followed because they are generally thought to be prone to shoplifting, and arrests prove the security personnel correct. Similarly, evidence for black women and not black men (and vice versa) is provided in the two neighbouring stores. Evidence can even be produced to show that women who dye their hair are more prone to shoplift. It is probable that 'proof' could be found for any group of people, however strange the criteria of selection, and that random selection would be just as successful, which perhaps goes some way to explain why Arabs were so prevalent in the late 1970s.

When they screen customers, then, store detectives rely on a number of factors in deciding whom to follow. First, and rarely, there are those people who are spotted by chance, the ones who are caught during an attempt to steal by the fortuitous location of the store detective. Secondly, and more generally, store detectives operate with a complex categorisation of the 'typical shopper', which locates a customer in terms of sex, age, appearance and the type of merchandise they are interested in. Any variation from this categorisation of the 'normal' shopper, unless it is 'too obvious', becomes suspicious and warrants further investigation. Finally, there are those people who are watched because they are stereotypically believed to be shoplifters, and disturbingly, this category would seem to be restricted largely to young black people. Having discussed what store detectives look for it is now possible to proceed to study how they operate to control the shoplifting population.

Controlling the potential shoplifting population

(i) *Banning and exclusion.* The simplest method of controlling the potential shoplifting population is to exclude all people considered to be a risk. Thus it has been seen that gangs of children and vagrants will frequently not be allowed to enter the store, or will be made to leave once inside. In addition, people who have previously been caught shoplifting will be banned from the shop, and will be asked to leave if they do return. In practice, it is difficult to see how a rigid policy of banning all previous shoplifters could be policed effectively.

However, the only case of adult exclusion which occurred during the fieldwork concerned a man who had previously been caught shoplifting. On this occasion, the store detective recognised a man that he had previously caught and banned, approached him and asked him to leave. The man refused to do so, saying it was a public place. The store detective, secure in the knowledge that legally a shop is *not* a public place, insisted that the man leave or the police would be called and he would be prosecuted for trespass. With much grumbling, the man eventually left, whereupon the store detective pointed out a pair of jeans which he said the man had been folding in preparation to steal them.

In addition, there were many instances of children being ejected from stores. For example, in one store, two boys were playing on the escalator rail and were admonished by the store detective, 'Here get off and get out.' He explained that they were the type of 'toe rags' they got in the store and the ones they tried to get rid of. In another shop, 'Truants are always put out because they are always trouble.' In yet another store, the detective came across two 'toe rags' and stared at them, until a saleslady independently chased them out, but not before they were chastised for not being at school and warned not to return. Morris points out that shoplifting has a game-like excitement for children, who often steal purely as a 'dare'.[85]

One store detective in a record shop explained how he dealt with 'troublesome' youths: 'I use different tactics with different groups. If a person is respectable, I'm diplomatic and polite. If they are rough kids, I'll use language that they will understand.' He said that if he found kids playing in the lifts he would say, 'Why don't you piss off?' and they would, But if he said 'Why don't you behave yourself?', they would laugh at him.

Juveniles were not always treated in this way, however, and often the police would be called. For example, in one boutique the store detective spotted three girls, one of whom had a blouse in her shopping bag and a top hidden in her coat. When she was taken to the interview room, she threw an hysterical fit and claimed that her father would kill her this time. She admitted that she had shoplifted before. The other two girls, sisters aged 15 and 12, continued to cry. The store detective decided to call the police, which caused even more distress among the girls. A policeman and woman arrived and listened to the evidence. They decided to let the two sisters go as they had not actually stolen anything. The girl 'shoplifter' had £20 on her at the time, which she claimed was a Christmas present from her mother. The store detective refused to let her pay for the goods, and the girl was led off to the police station, crying. The sisters were warned by both the detective and the police never to go into the store again.

While a policy of exclusion may be practised against certain 'undesirables' — groups of children, adolescents and previous shoplifters — it obviously cannot be applied systematically, for after all, management want customers. Consequently, store detectives attempt to control

148

most of the shoplifting problem within the store, usually by attempting to apprehend potential shoplifters.

(ii) *Making apprehensions.*   Some store detectives stationed themselves at selected sites and waited for potential shoplifters to come to them. The majority, however, walked around the shopfloor, patrolling the various counters and gondolas, in the hope of discovering something untoward. Departments which sold bulky merchandise (carpets, furniture, washing machines, etc.) were not often visited, but most other sections were covered, particularly those considered high-risk areas. Sometimes store detectives were detailed to patrol particular floors or departments; sometimes they were allowed to choose where they went for themselves; and for many, the whole shop would be the target area.

Apart from being tiring on the feet, this constant walking could be monotonous, and when there was no shoplifting activity, morale tended to sag. The search for 'bodies' often took on a game-like quality, similar to that of the hunter and hunted, and when a suspected shoplifter was spied, the adrenalin began to flow, as the following extract reveals:

> As we walked around Pam said, 'Now you can see how
> exciting it is once things start happening. You can be as
> tired as anything, your feet aching, bored out of your mind,
> but then suddenly something happens, and you get excited.
> You forget all about being tired.'[86]

There was no evidence from the research to support the view that store detectives received bonuses for results, but there was generally a strong desire to produce 'bodies' to prove that they were being effective and also to relieve the tedium of walking around the shops.

There seemed to be an average period of about 20 minutes spent following a person who appeared suspicious. After that time, if they had not been seen to take something, they would be abandoned. This operation, though, was very flexible. If the store were not busy, and no other suspects appeared, the suspect might be followed till he/she left the store. On the other hand, if the store were busy the observation could be reduced, and this might happen also if the store detective were requested to assist elsewhere.

Once a person is discovered behaving suspiciously, the store detectives generally begin to think in terms of apprehension; adrenalin flows; hearts pump faster; minds begin to race. Cover must be maintained and so the detective hides behind displays and peers through gondolas. Often a wire basket with a few light articles is carried to create the impression of a normal shopper, so that the store detective can edge closer to the suspect. They must be close enough to see everything that is occurring, but not too near to alert the suspect. The store detective watches constantly, concentrating deeply, begins to make mental notes, anticipating that the suspect will take something. Once the suspect takes and secretes an article, the store detective is moving into an apprehension context, and this has several serious implications. Before examining the circumstances of making an arrest, however, it is necessary to consider the two dangers that store detectives face in such a situation: the risk of violence and the possibility of false arrest.

In Chapter 5, it was seen that most security officers considered that violence was increasing and although little was observed in the fieldwork, a number of cases have been reported in the press, of which the following are an example.

Shoplift Thugs who Beat up Detectives

One in five of P.'s security guards, men and women, were attacked last year.[87]

The Perils of Being a Store Detective

Peter is 37, stands 6 ft 2 in in his socks and weighs 14 stone. In his job as store detective, he has been attacked 25 times in 18 months, ending up in hospital eight times. He has lost all of his teeth and has a steel plate in his jaw. His nose has been broken twice, he has had five fractured ribs and cracked bones in his feet. 'Black eyes?' he said, 'I've lost count.'[88]

Tougher Lines on Shoplifting

Jean talked about the violence she was as a matter of course involved in. Her hands still showed faint traces of the sixteen weals she had received months ago when a woman clawed her. 'I noticed her in our store, then followed her into another. Because she had not been caught here, her confidence was bolstered — she could hardly get everything into her bag quickly enough. When the detective from the other shop went up to her (she was a woman in her late 50's) she went berserk — said her husband was dead and started hurling packets of biscuits at her.' When the detective bent down to pick up some of the stuff, she lifted her arm to bang her on the back of the neck, and when I held her back she tried to bite me. Then when the other detective in turn tried to get her off and make her pick up her bags, she clawed me.[89]

Other incidents of violence were particularly gruesome.

Making it Hotter for Shoplifters

The store detective to whom my colleague was assigned to go round the store and see how detectives work, 24-year-old Mr L. had scars on neck and wrists. Eighteen

months ago his throat was cut and his wrists were
slashed by a man who had stolen a suit.[90]

The researcher subsequently met this store detective and verified the
scars on his body.

Although the next case does not involve store detectives, it demonstrates the lengths to which some shoplifers will go, and while store
detectives may perhaps over-emphasise the threat of violence to glamorise their jobs, it is clear that the possibility of injury is real.

Yells Saved PC from Axe Attack

Desperate screams of a policewoman saved the life of
a young policeman who was about to be hit by a woman
brandishing an axe, a court was told yesterday. WPC J.D.
25, yelled in alarm as she saw shoplifter Mrs M., 35, raise
an axe over the head to bring down on the skull of PC T.B.
20, it was said at Winchester crown court. ... The court
was told that the two police officers went to M.'s council
flat ... and tried to arrest Mrs M. 35, mother of three, on
suspicion of stealing 16 packets of pork chops. But before
they could take her away her husband grabbed the axe
from the kitchen cabinet and attacked PC B.[91]

The second problem which has to be overcome by store detectives
when making an apprehension is the prevention of claims for false
arrest. Again, no actual instances of this occurred in the fieldwork and,
not surprisingly, security personnel were less forthcoming about this
topic than they were about violence. The media, however, provide some
examples of the repercussions involved in wrongful arrest.

Innocent but Shamed

This is what happened to these two ladies who went out
shopping .... Mrs B., 58, spent about £5 at T.'s in Salisbury.
It was her usual weekend routine. But this time she was
stopped by a young man from the shop as she left and asked
her to come back and have her shopping checked. 'He held
my arm to lead me back into the store,' said Mrs B. 'An office
manager winked at a colleague as if to say, "here's another
one!" ' Mrs B. was accused of stealing a piece of Stilton cheese
for which no receipt could be found. She was subjected to the
embarrassment of walking right through the store with a
policewoman, who escorted her to Salisbury police station.
There she was made to empty her handbag and was detained
for two hours before her innocence was established. The
cash-till girl had made a mistake. E.B. had paid for the

Stilton cheese. She sued T.'s and was awarded £102 damages.

It was the sentimental verses in two Easter cards that brought Lady G., 60, to the greatest crisis in her life. She too was accused of shoplifting. She had bought the cards at J. in Chelsea, a store where she had spent literally thousands of pounds. But she decided the verses in the cards were 'too sloppy' so she took them back to change them. The store was busy and she was kept waiting for over 15 minutes. Worried about her car parked outside, she decided to help herself to two new cards and put the first two back. The new cards were actually marked at threepence less than the others. But when she left the shop, Lady G. was stopped by two women store detectives. She was taken to the local police station and charged with stealing two cards. In court, the case was dismissed because the prosecution offered no evidence. Lady G. was cleared. Not guilty. Her character unassailed.[92]

Some recent cases emphasise the trauma experienced by customers and demonstrates the bad publicity which falls on the stores.

Innocent Woman's Shop Ordeal

Mother of five, R.W., was walking out of a supermarket last year when a woman store detective stopped her. What happened then still haunts her. She said yesterday: 'It was an experience I can never forget.' Mrs W. runs a dairy farm near Abergavenny, Gwent. On a shopping trip to Pontypool she went into a F. branch to buy cat food. The store didn't stock the brand she wanted, so she returned her wire-basket to the stack and walked out. Mrs W. said: 'Outside the store I was grabbed by the store detective and marched into the manager's office. The detective gripped me painfully by both arms.' Mrs. W.'s bag was searched. It was empty. Then the detective produced what she claimed was stolen bacon. Mrs W. was charged with theft and elected to go for trial at Newport crown court, where she was cleared. Since then she has contacted the Civil Counselling Service for Alleged Shoplifters, set up to help people charged with the offence. Mrs W. is also suing F.'s for unlawful arrest and unlawful imprisonment.[93]

Woman Accused of Stealing her own Gloves

A woman was accused of stealing her own gloves when she was arrested on a shopping trip. For five months, the charge

hung over 50-year-old housewife, M.L. — until yesterday
when a court cleared her. After the hearing, Mrs L. said:
'It's been an absolute nightmare. The whole business
nearly destroyed my marriage — gossip has been so rife
it even had my husband doubting my word.' Magistrates
at Doncaster, Yorks, heard that Mrs L. was arrested after
a store detective saw her putting a pair of gloves in her
shopping bag. After spending more than three hours at
a police station, Mrs L. 'confessed' to theft from L.'s
store. But then an expert called in by her solicitor
examined the gloves and found that they were not new.
Prosecutor P.B. asked for the case to be withdrawn. He
said:, 'The situation is so confused that it would be wrong
to put the matter before the court.' Mrs L. ... said after the
hearing: 'Now I may sue both the store and the police.'[94]

Store detectives may sometimes fail to distinguish between dishonesty
and inadvertance, but the most serious mistake they can make is to fail
to demonstrate the actual 'taking' of goods, as these two cases demonstrate.

When they make apprehensions, then, store detectives must overcome
the two problems of violence and false arrest. May puts the position as
follows:

By involving the security officer for the first time in a public
declaration of her suspicions it commits her, and the store,
to a course of action that may prove not merely unrewarding
but decidedly embarrassing and disagreeable for them both.
And once embarked upon, withdrawal cannot be accomplished
without at best a serious loss of face. So the decision to
apprehend has the paradoxical effect of reducing the security
officer's power at the very moment she first chooses to exercise
it.[95]

The following two cases, taken from fieldwork notes, provide a focus
for discussing how security staff attempt to control the threat of violence.

Case I: Whilst walking around the store, two detectives
working together observed a woman removing a
cashmere sweater from its protective polythene
wrapper and place it over her own bag. She
ascended to the first floor via the escalator, and, as
she moved towards the lift, was seen to take the
garment with her right hand and place it in her bag.
She got into the descending lift and left the shop from

the ground floor. She was then apprehended by the male and female store detectives by placing their hands upon her shoulders. The male security officer then said, 'Hello love, I think you've got a jumper in your bag which you haven't paid for.' He identified himself as a store detective and produced his identity card. He asked the woman if she could speak English, to which the woman assented. She was then taken by a back route to the interview room, whereupon the chief security officer was called.

The interview stage of this arrest will be discussed later.

Case 2: Two 'black' youths were seen to be acting suspiciously in the jeans department. They each took several pairs of jeans into the changing rooms. Meanwhile, the store detective used his two-way radio to call for assistance for 'Help with some "sooties".' Several male store detectives quickly arrived on the scene. The two youths emerged from the changing rooms and placed several pairs of jeans back on the racks. However, it was obvious that whilst in the changing rooms they had put a pair of jeans under their own trousers, for the denim showed beneath the bottom hem of one of the youth's trousers, and the other looked as if he had several bandages around his knees. The youths were allowed to leave the store, but as soon as they had taken a couple of paces, four store detectives grabbed them and held their arms behind them. As the youths were being taken back into the store the detectives identified themselves.

Although these two cases differ markedly, they do have a number of features in common. The first thing to notice is that the security personnel will try to ensure that the suspected shoplifter is outnumbered by staff. In the first case, two store detectives arrested one woman, and in the second, four apprehended two youths. When there are insufficient store detectives, the arresting detective will try to ensure that a uniformed guard or other member of staff is available as a back-up. In addition, when approaching the suspect, it is customary for the security staff to position themselves on either side of the suspect, thus reducing the possibilities of flight. Security staff, then, will attempt to ensure that if there is an altercation, they will be in a physically superior position.

However, no store detective wants to be involved in brawling in front of their store — it creates a bad image, they might get hurt, and if the suspect is innocent, the repurcussions will be even more serious. So while it is comforting to have the assurance of physical support, store detectives rely more heavily on psychological weapons. They want to ensure that the suspect returns to the store as quickly and quietly as possible, and although the physical presence of several security person-nel may foster compliance, overt acts of force are just as likely to provoke aggression in the suspect. Perhaps because of their limited authority and lack of community support, store detectives, unlike uniformed police officers, have a strong desire to move the suspect to a private place to reduce their vulnerability. It must be noted that the vast majority of arrests correspond closely to the first case; few rely on the direct force exhibited in the second example.

What are these psychological advantages that store detectives possess? The first, and most obvious, is that store detectives are experienced in making arrests. They have done it many times before. In all probability, it is the suspect's first time at being caught. Secondly, the store detec-tive has a specific purpose in the encounter: to get the suspect to return, and knows how best to achieve this. The timing of the apprehension is significant here. Suspects are usually permitted to take several steps out of the shop (generally required to demonstrate the 'intent' aspect of theft). If the suspects are frightened of being arrested they will be expecting it to occur immediately they leave; once they have taken several steps they believe that they have avoided attention and have escaped. It is then that they are stopped. Psychologically, it is a critical moment, which takes them from elation to despair in a fraction of a second.

As they identify themselves and their reasons for making the appre-hension (though the word is never used), the store detectives will already have a hand on the suspect's elbow and will be leading them back into the store. In addition, as case 1 shows the arrest will be conducted in a calm and non-threatening manner. Rarely will security staff mention the word 'theft' and instead will intimate that a mistake might have been made or that there might be a problem which would be best dealt with in the manager's office. Any arguments by the suspect will be answered with the firm response that the manager's office is the best place to discuss the matter. By now, any opportunities for flight will have been excluded. As the customer prevaricates between the possibil-ities of denial and bluster, or the hope of leniency, he will be led inexorably back into the store. Even now, the situation is being present-ed as an internal matter, between the customer and the shop. The sus-pect hopes that even if he fails to talk his way out of the situaiton, he will be allowed to pay for the goods or will escape with a reprimand. The possible serious consequences have not yet occurred to the custom-er and the security personnel rely on this ignorance and hope in making a peaceful arrest. Critically, no threat of calling the police is ever made at this stage (unless the suspect is recalcitrant or struggles), and the likelihood of prosecution for theft in court is a remote possibility. Once in the security of the interview room, the store detectives know that they have control of the situation and most of the battle has been won.

Attention will now be focused on how store detectives manage the threat of false arrest. Avoiding the possibility of providing grounds for false arrest is more complicated than preventing violence when making an apprehension. At a minimum, the store detective must be able to show (a) that he/she did not act illegally, and (b) that the customer did in fact take the property of the store without paying for it *(actus reus)*. If the store detective cannot demonstrate the *actus reus,* then his/her professional competence will be questioned, and he/she will be liable for legal action. In practice, the security officer is also concerned with proving that the suspect intended to take the goods.

The best outcome from the store detective's point of view is for the suspect to admit the offence. Then the store can either act as if the offence did not happen and let the customer go with a warning, or if the case goes to court, it will not involve the detective in too much extra effort or time. If the suspect cannot be persuaded to admit guilt, then the store detective should be able to demonstrate guilt to a court, but this demands more effort. A lesser option for security staff is where a court accepts that the *actus reus* occurred, but rejects that intention was involved. Many store detectives view such a verdict as a waste of their time if they believe that the customer meant to steal. This outcome, however, does not undermine the correctness of the store detective's actions. The worst possible result for the store detective is where the *actus reus* of the case is not established.

The problem facing store detectives is that they do not know the outcome of the arrest: that is, whether the suspect will admit or deny the accusation. Although only a small percentage of suspects ever plead not guilty, store detectives must act as if they all would and be in a position to defend their actions in court. A sound case also has the advantage of encouraging the suspect to admit guilt. Hole argues that, 'the first obligation of the security officer is to see that proof of all elements of the crime he is claiming against the individual apprehended are established.'[96] Earlier chapters emphasised the need for the store detective to watch the whole action from beginning to end: the approach to the counter, taking an article without paying, and leaving the store. Only then can the *actus reus* of the theft be demonstrated. If the suspect is not seen to approach a counter, they could conceivably be matching their own property against the store's for colour or size. Similarly, if the suspect is not observed throughout the episode, they may have returned the goods or passed them to an accomplice.

Baker shows how a typical store detective would describe an arrest.

> I was on duty when I saw a woman walking round the store.
> I noticed that she was putting various items into her bag.
> I saw two books, a pair of scissors and some toilet goods
> going into her own shopping bag. She left the store after
> paying for a tube of toothpaste. I did my usual stuff, 'Excuse
> me, madam, I am a store detective and I have reason to
> believe you have some items not paid for.' (She claimed it
> was a mistake.) A year earlier this might well have worked.
> This is typical of a case I would have lost when I first started,
> but I left nothing out. I noted every move — how she looked
> right and left before putting things into her bag: how, when
> she took the books, she walked into the clothing section and,
> whilst pretending to be looking at some raincoats, she dropped
> the books into her bag. I recalled that I had instructed a super-
> visor to stand at the till whilst she paid for a tube of toothpaste
> in order to note how much was paid. I produced the receipt
> that she dropped on the floor which showed that only one
> item was paid for. This was to forestall any pretence that she
> had paid for everything but had mislaid the receipt. I closed
> every loophole. She was fined £50 and £50 costs.[97]

Some of the store detectives in the study took brief notes whilst
watching suspects and expanded them later. Most, however, wrote their
reports from memory once the suspect had been detained, for fear of
missing some relevant act, losing sight of the suspect, or of alerting them.
Apart from the factors described by Baker, store detectives often
included other details such as what the suspect was wearing and carrying,
where they went, and what they said on arrest.

Proving the *actus reus* of the offence is usually straightforward. Each
store has its own style of goods and distinctive price tags and labels.
Receipts should be automatically placed in a bag along with the purchased item(s). The absence of a receipt and bag suggests that the customer has not paid. In practice, few people deny the taking of goods and
if the detective is proficient there should be no doubt about the *actus
reus*, but when the *actus reus* is not proven, the case often receives
extensive press coverage, as demonstrated above. If a person is going to
deny theft, then it is usually by denying intent, a far more contentious
area. Hole believes that, 'Intent to permanently deprive the owner of
his property is the most difficult theft element to prove.'[98] And Cox
states, 'The most common defence involves some degree of absent-mindedness.'[99] Although store detectives must be able to prove *actus reus*,
they are also eager to demonstrate the intention to steal. This is partly
because it helps in persuading the suspect to admit guilt and improves

the store detective's case if it is taken to court. It is also because the two elements of theft are inextricably linked. Full observations and a complete record of all the suspect's actions are required to demonstrate *actus reus*, and included in these will be details of whether the suspect looked around before taking goods, whether and where the items were placed, whether the suspect attempted to avoid detection, and if they tried to flee. Inevitably the rationality of the suspect will be emphasised: items will be 'selected' and then they will be 'secreted'. Method and daring will be stressed. Walking from counter to counter will be presented as progressive steps in a planned expedition of stealing.

As Hole points out a detailed report has several functions:

> A complete report prevents the defence attorney from casting doubts upon your qualifications or professionalism.... Another affirmative aspect of a good report is that defendants are encouraged to plead guilty in the face of it. [100]

This aspect is taken up by Griffin: 'Being able to name the item and place of concealment will go a long way towards convincing the shoplifter he has been caught red handed' [101] — an aspect which will be considered in more detail below. According to Scott and Lyman,

> Activities that are prohibited became legally actionable in the sense of a potentially successful prosecution of the deviant actor, only if it can be shown that the actor intended to commit the act and foresaw the consequences. A variety of other interpretations, which appear as accounts, with respect to the same event are possible. [102]

The task of store detectives, then, is to provide evidence which confirms the one account of a suspect's actions: that they intended to steal. Suspects may provide such alternatives for their actions as absentmindedness and being under the influence of drugs. The critical difference between these two sets of accounts is that the security officer's stresses rationality and full knowledge of action, while the suspect's emphasises irrationality or impaired knowledge. In court, the store detective relies on a carefully prepared and detailed report to emphasise that the suspect's actions were typical of somebody who *knew they were stealing and did not want to be caught,* in an attempt to deny any other account of impaired judgement.

Ideally, the store detectives would like the suspect to accept their account of the incident and plead guilty. Before seeing how security officers accomplish this in the interview, a small digression is necessary to discuss two kinds of shop thieves who pose different legal and practical problems to shoplifters: 'price-tag switchers' and 'refunders'.

Although 'switchers' and 'refunders' are both thieves, they are covered by different sections of the Theft Act 1968, and the restrictions on apprehension differ from those on shoplifting. Critically, 'price-tag switchers' and 'refunders' can be arrested immediately after their deception, i.e. they do not have to leave the store. Price-tag switchers are very difficult to combat. As one store detective declared, 'With price swaps, you can't do anything, they are too quick doing it to see them and at the till you can't prove that they have done it, so we just deter them.' 'Switchers' are combatted by deterrence and by other practical measures which include destructible price tags. Steiner *et al.*, from a sample of 20 self-confessed switchers, found that 'subjectively, price-tag switching was considered not really stealing'. 'Correspondingly, most persons felt that if they were detected, price-tag switching as opposed to outright theft would be more difficult to prove; they would be less likely to be prosecuted and if charges were brought against them they would be less severe.'[103] There does not appear to be much evidence that price-tag switching is very prevalent.

'Refunders' — people who shoplift goods and then return later, attempting to exchange the goods for cash — tend to be more professional than most shoplifters and can cause particular problems. Some stores do not allow goods under a certain value to be exchanged without a receipt. Consequently, thieves steal articles valued less than this limit from one shop in the chain and take it to another to obtain a cash refund. Even where shops insist on a receipt before making exchanges, they will often give refunds if the shopper provides a plausible explanation, e.g. the receipt has been lost, or the article was a present. It is unlikely that a security officer will observe everything involved in a deception and will therefore be unable to prove the case. Consequently, where they are suspicious, they will try to make it difficult for the suspect to obtain a cash refund. On the advice of the store detective, the sales assistant will attempt to obtain the suspect's name and address and offer to send the money. Delays can be explained by bogus stock-taking and audits. Refunders will be reluctant to provide their real names and addresses as they can then be traced, and if they give a false address they might not receive the money.

During the fieldwork one incident was observed when a refunder was believed to be operating. A man who had been followed in the morning suspected of stealing jeans, but who had been lost, returned in the afternoon and was spotted trying to obtain a refund for a pair of jeans. After some delay in asking him for his name and address, he was given a credit note. The store detective ostentatiously followed him out of the store hoping to scare him out of attempting to exchange the credit note.

It is now possible to examine the next stage in the sequence: the interview.

(iii) *The interview.* The interview of the suspect usually occurs in a secluded room, often the manager's office, or, in larger stores, in a specially designated security room. 'Interrogation of a suspect', says May, 'always takes place in the presence of at least two members of staff, to permit a close watch of the suspects so that they can't dispose of articles or injure themselves and to defer potential accusations of misbehaviour.'[104]

To provide a focus for the discussion of interviews, three cases taken from fieldwork notes, are presented. The first is the routine continuation of case 1 discussed above under *Apprehensions.* The other two cases both involve small sums of money, but are instructive in that they have different outcomes.

Case 1: 'Hello love, I think you've got a jumper in your bag which you haven't paid for.' He identified himself as a store detective and produced his identity card. He asked the woman if she could speak English, to which the woman assented. She was then taken by a back route to the interview room, whereupon the chief security officer was called. The girl said that she had never done this before and when asked by the CSO why she hadn't paid she replied that she didn't have any money. The store detective repeated what she had seen and the woman was charged with the evidence provided. The CSO asked if he could look into her bag. She agreed and he found nothing in there that appeared to have been stolen. [The jumper had already been removed.] He asked her various biographical details. She was nineteen and gave her occupation as a machinist pattern cutter in a couture house. She said that she had given up her job that morning and had an interview for another at 3.30 that afternoon. She had a very upper-class accent and the CSO asked whether her parents were 'monied'. She replied that her mother was ill and that she had sole responsibility for her welfare. She was asked to produce any other items she had taken, but there were none. The CSO told the detective to call the police. The woman then asked if she had to go through with it, and whether there was anything that she could do. He said that she had stolen, like anyone else, and he saw no reason to make an exception in her case. She said that it was a very foolish thing to do and she whole-heartedly admitted that she was guilty. After a plain clothes police officer had arrived and listened to the evidence he cautioned her and took her to the police station, where she was charged.

Case 3: The store detective saw a young black girl with her back to us. She saw furtive hand movements next to the soap display and into the girl's bag. The girl then went quickly out through an empty check-out and through the main entrance. The store detective hurried after her and apprehended her and said, 'I am a security officer for X and I have reason to believe you have goods in your bag which you have not paid for, would you please come back into the store?' Miss A. said, 'No, I have not.' She again said, 'Will you come back?' and she said, 'No, I won't.' The assistant manager who had come out with the store detective, helped her to bring the girl back into the manager's office. The store detective then cautioned the girl and asked her to empty her brown bag. This she did, and after taking out a skirt, she took out the two bars of soap. The detective then said, 'Empty the other bag', and the girl said, 'No I won't, they are mine.' The detective again said, 'Empty it or I will call the police.' The girl then took out a pair of jeans and two more bars of soap. She then said, 'You can let me go now.' She was asked her name and eventually said that it was 'Angela Davis'. She said that she was sixteen. Once she had surrendered the soap, Angela wanted to leave, but the store detective called the police. The girl went berserk shouting, 'You said you wouldn't if I opened the bag', to which the store detective replied, 'I never said I wouldn't.' The girl answered, 'What do you want to call the police for if you've got your bars of soap back?' Whereupon, she attacked the store detective, climbed over the office partition and had to be restrained by a storeman. Three men took her to a small storeroom and locked her in, but the detective said the door should be opened. The police quickly arrived, expecting a large commotion, and were quite amused to find a small girl. She was known to the police, not as Angela Davis, but under her real name and age [seventeen]. She had previous convictions for shoplifting. The police wanted the store detective to press charges for assault but she declined to do this.

161

Case 4:   An old lady was spotted taking cat food, cheese
and evaporated milk and putting them into her
shopping bag. The store detective stopped her
inside the shop and said, 'You've put some stuff
in your bag and you haven't paid for it.' She said,
'I know.' The store detective did not say that she
was a security officer and stopped her before she
left the shop because she was frightened the old
lady might 'flake out'. The old woman only had
eighty-five pence on her and offered to pay for some
things. The staff let her buy a tin of cat food and a
tin of evaporated milk. The value of the stolen goods
was £2.80. The old lady said she felt so ashamed and
cried. She also wet herself with the shock of it all and
was taken to the toilet. The woman was a regular
customer, and when questioned, admitted that she
had stolen before. She realised what was happening
and understood that she was barred from the shop.
She said, 'I won't be able to come back.' The police
were not called as the store detective was frightened
of the effect it might have on the woman and of the
publicity it might bring to the store. The woman was
released with a caution and caused the manager,
researcher and store detective considerable disquiet
afterwards.

According to Griffin, the interrogation has three functions: the
recovery of property, the production of a confession, and the signing
of a release for civil liability.[105] The interview has a number of other
functions, however, which will become apparent later. How does the
store detective achieve the goals of an interview? To begin with, the
participants in the interview situation are not equals. As Scheff says,

> Interrogator and client have unequal power in determining
> the resultant definition of the situation. The interrogator's
> definition of the situation plays an important part in the
> joint definition of the situation which is finally negotiated.
> Moreover, his definition is more important than the client's
> in determining the final outcome of the negotiation, princi-
> pally because he is well trained, secure and self-confident in
> his role in the transaction, whereas the client is untutored,
> anxious and uncertain about his role. Stated simply, the
> subject because of these conditions, is likely to be susceptible
> to the influence of the interrogator.[106]

There are a number of ways that store detectives can manipulate the situation so that it is favourable to themselves. These techniques are commonly employed by law enforcement agencies of all kinds as well as by people in positions of authority (e.g. head teachers, military officers, etc.). Store detectives may make the suspects wait for a while before beginning the interview, thereby hoping to increase the suspects' insecurity and uncertainty, and make them more malleable. Suspects are made vulnerable in the office, they are not allowed outside communication. Their shame at being caught is translated into anxiety about the outcome; their insecurity is maximised, and they are more prepared to plead guilty in the hope that the ordeal will all be over quickly.

Once the interview has commenced, the first task is to regain the stolen property, unless, as in cases 1 and 4 above, the store detective has already recovered it from the suspect. The procedure, as dictated by one security officer is as follows: 'When they are back in the office, they are cautioned and asked to produce the items they haven't paid for. If you know what they have got and where it is, they are more likely to produce it.' If the suspect declines to produce 'goods not paid for' the store detective says, 'What about the X in your pocket?' This usually has a devastating effect on the suspect and results in the goods being produced. As May says,

> Here is where the careful observation work prior to appre
> hension can be used to advantage. If the security officer
> knows where at least one of the stolen articles is hidden
> this may be sufficient to convince the suspect that continued
> protestations of innocence are useless.[107]

And in Griffin's words, 'it will go a long way towards convincing the shoplifter that he has been caught red-handed.'[108]

More generally, the interview is conducted under the assumption that the suspect is guilty and has taken articles without paying. Speaking of police investigations, Sudnow reports, 'The conceivable first question, "Did you do it?" is not asked because it is felt that this gives the defendant the notion that he can try the innocent pitch.'[109] Similarly, store detectives do not ask suspects whether they shoplifted but proceed straight to the details ('Where are the goods not paid for?'), when they usually know full well where they are hidden.

As the store detective quoted above said, 'Once they've produced the goods they've taken, you ask, "Is there anything else?" and often they bring out things you haven't seen.' (Cf. case 1.) Once the suspect has produced one item not paid for he has little to gain by pretending that other items have not been taken for if the goods are all from the same store, it is still only one offence of shoplifting.

'No private person, which includes security officers,' say Oliver and

Wilson, 'has the right to search anyone. Consent to do so must be given at the time.'[110] Store detectives, then, cannot force a suspect to be searched. If necessary, the usual procedure is to ask the suspect authoratively to turn out his/her pockets. In case 1, the CSO politely asked if he could look in the girl's bag. This in effect, was a search, but done in such a low-key fashion as to be unremarkable.

By this stage, it is unusual for suspects not to have handed over any stolen goods, and admitted their guilt, but if they have not, store detectives have an effective tactic to ensure cooperation. As May says, 'they do so by holding out the promise of rewards for cooperation or hinting at the unpleasant consequences that will follow continued non-cooperation.'[111] The critical power possessed by store detectives is the discretion to call the police or let the suspect go. Although the store detective may already have decided to call the police — or indeed, it may be store policy in all cases — the suspect will not know this, and will be hoping for leniency. Threats to call the police, then, will almost always ensure compliance, as no suspect wants the police involved. In case 3, for example, the recalcitrant girl was manipulated into compliance by the threat to call the police.

The store detective's phrasing in this case is interesting as it holds out the implicit promise not to call the police, while at the same time not denying that option to the detective. Indeed, the fact that the suspect needed to be threatened to ensure cooperation will *increase* the probability that the police will be called. Ironically, as the store detective in case 3 said, if the girl had been cooperative she would have let her go.

A method used by one store detective to gain cooperation was to threaten to check the till roll:

> When a suspect is brought back and will not confess, I often
> threaten to check the till rolls, having already asked where
> the suspect bought the items and at what till point. This is
> usually a bluff because unless the item is unusually priced,
> there is no way it can be distinguished from many others.
> The purpose is to soften up the suspect so they confess.

It is doubtful whether a watertight case of shoplifting could be based on evidence supplied solely from till rolls. However, Robert Adley, MP, cites one case where, 'a man who had served almost 30 years with the Hampshire constabulary was convicted of shoplifting almost solely on the evidence of the till roll.'[112] Where till rolls are used, it is more usually as a 'softening-up' technique.

A form of plea-bargaining may occur when the suspect has struggled to avoid apprehension: In the words of one store detective, 'I bargain with the suspect if there has been a struggle, I say I won't mention it to keep them quiet and to get them to confess.' But he believed that merely by talking nicely to suspects you would get them to confess anyway.

Thus far, the strategies employed by store detectives have been geared to ensuring the shop's property is returned and that, implicitly or explicitly, the suspect confesses (at least to the *actus reus*). If the store detective intends calling the police, waivers against liability are not necessary, as these are only required when the suspect is released with a warning. The interview does have other functions, however.

Another aspect of the interrogation is the status degradation of suspects — they are made to think of themselves as thieves and not just people who take things, or even as shoplifters. This is to make the task of eliciting a confession easier and to make the experience more traumatic. By acting as moral arbiters, and decrying the suspects' actions, store detectives hope to make the whole experience unpleasant and unforgettable for the suspects, so that they are deterred from ever stealing again. Most security officers act in this fashion even if they have decided to call the police, but are even more stern when they have decided to let the suspect go. These transformations of status are begun by the store detectives, continued by the police, and reach their public end in the courtroom, and perhaps even appear in local and national newspapers. As Cameron says, 'Arrest forces the pilferer to think of himself as a thief.' She continues:

> In the course of all this investigation, it becomes increasingly clear to the pilferer that he is considered a thief and is in imminent danger of being hauled into court and publicly exposed as such. This realisation is often accompanied by dramatic change in attitudes and by severe emotional disturbance.[113]

For example, in cases 1 and 3, the suspects became agitated when they realised that the police were to be involved. The feeling of shame is again expressed in cases I and 4; and the realisation of their actions and confessions are again verbalised in these two cases. Gusfield,[114] Goffman[115] and Garfinkel[116] all deal with status degradation and the ensuing stigma which is attached to the label of thief, and these will be discussed more fully in Chapter 7.

Making the suspects break down or cry is often seen as an end in itself: it signifies shame and is taken as a symbol of remorse. Suspects often apologise profusely, and this may be seen as a necessary precondition for leniency. The reverse is certainly the case: if a suspect does not accept the opprobrium of stealing and shows no remorse, the store detectives are more likely to call the police.

In the previous chapter, the outlines for discretion were discussed, and although there was variation, it was generally accepted that leniency would be shown to the old, young, sick and pregnant. There were exceptions to these guidelines as the following extracts from one retailer suggests:

a. Woman, aged 71, detected by security stealing goods valued at £2.11.
Police dealing.

b. Boy aged 13, detected by security stealing goods valued at 63p.
Warned by the police.

Note in both these cases the amounts stolen were small and the suspects would usually have been warned by virtue of their age.

As a general rule, the old and the young are not referred to the police; however, a number of other factors emerged during the fieldwork which affected the decision to call the police, as the following examples illustrate.

A boy of 14 was caught stealing goods of low value, but when questioned by the store detective refused to give his name and was generally uncooperative, so the police were called (cf. case b. above). In a similar case, a man was caught with a 59p tin of spam in his possession. When questioned, he said he was 105 years old and gave his name as Cliff Richard. Again the police were called. In situations such as these, cooperative suspects would often be shown leniency, the police are called, however, because the suspects are not taking the situation seriously, are not being cooperative, are not demonstrating remorse, or are not being respectful. Critically, without the suspect's cooperation, store detectives cannot obtain their names and addresses or their admission of guilt. The store cannot let such suspects go free as this will invite prosecutions for false arrest; consequently they have to call the police. Moreover, as case 3 demonstrates, when cooperation has to be gained by threats of calling the police, the probability of police involvement is greatly increased.

In addition, if a suspect, who would normally have been released, exhibits a degree of professionalism, then the police will often be called. For example, when two 13 year-old girls were caught, because of the number of goods they had taken, and the expertise they had shown in stealing, they 'had to be referred to the police'.

Conversely, people who might ordinarily expect to be referred to the police are occasionally shown leniency because of various mitigating circumstances. For example, in one store a consultant surgeon was caught stealing two 'girlie' magazines, because, as he said, he was too embarrassed to buy them. He was allowed to pay for the magazines as the store detective believed that calling the police 'would have ruined him and I did not want to see such a man destroyed over such a trivial affair.'

Sections (ii) and (iii) above have dealt with the apprehension and interview of suspects who would generally be referred to the police unless they fell into certain discretionary categories or were affected by special factors. The option for apprehension/interview/police referral, however, is not always an available or desirable one. Section (iv) examines some of the methods store detectives employ to control shoplifting when apprehension is not viable; it also discusses the reasons behind these tactics.

(iv) *Alternatives to apprehension — 'informal methods'.* On many occasions, the apprehension/interrogation/police referral model may be either inappropriate or unavailable. Security personnel will be concerned to retrieve the store's goods without invoking the problems of false arrest, and to this end they adopt a number of tactics or 'informal methods' for controlling shoplifting. There are various reasons for not arresting suspects and different informal tactics may be used for each reason.

Small shopkeepers, who often do not have the time or resources to institute arrests, adopt tactics best suited to their situation. Cameron discusses one grocer who adds $5 to the bill of shoplifters and, if they query it, answers deliberately 'You know' (what it is for).[117] Another small shopkeeper offered to wrap 'the rest' of the customer's goods, a tactic also reported by Walsh.[118] Occasionally, shoplifters were threatened with physical violence. In one small boutique, the researcher noticed the sign, 'I don't prosecute shoplifters — I break their arms', and although of dubious legal status, it was evidently effective. Walsh cites the case of one shopkeeper who said, 'I administer the law by myself, because the law is not doing its job. I caught one and bashed him in the face. I said, "Are you coming in here again?" He said, "No". I bashed him in the face again, and I let him go. He has not come back.'[119] Fortunately, such pugilistic stratagems are rare.

In the larger shops and stores, where arrest is the normal routine, the first reason for adopting an informal approach is because there is insufficient evidence to support an apprehension. A suspect may have been seen secreting an article, but may not have been observed approaching a counter; or the store detective may have momentarily lost sight of the suspect during the incident. The threat of a false arrest is too great a risk, and yet the security officer is convinced that the store's goods are about to be taken. Baker describes one tactic, which he calls 'ghosting', that he adopts in such situations:

> Occasionally one catches a glimpse of a thief at work, but there is insufficient evidence to stop that person outside.

What can you do about it? The recovery of the goods is the first priority.... I caught such a glimpse. As I turned the corner of the counter, I saw what appeared to be a box of fancy candles going into a bag. I kept the woman under observation but she went towards a checkout with a couple of items in the store's wire basket. As she stood in the queue, I went back to the counter, picked up a similar box of candles and stood at the far end of the checkout with these in my hand. I stared at her, I stared at her shopping bag and I tossed the box several times into the air. After having the goods in her wire basket checked out she walked around the checkout, picked up another basket, put seven items from her shopping bag into the basket and went back through the checkout. The items, including a box of candles, had a total value of almost £5. However, I would not have stopped her outside, my evidence was too flimsy.[120]

An alternative method is discussed in *The Guardian:*

One of the girls said, 'It can be frustrating but there is nothing much you can do about it. Sometimes when I see someone has something they haven't paid for I follow them out of the shop, stare at the item in their hand or bag, and say things out loud like, "Tut, tut, I think it's disgraceful the way people steal things from M.'s' ". You'd be surprised how often that works. They lose their nerve and go back and pay for it.[121]

A similar tactic was observed during the fieldwork. A man was seen furtively holding a pair of socks, but the store detective had not seen him take them from the gondola, though she suspected that he had. Consequently, she made it obvious that she was watching him and 'put the frighteners on him', so that he eventually replaced the socks and left.

On occasions, store detectives will enlist the support of other shop staff to deter shoplifters. For example, two women were observed handling a tablecloth suspiciously but the store detective's vision was obscured and she was unable to see if they had taken it. The women eventually attempted to purchase four large wicker baskets, in one of which the store detective suspected was hidden the tablecloth. Consequently, she asked one of the cashiers to examine the baskets; the tablecloth was duly 'discovered' and, with considerable embarrassment, was paid for.

A similar approach was described by one store detective: 'If you're not certain, but sure, you get a manager to "pack" the shopper's bag for them, and as he starts to place the purchased items in the shopping bag, he "discovers" the secreted goods already hidden in the bag.' An even more subtle method entailed getting a supervisor to stop the suspect once they had passed through the checkout by saying 'Excuse me, I'm doing a price-check to test that the cashiers are working correctly.' The manager would then check the goods purchased against the receipt, and any articles which had not been paid for would become evident. The cashier would then be blamed for the 'mistake', the shop would regain its goods, the store detective would not have risked a controversial arrest and, hopefully, the suspect would have been deterred from future thefts.

A second reason for not apprehending suspects is that it might interfere with the domestic arrangements of security officers. Arresting a suspect, waiting for the police to arrive, accompanying them to the police station, and making a statement can all take several hours. Consequently, some store detectives will be reluctant to arrest 'trivial' shoplifters near to closing time, particularly if they have planned an evening's entertainment. (Conversely, others will be more eager to make apprehensions late in the day solely for the overtime pay.) As one respondent phrased it: 'Prosecution depends upon the time of day — you do not want to get stuck at the police station at closing time if you're going out.' On another occasion, late in the day, the researcher and a store detective came across a very suspicious party of boisterous French children. However, the store detective quickly walked on, declaring, 'I've got enough aggravation this time of night without "nicking" French kids and taking them all to the station, with their teacher and an interpreter.'

Similar occurrences were witnessed in other stores. In one, a man was seen secreting a vest, but the store detective asked a supervisor to approach the man and tell him, 'We're closing now, the cash till for the vest is over there', whereupon the man paid. The detective explained that it was not worth the trouble to go to the police station at 5.30 p.m. for a vest. On a different day, with a different security officer, but in the same store, a well-dressed man was spotted acting suspiciously in the food hall. His bag was held awkwardly, and as we watched, he proceeded to slide a bottle of whisky into it. The store detective employed the same tactic, asking a supervisor to point him to a cash desk, 'as we're closing', and the man subsequently paid. The detective said she did this for two reasons. First, thefts of drink had to be notified to head office, which would be difficult at 5.30 p.m., but, more importantly, it was late and she did not want to be kept behind that particular night.

Groups of suspected shoplifters, be they children, adolescents or professionals, are a particular problem for security personnel and are a third reason for preferring informal methods. This is because the security officer is unlikely to know which member of the gang has taken the articles and where they are located. Additionally, if she waits until the suspects are leaving (often by separate exits), she will not know which one to stop, and will not be able to apprehend them all if they run. This dilemma is aptly illustrated in the next case.

The store detective and researcher were confronted by three adolescent boys each in the process of taking two cashmere sweaters. The store detective was by herself and could not obtain assistance quickly. She reasoned that she would not be able to follow all three boys out of the store, apprehend them and make them return, as she believed that they would separate and run. If this occurred, the best outcome would be one arrest but with a consequent loss of expensive merchandise. Rather than risk this, the store detective approached the three boys as they stood by the counter and ordered them to return the sweaters. The boys did this and then ran from the store. Three apprehensions had been lost, but the cashmere sweaters had been saved. The policy of deterrence for groups of suspected persons was ubiquitous. In one store, the manager said, 'Gangs of adolescents used to be big trouble, but we used to surround them when they came in and breathed down their necks till they left.' Another respondent declared, 'If there is a big gang you can only deter.' In another store, continental quilts were continually disappearing and so every time a group of people approached the quilts, store detectives and sales staff surrounded them and made it obvious that they were under observation until they left.

The same tactic of acting as visible, overt deterrents was often adopted when security resources were pressurised, as at sale times, during the pre-Christmas rush and on Saturdays. The chief security officer of one store spent Saturdays and lunchtimes at the main entrance, which opened on to a shopping precinct, acting as a very obvious deterrent. In another store, the detective said that he spent most of his time behind a two-way mirror screening the customers for potential thieves, except on Saturdays when he had to get out on the floor and act as a visible deterrent. In a third chain of shops, the declared policy was: 'On Saturdays, everybody works on the shopfloor as deterrents'. Store detectives here made themselves very obvious and would approach suspected shoplifters and stare at them until they left. Occasionally, they would use the more obvious tactic of informing the customer that, 'the till's over there.'!

The reasoning behind these approaches appeared to be based on the assumption that store detectives would be able to control shoplifters by a policy of arrest and police referral during weekdays, even though this was time-consuming. During busy periods, however, the number of shoplifters might quickly overwhelm the security staff and while they were at the police station with people arrested for stealing small items the store would be vulnerable to the attacks of more avaricious thieves. In all those cases, while arrest and police referral are the preferred policy of the stores, in practice such situational contingencies as, insufficient evidence, domestic arrangements and pressure on resources produced exemptions.

The next cases differ in that the arrest/police/referral model was not the preferred policy, rather it was the option of the last resort. Retail chain 1 in Table 5.3 was one of only two retailers in the research to favour managing shoplifters informally. Ideally, for these two chains, tactics would be employed to prevent a situation where an arrest had to take place. Security officers were instructed to apprehend only those people who ignored or rejected all attempts at informal management. Once arrested, however, the suspects were referred to the police and prosecuted. The following cases exemplify how suspects were given every opportunity to avoid being categorised as shoplifters.

A man was seen to put on a leather jacket underneath his coat. The store detective approached the man, touched his sleeve, and said 'Gonna pay for that jacket?', whereupon the shocked man nodded and returned to the cash desk. This store detective had an excellent reputation with the local police as there were never any difficulties with the few shoplifters she referred to them. On another occasion, the same woman observed a man throw away a price tag from a raincoat. The man loitered around the coat on the coat-rack, and eventually put it on. The store detective picked up the tag, stopped the man just as he was about to leave the store and said, 'Take it off or pay'. The man took back the raincoat and replaced it on its hanger. The interesting thing to note about these two cases is that they involved expensive items, and in almost any other shop, the suspects would have been allowed to leave the store and then been arrested. Instead, they were permitted to replace or pay for the items. This practice relies on the shock of being stopped by a store detective being a sufficient deterrent to all but the most determined thieves. It has the advantage also of maximising security cover on the shopfloor, as the detective rarely has to go to the police station.

Comparison of this chain of retailers with department store 5 in the table, is misleading, as they appear to have fairly similar numbers of apprehensions referred to the police each year. However the figures for the chain represent arrests in hundreds of outlets, while those for the other are from one outlet only. Critically, then, police referral rates are minimised with the informal approach. The retailers themselves justify this approach as taking responsibility for the temptation presented by self-service: they believe that they have an obligation to deal leniently with their customers. It was also felt that the very fright of being stop-ped by a store detective was often deterrent enough. Additionally, it was pointed out that most stores adopted these tactics on occasion anyway; they were merely being more systematic about it.

Having looked at the various methods used to control shoplifting, it is now possible to consider the work of store detectives more schematically.

(v) *Store detectives — their three roles.* Describing the ways in which the police keep order on 'skid row', Bittner identifies two methods of operating, which he terms the 'law-enforcement' model and the 'peace-keeping' model. [122] Officers following the law-enforcement model seek to arrest, charge and prosecute violators, however trivial the circumstances. On the other hand, officers acting under the peace-keeping model, tend to ignore minor infractions of the criminal code in the hope of calming the situation and restoring the *status quo.* For example, a law-enforcer, when confronted with two drunks fighting, will arrest them both for being drunk and disorderly, or for a breach of the peace, and take them to the police station to be charged. When confronted with the same situation, the 'peace-keeper', on the other hand, will separate the fighting men, attempt to find the cause of the trouble, and settle the dispute there and then, whenever possible. The disturbance is pacified by both methods, but the repercussions for the drunks will be more serious if they are arrested. The time spent by the officers patrolling the beat will vary according to the model adopted. As Chatterton points out, the power of arrest is used as a resource to strengthen the probability of achieving a settlement. Critically, the effectiveness of the peace-keeping role depends upon the availability of the law-enforcer role. [123]

Analogously, the two models can be applied to store detectives, albeit in a more restricted sense. The store detective who pursues the 'law-enforcer' role will be intent on discovering, apprehending and interrogating suspected shoplifters and referring them to the police with a view to prosecution. Correspondingly, the store detective who prefers the 'peace-keeper' role, concentrates on the protection of goods and will attempt to control the shoplifting population without recourse to prosecution. The latter may be achieved by arresting suspects and interviewing them, but allowing them to leave without calling the police. More commonly, store detectives will attempt to manipulate the various categories of customer in order to prevent a 'shoplift' from occurring.

It was pointed out too that the 'peace-keeper' role will only usually be adopted when the 'law-enforcer' role is unavailable or undesirable. For some stores, this method is the preferred means of controlling shoplifting. Significantly, for the police officer and the store detective, the two roles are interchangeable, even when one has already been adopted. For example, the police officer following the 'law-enforcement' model, may arrest the two drunks and take them to the police station, but may decide not to press charges, and let them off. The 'peace officer', on the other hand, may decide to arrest the two drunks if they continue fighting or do not accept him as an arbiter. Likewise, the store detective who adopts the 'law-enforcement' role may arrest and interrogate a suspect, but may decide not to proceed further for a number of reasons (cf. the consultant surgeon who was arrested for stealing 'girlie' magazines and interviewed, but was released). Similarly, the store detective who would normally adopt the 'peace officer' role may be forced into the 'law-enforcer' role by a variety of circumstances. The lack of cooperation of 'Angela Davis' and the man who claimed he was 'Cliff Richard' forced a store detective who would normally have operated as a 'peace officer' into a 'law-enforcer'. Again, the store detective controlling the leather jacket incident would always try to adopt the 'peace-keeping' role unless extreme provocation pushed her into the 'law-enforcer' role.

Both the 'law-enforcer' model and the 'peace officer' model are available to store detectives, and while one may be the preferred, the other is always present if needed. There would also appear to be a middle-ground where either model may be adopted depending upon the circumstances. For example, during sale times and on Saturdays, many store detectives will adopt the 'peace-keeping' role, but may occasionally be forced into the 'law-enforcer' role when confronted with determined and avaricious thieves.

These two roles are not the only ones available to the police or store detectives; Bittner alerts us to a third possibility:

> Policemen often do not arrest persons who have committed minor offences in circumstances in which arrest is technically possible [the peace officer role] .... It is less well appreciated that policemen often not only refrain from invoking the law formally but also employ alternative sanctions. For example, it is standard practice that violators are warned not to repeat the offence. [124]

Police officers may become, in addition to their other roles, 'moral entrepreneurs', acting as representatives of society's values and as arbiters of morality. In Garfinkel's phrase, they are 'professional degraders'. [125]

Store detectives similarly adopt this role of moral entrepreneur, although for them it is bounded by considerations of theft. As has been shown, and as Bittner suggests, violators are often warned not to repeat the offence when they are being released. Typically, when store detectives have decided not to refer the case to the police they emphasise their role of moral entrepreneurs to accentuate the unpleasantness of the situation for the suspect. This may occur on the shopfloor (especially when dealing with children and adolescents) or during and after the interview, following apprehension. Store detectives may adopt the role of 'professional degraders' even when they have decided to call in

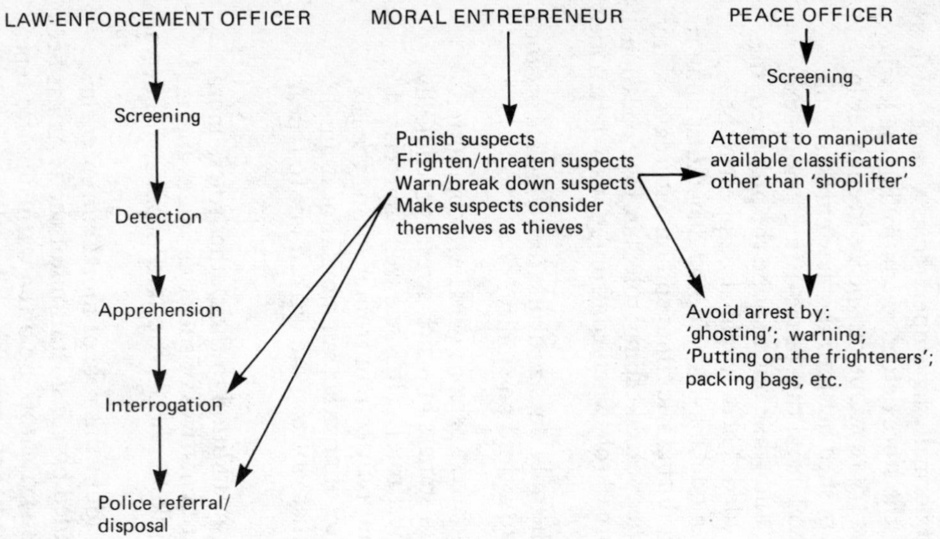

LAW-ENFORCEMENT OFFICER

Screening

↓

Detection

↓

Apprehension

↓

Interrogation

↓

Police referral/
disposal

MORAL ENTREPRENEUR

Punish suspects
Frighten/threaten suspects
Warn/break down suspects
Make suspects consider
themselves as thieves

PEACE OFFICER

Screening

↓

Attempt to manipulate
available classifications
other than 'shoplifter'

↓

Avoid arrest by:
'ghosting'; warning;
'Putting on the frighteners';
packing bags, etc.

Figure 6.1: Store detective roles

the police. This may be to emphasise the wrongness of the suspect's actions and get them to think of themselves as thieves. It may also be an attempt to break the suspect down to get a confession. These three roles are represented diagrammatically in Figure 6.1.

Thus, the store detective may adopt one of three roles: law-enforcer (arrest/interview/referral to police for prosecution); peace officer (no arrest of suspects/situation dealt with on the shopfloor/preservation of the *status quo*); or 'moral entrepreneur' (normally in conjunction with one of the other two, but sometimes adopted for dealing with rowdy children and adolescents). These roles are not exclusive and may be operationalised in tandem — the moral entrepreneur role is typically used as a reinforcer at the interrogation stage or at the warning stage (expressed by arrows in the figure). Once adopted, a role is not fixed for that incident: store detectives may switch from one to another, wherever circumstances dictate.

It is now possible to offer a step-by-step analysis of the decision-making processes engaged by store detectives.

Figure 6.2 represents the options available to store detectives in controlling shoplifting at each stage. The left-hand side corresponds to the decisions available to the law-enforcer, and the right, the decisions available to the peace officers. The moral entrepreneur role may be engaged under either model, but is typically used to warn or frighten suspects or to ensure compliance.

Before the store detective begins operating, the shop will often be organised to manipulate people into the customer role by providing them with shopping baskets, and assistants proferring help.

Stage 1 consists of screening the customers to exclude such potential trouble-makers as gangs of adolescents, vagrants and previous shoplifters. This practice may be adopted by store detectives preferring either the law-enforcer role or the peace-keeping one.

Stage 2. The store detective notices something suspicious. The decisions now taken by store detectives differ according to which role they adopt. The peace officer will begin considering tactics to prevent the situation developing into shoplifting, and will decide which is the more appropriate. The potential shoplifter is thus manipulated into a customer role and made to pay for the goods or return them, and then leave. The situation is more complicated for the law enforcers, however. For them, apprehension is the next step.

Stage 3. The store detective must begin to consider how to present evidence and how to avoid the threat of false arrest. Here, store detectives will be mindful of proving the *actus reus* (the taking aspect) as well as demonstrating that the suspect knew what she/he was doing (*mens rea*), by stressing the rationality of their actions. (On occasions, the law-enforcer will switch to the peace officer at this juncture and give

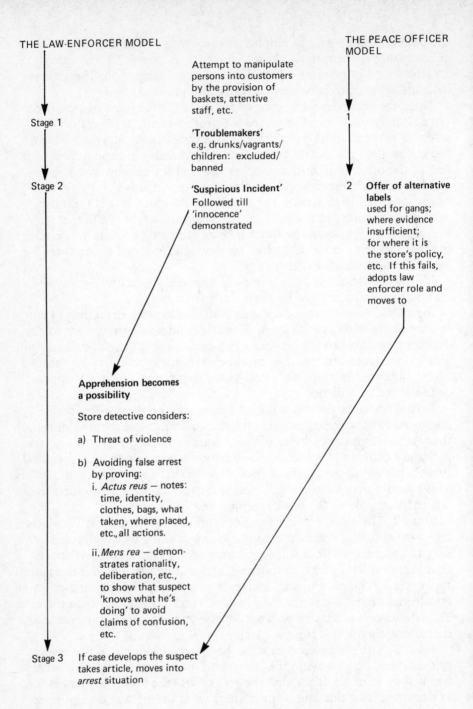

THE LAW-ENFORCER MODEL

THE PEACE OFFICER MODEL

Attempt to manipulate
persons into customers
by the provision of
baskets, attentive
staff, etc.

Stage 1

1

'Troublemakers'
e.g. drunks/vagrants/
children: excluded/
banned

Stage 2

'Suspicious Incident'
Followed till
'innocence'
demonstrated

2 Offer of alternative
labels
used for gangs;
where evidence
insufficient;
for where it is
the store's policy,
etc. If this fails,
adopts law
enforcer role and
moves to

Apprehension becomes
a possibility

Store detective considers:

a) Threat of violence

b) Avoiding false arrest
by proving:
i. *Actus reus* — notes:
time, identity,
clothes, bags, what
taken, where placed,
etc., all actions.

ii. *Mens rea* — demon-
strates rationality,
deliberation, etc.,
to show that suspect
'knows what he's
doing' to avoid
claims of confusion,
etc.

Stage 3 If case develops the suspect
takes article, moves into
arrest situation

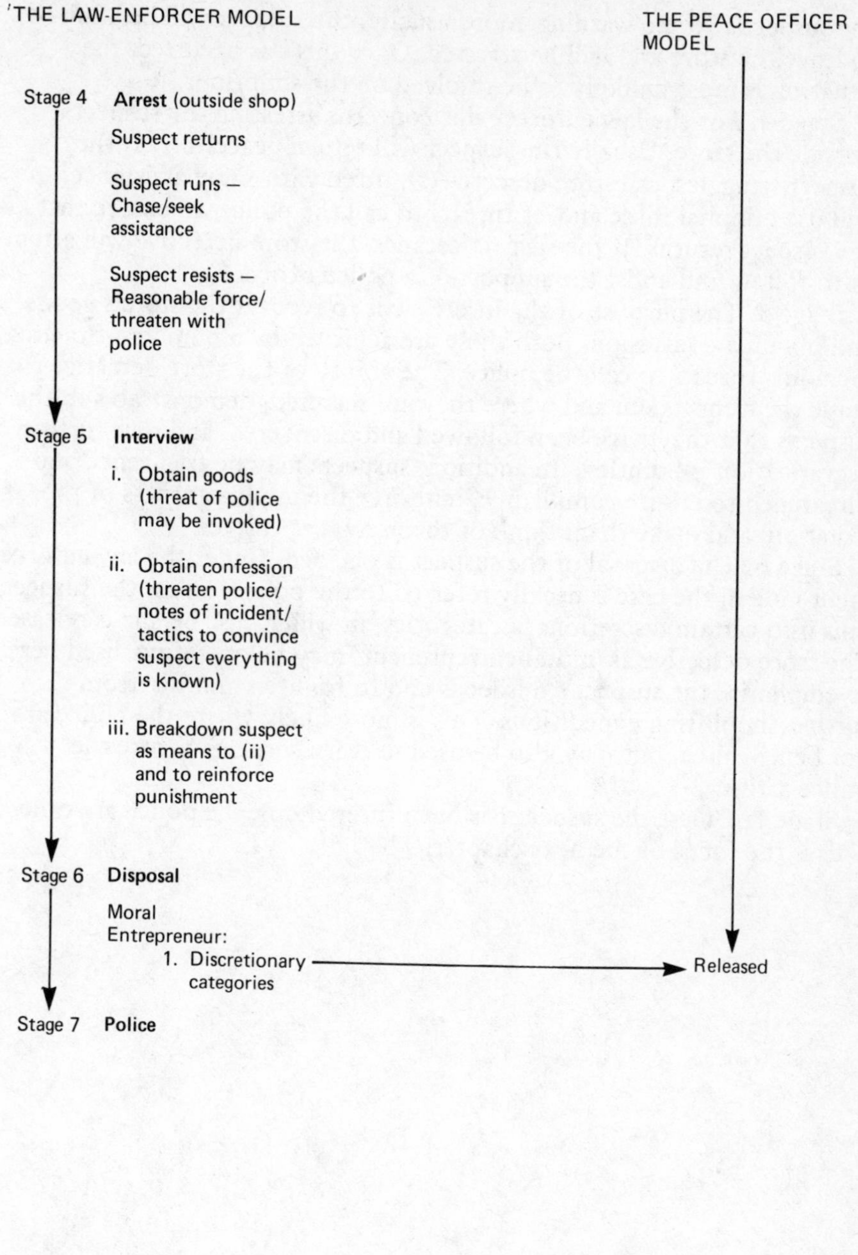
'THE LAW-ENFORCER MODEL
THE PEACE OFFICER MODEL
Stage 4 Arrest (outside shop)
Suspect returns
Suspect runs – Chase/seek assistance
Suspect resists – Reasonable force/ threaten with police
Stage 5 Interview
i. Obtain goods (threat of police may be invoked)
ii. Obtain confession (threaten police/ notes of incident/ tactics to convince suspect everything is known)
iii. Breakdown suspect as means to (ii) and to reinforce punishment
Stage 6 Disposal
Moral Entrepreneur:
1. Discretionary categories
Released
Stage 7 Police

Figure 6.2: The progressive selection/rejection/clarification involved in the store detective's decision-making process the suspect a severe warning. More usually, the suspect will be allowed to leave the store and will be arrested. Once this has occurred, the situation is most unlikely to be resolved on the shopfloor.)

Stage 4. For the law enforcer this concerns arresting the suspect outside the store. Usually the suspect will return peacefully. If the suspect struggles, the store detective(s), often with some assistance, will use minimal force and/or threats to call the police, to ensure that the suspect returns. If the suspect escapes, the store detective will attempt to follow and enlist the support of a police officer.

Stage 5. The purpose of the interview is to recover the store's goods and obtain a confession. Both these are achieved by a number of tactics, including threats to call the police. The ability of the store detective to name the items taken and where they are secreted, demonstrates to the suspects that they have been followed and discovered, and that further prevarication is pointless. In addition, suspects may be frightened and threatened to ensure compliance, reinforce the unpleasantness of the situation, and make them think of themselves as thieves.

Stage 6. The disposal of the suspect is decided. Under the law-enforcement model, the case is usually referred to the police, unless the suspect falls into certain discretionary categories, in which case he/she is released. The store detective as 'moral entrepreneur' may be operationalised here to emphasise the suspect's misdeeds and to frighten him/her from further shoplifting expeditions. This is more likely where the police are not being called, but may also be used to warn suspects before the police arrive.

Stage 7. Unless the suspect has been filtered out, the police are called. This is the focus of the next chapter.

Notes

1. *Evening News*, 12 May 1977.
2. Baker, L.L., *They Always Come Back* (Bognor Regis: New Horizon, 1979)., p. 48.
3. Cohen, S., *Folk Devils and Moral Panics* (London: Martin Robertson, 1972), p. 9.
4. Cohen, S. and Young, J., *The Manufacture of News, Deviance, Social Problems and the Mass Media* (London: Constable, 1973), p. 343.
5. Cohen, *op. cit.*, p. 17.
6. *Evening News*, 8 November 1976.
7. *Daily Telegraph*, 7 November 1976.
8. *Daily Mirror*, 9 November 1976.
9. *Evening Standard*, 15 August 1977.
10. *Daily Mirror*, 21 April 1977.
11. Chapman, D., *Sociology and the Stereotype of the Criminal* (London: Tavistock) 1968.
12. *Daily Mail*, 19 August 1978.
13. *Sunday Telegraph*, 27 August 1978.
14. *Daily Mail*, 26 September 1979.
15. *Daily Star*, 26 September 1979.
16. *Sunday Express*, 20 August 1978.
17. *Daily Mail*, 12 October 1979.
18. *Evening News*, 15 November 1977.
19. *The Times*, 6 July 1978.
20. Home Office, *Criminal Statistics. England and Wales* (London: HMSO, 1983).
21. Roshier, B., 'The Selection of Crime News by the Press', in Cohen, and Young, *op. cit.*, pp. 28–39.
22. *Daily Telegraph*, 4 October 1978.
23. *Evening Standard*, 15 May 1984.
24. *Daily Mirror*, 9 February 1979.
25. *News of the World*, 3 June 1979.
26. *Daily Telegraph*, 19 August 1978.
27. *Daily Star*, 1 June 1979.
28. *Daily Mirror*, 21 April 1977.
29. *Sun*, 1 April 1979.
30. *Sunday Telegraph*, 14 August 1977.
31. *The Guardian*, 15 May 1980.
32. Ibid., 29 March 1979.
33. Ibid., 29 May 1978.
34. *Evening News*, 18 November 1977.
35. *Daily Mail*, 27 May 1978.

36. *Daily Telegraph*, 14 December 1978.
37. *Sunday Telegraph*, 25 February 1979.
38. *Daily Star*, 20 September 1979.
39. *Daily Mirror*, 10 June 1978.
40. Verill, A.H., 'Reducing Shop Losses', in *Combating Crime Against Small Business*, ed. Post, R. (Springfield, Illinois: Charles C. Thomas, 1972), p. 119.
41. Post, R., *Combating Crime Against Small Business* (Springfield, Illinois: Charles C. Thomas, 1972), pp. 56—7.
42. Cameron, M.O., *The Booster and the Snitch. Department Store Shoplifting* (Glencoe, Free Press, 1964), p. 39.
43. Sutherland, E.H., *The 'Professional' Thief — By A Professional Thief* (Chicago: Chicago University Press, 1937), pp. 3—40.
44. Edwards, L.E., *Shoplifting and Shrinkage Protection for Stores* (Springfield, Ill: Charles C. Thomas, 1978), p. 16. (First published 1958.)
45. Cameron, *op.cit.*, p. 40.
46. Gibbens, T.C.N. and Prince, J., *Shoplifting* (London: ISTD, 1962), p. 31.
47. Walsh, D. P., *Shoplifting: Controlling a Major Crime* (London: Macmillan, 1978), p. 73.
48. *The Guardian*, 1 February 1977.
49. *Daily Telegraph*, 6 February 1979.
50. Ibid., 6 December 1978.
51. Francis, D.B., *Shoplifting, The Crime Everybody Pays For* (New York: Elsevier/Nelson Books, 1980), pp. 14—15.
52. Lehr, K., 'Shoplifting By a Gang', *Kriminalistik*, Vol. 23, No. 8. (1969), pp. 433—6.
53. Baker, *op. cit.*, pp. 36—7.
54. de Rham, E., *How Could She Do That? A Study of the Female Criminal* (New York: Clarkson N. Potter, 1969), p. 59.
55. *Daily Mirror*, 18 August 1978.
56. *Daily Telegraph*, 8 September 1977.
57. Ibid., 8 September 1978.
58. Ibid., 26 September 1978.
59. Ibid., 16 September 1977.
60. Ibid., 23 September 1978.
61. *Sunday Mirror*, 12 December 1977.
62. Smigel, E.O. and Ross, H.L. (eds.) *Crimes Against Bureaucracy.* (New York: Van Nostrand, Reinhold, 1970), p. 5.
63. Robin, G.D., 'The Corporate and Judicial Disposition of Employee Thieves', in Smigel and Ross (eds.), ibid. p. 125.
64. Martin, J.P., *Offenders as Employees.* Cambridge Studies in Criminology (London: Macmillan, 1962), p. 87.

65. *Daily Mail,* 19 November 1976.
66. *Daily Mirror,* 3 January 1979.
67. Ibid., 13 February 1978.
68. Ditton, J., *Part-Time Crime: An Ethnography of Fiddling and Pilferage* (London: Macmillan, 1977), p. 116.
69. Ditton, J., *Controlology* (London: Macmillan, 1979), p. 78.
70. Dickenson, S., 'Theft and the Retailer', *Security World* (April 1970), pp. 171–6.
71. Ibid.
72. Keeton, G.W., 'The Hand in the Till', *Justice of the Peace* (22 October 1977), pp. 623–6.
73. May, D., 'Juvenile Shoplifters and the Organisation of Store Security: A Case Study in the Social Construction of Delinquency', *International Journal of Criminology and Penology,* No. 6. (1978), pp. 137–60.
74. Ibid.
75. Cameron, *op. cit.,* p.30.
76. Edwards, *op. cit.,* pp. 212–13.
77. *Evening Standard,* 14 December 1981.
78. *Sun,* 23 September 1977.
79. *The Guardian,* 12 December 1977.
80. *Evening Standard,* 15 August 1977.
81. Baker, *op. cit.,* p. 15.
82. Meek, V., *Private Enquiries* (London: Duckworth, 1967), p. 50.
83. Edwards, *op. cit.,* pp. 33–51.
84. Store detective classifications though, tended to be inconsistent.
85. Morris, T., *The Criminal Area* (London: Routledge & Kegan Paul, 1957). See also idem., *Deviance and Control: The Secular Heresy* (London: Hutchinson,). Also, personal communication.
86. *The Guardian,* 12 December 1977.
87. *Daily Mirror,* 23 March 1982.
88. Ibid., 24 March 1982.
89. *Sunday Telegraph,* 28 March 1982.
90. *Sunday Telegraph,* 8 February 1976.
91. *Daily Telegraph,* 24 January 1979.
92. *Sunday People,* 5 February 1978.
93. *Daily Mirror,* 24 March 1982.,
94. Ibid., 1 April 1982.
95. May, *op. cit.*
96. Hole, R.R., 'Shoplifting Apprehensions Can Be Made to Stick', *Security World,* Vol. 9, No. 1 (1972), pp. 26–8; Vol. 9, No. 2., pp. 32–46.
97. Baker, *op. cit.,* pp. 13–14.
98. Hole, *op. cit.*

99. Cox, A.E., 'Shoplifting', *The Criminal Law Review* (1968), pp. 425–30.
100. Hole, *op. cit.*
101. Griffin, R.K., 'Shoplifting Policy for Retailers', *Security World*, Vol 10, Part II (1973), pp. 34–6, 41–4.
102. Scott, M.B. and Lyman, S.M., 'Accounts, Deviance and Social Order', in *Deviance and Respectability* ed. Douglas, J.D. (New York: Basic Books, 1970), pp. 102–3.
103. Steiner, J.M., Hadden, S.C. and Herkomer, L., 'Price-Tag Switching', *International Journal of Criminology and Penology*, Vol. 4 (1976), pp. 129–43.
104. May, D., 'The Management of Juvenile Shoplifters' (University of Aberdeen, unpublished paper 1974), p. 78.
105. Griffin, *op. cit.*
106. Scheff, T.J., 'Negotiating Reality: Notes on Power in the Assessment of Responsibility', *Social Problems*, Vol. 16 (1968), Summer. pp. 3–19.
107. May, *op. cit.* (1974), p. 81.
108. Griffin, *op. cit.*
109. Sudnow, D., 'Normal Crimes: Sociological Features of the Penal Code', *Social Problems*, Vol. 12 (1965), pp. 255–70.
110. Oliver, E. and Wilson, J., *Practical Security in Commerce and Industry* (Epping: Essex Gower Press, 3rd edn, 1978) p. 97.
111. May, *op. cit.* (1974), p. 81.
112. Adley, R., 'Take It or Leave It. An Independent Study of the Cause and Effect of the Increase in Shoplifting' a pamphlet produced by the Adley Working Party (1978), p. 6.
113. Cameron, *op. cit.*, p. 162.
114. Gusfield, J.R., 'Moral Passage: The Symbolic Process in Public Designations of Deviance', *Social Problems*, Vol. 15, No. 2 (1968), pp. 75–188.
115. Goffman, E., *Stigma: Notes on the Management of Spoiled Identity* (Harmondsworth: Penguin Books, 1968).
116. Garfinkel, H., 'Conditions of Successful Degradation Ceremonies', *American Journal of Sociology*, Vol. 6 (1956), pp. 420–4.
117. Cameron, *op. cit.*, p. 16.
118. Walsh, *op. cit.*, p. 79.
119. Ibid., p. 79.
120. Baker, *op. cit.*, p. 83.
121. *The Guardian*, 12 December 1977.
122. Bittner, E., 'The Police on Skid Row: A Study of Peace-Keeping', *American Sociological Review*. Vol. 32 (October 1967), pp. 699–715.
123. Chatterton, M., 'Police in Social Control', In *Control Without Custody*, ed. King, J.F. (Cropwood Round Table Conference, 1976).

124. Bittner, *op. cit.*
125. Garfinkel, *op. cit.*

7 Shoplifting and the police

Introduction

In terms of its effect on police resources, shoplifting is a significant offence. It constitutes 14 per cent of all offences of 'theft and handling stolen goods' recorded by the police, and approximately 7½ per cent of all notifiable offences (previously 'serious offences', and called 'indictable offences' before the implementation of the Criminal Law Act 1977) recorded by the police in 1981.[1] As most offences of shoplifting are only discovered when an offender has been arrested, the 'clear-up rate' for detected offences is high (89 per cent in 1981),[2] and consequently makes a valuable contribution to the percentage of offences which are cleared up overall. Nevertheless, police involvement with the detection of shoplifting offences is minimal: their role is largely one of processing offenders detected and arrested by private citizens, usually store detectives. As one police officer put it. 'Shoplifting creates a lot of work and no job satisfaction. It's not really police work — just clerking. Shoplifters are just "handovers".' The police role in the control of shoplifters, then, is small, and is at variance with the popular mythologies of police operations, as well as the more academic explanations of police activity.

This chapter does not review the literature on police practice and theory, as that is provided elsewhere,[3] and is not germane to a discussion of shoplifting. Instead, it examines first the variations in the way shoplifters are prosecuted and the different policies relating to cautioning; and second, concentrates on what happens to shoplifters after the police have been called and they are taken to the police station.

Prosecution and cautioning policies

Unlike Scotland, the USA and many European countries, there is no independent prosecuting body in England and Wales; most prosecutions in criminal courts are conducted by the police or by a lawyer acting for them.[4] Before police forces were established in the early nineteenth century, the onus of bringing prosecutions rested with the private individual. Despite provision for assistance in the costs of making a prosecution, taking legal action was an expensive business and so prosecuting societies were formed to aid the individual. As police forces were established they began to take on the prosecutory role and prosecution societies gradually died away. However, the legal principle of an individual's right to bring a private prosecution was not questioned and remains an important aspect of English democracy. As Lidstone *et. al.* say,

> The present situation is therefore a complex one. The private citizen is theoretically free to prosecute anyone he wishes, though careful perusal of the statutes shows that this freedom is much more restricted than is sometimes supposed. Meanwhile, the failure of the nineteenth-century moves for a public prosecution system have left the police, in theory, still prosecuting each and every case they bring to court only as 'private citizens'.[5]

Most offences which are prosecuted by individuals and agents other than the police concern infringements of government department or local authority regulations and are mainly non-indictable (i.e. are not recorded as notifiable offences). Shoplifting is a major exception in that it is a notifiable offence. The various ways shoplifters can be prosecuted then, derive partly from historical developments, and, as will become apparent, from practical exigencies.

According to a report of a working party appointed by the Association of Chief Police Officers there are three different procedures which can be adopted for prosecuting shoplifters: private prosecution, arrest by police and summons by police.[6] In the evidence presented to the working party, it emerged that the majority of police forces favoured only one procedure and cases where different policies were practised in the same police force were rare.

The procedure of the private prosecution is considered important as it is the means by which an individual citizen may make an arrest without a warrant. The store detective or other personnel arrests a person whom they suspect of stealing. The police are then called. The attending officer ensures that there are reasonable grounds for making the arrest, and having cautioned the suspect and given him the opportunity to speak, takes him to the police station. In effect, the store detective is giving the prisoner 'into the custody' of the police officer: the police assist in the processing of the suspect but the onus for the prosecution rests with the store detective. Once at the police station, the store detective makes a statement to substantiate the arrest and accusation. By placing an individual into the custody of the police, the private citizen can insist on police cooperation in bringing the accused before magistrates, provided that the arrest had been made lawfully and that there were reasonable grounds to support the charge. Consequently, if the arrest were not lawful, only the private citizen would be liable in law, and not the police. If an individual places a suspect in the custody of a police officer, that individual may insist on the right to prosecute. In practice, few individuals insist on this right, but in some police forces they may be encouraged to do so.

Of the 43 police forces in England and Wales, seven considered the arrest of a shoplifter as an 'arrest by a private person' who 'gives a prisoner into custody', but five of these normally undertook to prosecute the suspect themselves. Private prosecution was the accepted means for the Metropolitan Police of bringing suspected shoplifters to court, and, except in certain circumstances, the responsibility for bringing the prosecution rested with the store. The store would then have to bear the costs of the prosecution but was usually granted costs by the magistrate to cover expenses. This practice will be questioned below, but for now, it can be seen that the effects of private prosecution are that it enshrines an individual's historic right to bring a prosecution without a warrant; restricts liability for false arrest to the shopkeeper; and where the store undertakes the prosecution, it saves police resources.

The second procedure for bringing prosecutions against shoplifters is the more customary one, termed by the working party 'arrest by police'. Again, the store detective arrests a suspect for shoplifting and calls the police. The police officer attending the store listens to the evidence provided by the store detective and determines whether there were sufficient grounds to justify an arrest. Once satisfied, the officer cautions the suspect and listens to the evidence. Unless there are some glaring inconsistencies, the police officer 'adopts' the arrest by informing the suspect that he/she has now been arrested by the police and will be taken to the police station to be charged. The implication of this procedure is that if the grounds for arrest are found to be insufficient, both the store detective and the police officer are liable in law. Where a suspect is arrested by the police then they take responsibility for prosecution, and provided that the store detective's statement is complete and the suspect pleads guilty, the store detective may not have to attend either the police station or the magistrates' court. The costs of the prosecution are, of course, borne by the police.

The third procedure which may be adopted is 'summons by police', which gives the police time to consider the exercise of discretion and/or gather more information. This procedure of 'laying an information before a magistrate' is also available to the officer in charge of the police station, once a person has been arrested by the police or arrested by a private citizen (provided that the individual does not insist on prosecuting personally). Once again, the store detective arrests a suspected shoplifter and calls the police. The police officer attending the incident investigates the offence, and provided that the name and address of the suspect are known, may decide to proceed by taking out a summons. The suspect is allowed to leave the store, the police officer returns to the police station and furnishes a senior officer with the information, to decide whether a prosecution is supportable or advisable. If a prosecution is undertaken, the police will conduct it. This policy is often adopted to deal with juveniles and also has the advantage of saving time when the police station is a considerable distance from the shop where the incident occurred. This disadvantage is that it is difficult to conduct personal searches if the suspect is not taken back to the police station. The majority of police forces usually charge offenders but will use the summons procedure if they require to consider the case more. A few police forces, instead of using a summons, might bail a suspect to give them time to consider the most appropriate action.

Of the 43 police forces in England and Wales, the majority (38) informed the working party that they undertook all prosecutions for shoplifting; four police forces reported that a small proportion of shoplifting offences were prosecuted by private individuals;[7] while in the Metropolitan Police Force prosecution by private individuals was the standard process, and although no figures are available on the exact numbers of private and police prosecutions, the vast majority were brought by private citizens. As the Metropolitan Police dealt with approximately 12 per cent of all shoplifting offences in England and Wales, a considerable variation in police practice was apparent.

The reasons behind the Metropolitan Police policy were set out by the Commissioner in his evidence to the Royal Commission on Criminal Procedure, and are discussed by Lidstone *et al.* The first reason the Commissioner gave was to reduce the pressure on the

Metropolitan Police, citing the 27,348 shoplifting offences in 1977, with 24,815 arrests. Secondly, the Commissioner believed that because of their self-service, open-shelf marketing policy, stores were tempting customers and encouraging theft, and consequently ought to take some responsibility for the control of shoplifting.[8]

Lidstone *et al.* agree that London has particular problems with shoplifting, but argue that this should be considered in the light of police manpower in the capital. Comparing the number of recorded offences of shoplifting with police manpower, they demonstrate that other police forces have a burden as heavy or heavier than that of the Metropolitan Police. Six provincial forces were compared with the Metropolitan Police, and all had a higher ratio of recorded shoplifting to police strength than the Metropolitan Police.[9] When considered in this way, the argument that the Metropolitan Police faces special problems is not upheld.

The second reason forwarded by the Commissioner is more complex. Certainly, the policy of self-selection makes shoplifting easier (though note it exists even where there are many assistants serving behind counters) and modern marketing techniques are geared to tempt the customer. Self-service also permits stores to reduce staff costs and increases turnover. There does seem to be a rationale for shops to accept some responsibility for their sales techniques, although the stores themselves would argue that they are encouraging customers to buy but not to steal and that the benefits of self-service permit them to keep prices down, to the advantage of the customer in general. What is clear is that self-service and open shelves are here to stay. The position, however, is complicated because if one believes that stores have some obligation to accept the onus of modern marketing practice, by prosecuting shoplifters themselves, then the principle can be extended to other groups. Should not householders who do not lock their windows take responsibility for subsequent burglaries? and similarly, car-owners leaving the windows of their car open? As Lidstone *et al.* say, 'these issues clearly deserve a more thorough debate than they have yet received', and it is to be hoped that public discussion will be encouraged on this topic.[10]

More specifically, Lidstone *et al.* believe that the legal position of the Metropolitan Police in encouraging stores to conduct their own prosecutions is ambiguous. In R. vs. the Commissioner for Police for the Metropolis *ex parte* Blackburn, it was argued that there was no statutory obligation on the police to prosecute (the present practice having arisen out of historical developments rather than deliberate policy). The Court of Appeal rejected this argument and declared that there was a responsibility on the police to prosecute, but there was also recognition of residual cases where police discretion was accepted.

In London, most stores are willing to accept responsibility for prosecuting shoplifters, but legal difficulties could arise if shops were discouraged from prosecuting shoplifters and the offence were allowed to go 'unchecked'.

Having discussed the various policies available for prosecuting shoplifters, it is now possible to examine the different policies with regard to the cautioning of shoplifters. As Ditchfield states,

> the formal police caution is officially regarded as an alternative to prosecution. For indictable offences, it almost invariably takes the form of an oral warning by a senior uniformed police officer about the offender's conduct and about the possibility of future prosecution if a further offence is committed.[11]

Before the possibility of a caution can be considered, four conditions have to be met:

1. the offence must be admitted fully and in keeping with the evidence;
2. the offence must be trivial;
3. the offender must not have been recently cautioned or convicted for a similar offence;
4. the aggrieved party should be consulted.

According to the *Criminal Statistics,*

> In 1981 about 150,000 offenders were cautioned, the highest number recorded; most of the increase was in the use of cautioning for summary offences which reached a peak of 50,000, the number for indictable offences (104,000) being similar to those in the previous three years and less than the peak number of 111,000 in 1977. There was a considerable increase in the number of persons cautioned up to 1974, but from 1975–80 the numbers fluctuated around 140,000. For indictable offences, over a quarter of those cautioned were females and 84 per cent were under 17. [12]

The decision by police to exercise discretion and caution suitable offenders varies widely from force to force. The general pattern of cautioning for shoplifting throughout England and Wales is that it is mainly applied to young people under 17, and, to a lesser extent, to people over retirement age, as Table 7.1 and Figure 7.1 show.

Figure 7.1 shows the relative proportions of offenders who are prosecuted or cautioned, by three age groups, [13] and it is apparent that few people aged between 17 and 64 were cautioned only for

Table 7.1:   Shoplifting Offenders Cautioned in 1981
by Age and Sex

Age:	10–14	14–17	17–21	21+	Total
Males	13,652	9,330	297	2,763	26,042
Female	9,196	8,024	277	3,904	21,401

shoplifting: 96 per cent were prosecuted. By contrast, just under a quarter (23 per cent) of juveniles were prosecuted, with 77 per cent receiving cautions. Over half of the 65-year-olds were also cautioned: 'In short, most adult shoplifters [were] prosecuted, but even in the age groups where cautioning is deemed appropriate, a significant minority are prosecuted in court.'[14]

The reasons why all pensioners and juveniles are not cautioned is partly explained by a history of previous convictions, the seriousness of the offence or the failure to admit guilt. The disparity between pensioners and juveniles is also partly due to the policy of some police forces not to caution any adults for theft and other indictable offences. The ACPO Working Party of 1975 recommended to chief constables that they should be prepared to exercise discretion not to prosecute adults (including pensioners) given that the usual criteria were satisfied. It was also recommended that collators should keep a record of all adults cautioned for shoplifting for three years. The Metropolitan Police, however, disagreed with these recommendations as they doubted the wisdom of dealing with theft by use of a warning for any save juvenile offenders. Approximately 12 per cent of shoplifting offences are recorded by the Metropolitan Police, and their decision not to caution adults and pensioners affects the total prosecution/caution ratio.[15]

If discretion were to be considered for shoplifters in general, then the numbers who might possibly be eligible for a caution are surprising. In 1981, there were 225,342 offences of shoplifting recorded by the police, with 123,276 offenders found guilty at all courts or cautioned by the police (note some offenders will be found not guilty, but, more significantly, some offenders will be responsible for more than one shoplifting offence). The average value of the property stolen was £31, but this figure was obviously inflated by the more serious cases of shoplifting — for example, in 1981, two offences of shoplifting involving over £50,000 were recorded, as well as 536 offences involving sums

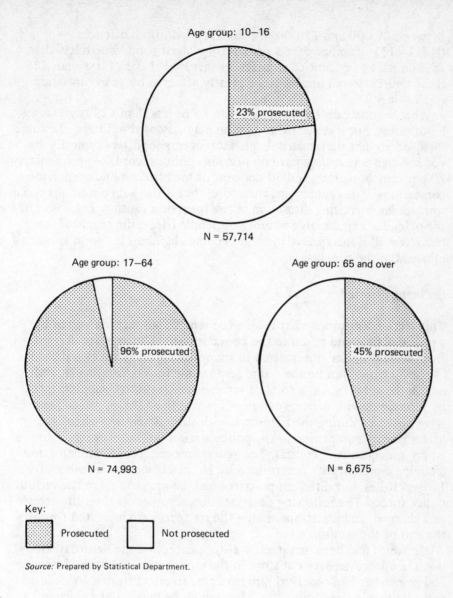

Age group: 10—16

23% prosecuted

N = 57,714

Age group: 17—64

96% prosecuted

N = 74,993

Age group: 65 and over

45% prosecuted

N = 6,675

Key:

Prosecuted   Not prosecuted

Source: Prepared by Statistical Department.

Figure 7.1: Shoplifters cautioned or prosecuted in England
and Wales in 1977, by age group: 10—16, 17—64, 65 and over

between £1,000 and £5,000. By contrast, half of all offences (N=114,131 offences, 50.65 per cent) involved goods worth less than £5, and 83.42 per cent of all offences involved thefts of less than £25; these figures do not appear to be greatly affected by yearly inflation (cf. Table 4.2).

Whether one calls thefts of less than £5 or less than £25 trivial is a moot point, but it is clear that for the majority of shoplifters, the sums involved are not particularly large. Moreover, shoplifters typically are not recidivists (i.e. they have no previous police record). Approximately 70 per cent of women and 50 per cent of men had no known previous convictions.[16] It is apparent, therefore, that if the police were prepared to consider exercising discretion in the form of a caution, regardless of the offender's age, a large number of people (depending on how the term 'trivial' is interpreted) would become eligible. This point is taken up again in the conclusion.

On being arrested

This section examines what is involved when a suspect is arrested by a police officer and taken to the police station. The data are derived from several weeks' observation in six police forces (with two divisions of the Metropolitan Police — one responsible for Oxford Street, and one in the suburbs, i.e. a total of seven police stations), supplemented by interviews with officers of various ranks. In addition, police practices were observed during the fieldwork with store detectives when shoplifters were accompanied to the police station (and subsequently followed up in magistrates' courts). The general procedures for arresting and charging a prisoner are determined by Home Office regulations and Judges' Rules, but different practices may be operational in the various police forces. The following describes how a suspect is typically arrested and charged, and variations among the six forces are indicated towards the end of the section.

Mr Smith had been arrested by a store detective one Saturday afternoon in a large department store in the city centre. The store detective and researcher had observed him take two sweaters from a gondola and secrete them in a shopping bag, after which he purchased a shirt and a pair of socks. Once he had taken a few steps outside the exit, he was stopped by the store detective, who identified herself and asked him to return to the manager's office, which he did calmly. In the office he was asked to place the stolen items on the desk, and after some hesitation and denial, he took out the two sweaters, and then placed the remainder of the contents of the bag on the table. As Mr Smith was outside the boundaries where discretion was usually considered, the assistant manager decided to refer the case to the police.

192

After about 40 minutes, a young man in casual dress came through the door. The store detective recognised him as a CID officer as they had had many dealings together in the past. The CID officer produced his warrant card and showed it to the suspect, saying at the same time, 'I'm Detective Constable Jones'. DC Jones then ensured that Mr Smith could speak English (if Mr Smith had been foreign there would have been delays while interpreters were located) and told him that he was going to ask the store detective what had happened, after which Mr Smith would have an opportunity to speak. The store detective related the story in some detail to the police officer. The officer then asked Mr Smith if he had anything to say, and formally cautioned him: 'You are not required to say anything unless you wish to do so, but anything you say will be taken down in writing and may be used in evidence.' The officer then asked Mr Smith if he understood and if he wished to say anything. Mr Smith signified that he understood and merely said, 'I'm sorry', which was duly recorded.

This procedure is in accordance with that described by Oliver and Wilson.

> When police assistance is called for, following an arrest by a private person, the officer attending will ask to be told, in the presence and hearing of the person detained, what is the evidence that he has committed an offence.... The person responsible for stopping the suspect and who recovered, say, company property from him, would then tell the officer what he saw, what he did, what he said to the suspect and what the suspect replied. The identification of any property allegedly stolen and its value would be required by the officer from a competent witness. The officer then will ask the suspect whether, having heard what has been said, he wishes to say anything. He will caution him that he is not required to say anything unless he wishes to do so but what he does say will be taken down in writing and may be given in evidence. The officer will record in writing anything he says. On the assumption that the evidence shows a *prima facie* case against the suspect the officer will then tell him he proposes to arrest him and for what offence and then take him to the police station accompanied by witnesses.[17]

Next, DC Jones told Mr Smith that he was going to arrest him under section 1 of the Theft Act 1968, and that they would have to go to the police station. By this stage, Mr Smith looked extremely miserable and forlorn. The officer and his prisoner, accompanied by the store detective and researcher (whose presence and credentials had privately been verified by the police officer) left the store by a back stairway and got into DC Jones' unmarked police car. Little was said in the car, the only sound being the two-way radio. The police station was soon reached and the car turned into the park at the back of the building. Detective Jones rang a bell in a solid steel door and access was gained to the charge room and cell area.

The charge room was a large room with a counter at one end, behind which stood a police sergeant and constable (the jailer). To the side of the counter was set a steel gate leading to the cells. The room was bare, there were no seats, tables or any other movable objects. There was a waiting area adjoining the charge room with two wooden benches fixed in the concrete floor. DC Jones approached the charge counter with Mr Smith and related the reasons for the arrest to the sergeant. Mr Smith was formally cautioned again, and asked if he had anything to say, to which he replied 'No'.

Mr Smith was now a 'prisoner in custody' (PIC) and the procedures for dealing with him were the same as for any prisoner. Details of his name and address were taken, verified and checked with the police computer to see if he were wanted for any outstanding offences and if he had any previous convictions. Next Mr Smith was searched: he was asked to empty his pockets and take off all rings, jewellery and his watch. His tie and belt were also taken, as they could be used as weapons to injure himself or the police. All the items of personal property were listed on the charge sheet and were placed in a bag which could then only be opened by destroying a unique seal. The whole procedure was explained to Mr Smith and once he had been searched by an officer to ensure that nothing was concealed, he was asked to sign for his property.

Mr Smith was informed that he had a right to notify a person of his choice of his whereabouts. He was then led away to be fingerprinted and photographed and then taken to a cell by the jailer and locked in. After a short time, DC Jones took Mr Smith to an interview room and took his statement. His 'antecedents' of age, occupation, income, HP commitments, dependants, etc. were also elicited to help the magistrates in deciding their sentence. Mr Smith was returned to his cell. Finally, he was brought before the station sergeant and the charge against him was read out 'that you did steal two sweaters the property of X, value at £16 on Saturday the 15th of May at 4.30 p.m., contrary to section 1 of the Theft Act'. Mr Smith, still under caution, was asked if he had anything to say, to which he replied 'No'. His personal property was returned and he was asked to check it and sign that it was all in order. He was informed that he had been bailed to appear at the magistrates' court at a certain date and the penalties for non-appearance were explained. Mr Smith was then given a carbon copy of the charge sheet, specifying details of the offence, the date of the court appearance and was allowed to leave the police station.

The procedures used by the police in arresting and charging a suspect are generally the same regardless of the nature of the (notifiable) offence. Although shoplifters might be considered a nuisance by the police, they are treated the same as any other offenders and become part of a routinised, bureaucratic process. This typical ('normal') process demonstrates to the shoplifter that he/she is being treated like any other criminal, and the full implications of their actions are emphasised. Usually, any knowledge the shoplifter has of police practices is derived from television and films and it is a shock to realise that the clichés of, '...anything you say', etc. are actually used and, more significantly, are being applied to themselves. Each successive step in the arrest/charging process further degrades the suspect, destroying his previously held self-image, and bringing home the fact that he is being treated as a criminal.

The journey from the department store to the police car is an anxious one for suspects lest anybody recognises them. There will be little or no conversation in the car, often the only sound being that of the police radio. If the suspected shoplifter has ever been to a police station, it is likely to be via the front entrance. This time it is by the back entrance, leading to the charge room and cell block. Cell blocks at best are bare, antiseptic and unwelcoming; at worst, they can be grim and frightening, often with a characteristic smell of alcohol, disinfectant and urine.

Once inside the cell block, the suspect becomes a 'prisoner in custody', his/her status has now been completely transformed from shopper to arrestee to prisoner. He is searched, and made to empty his bags and pockets. He has to sign for his property. Elsewhere, Goffman has noted the symbolic rites of passage attending such personal humiliations.[18] Nothing the suspect says will be accepted at face value, all statements will have to be verified: he has to prove his identification and address. He will be fingerprinted, which entails each pad of each finger and thumb being inked and pressed hard on a sheet of paper: a messy business, and the ink is difficult to wash off. He will be photographed, front and profile and will carry a plate with his name and number on. He may then be placed in a cell and left for a short time in isolation: a frightening and humiliating experience for most people. He will be interviewed about the offence and asked to make a statement. He will then be charged and bailed to appear before a magistrates' court, and finally allowed to leave. The next crisis will be the court.

One pervasive aspect of the whole event is that for most alleged shoplifters (even for suspects who have been arrested before), it is a critical situation, but for the police it is all part of their normal, bureaucratic routine. In the store, the suspect may still think of himself as a 'respectable' person, while the store detective attempts to change his self-conception to that of thief. By the time the police are involved, there is no question of trying to preserve his image — not only is he conceived of as a thief and criminal, more importantly he is *treated* as one.

The way in which the identity of the shopper is transformed has been described by Garfinkel as 'status degradation': [19]

> The transformation of identities is the destruction of one
> social object and the constitution of another.... It is not
> that the new attributes are added to the old 'nucleus'.
> He is not changed, he is reconstituted. The former identity,
> at best, receives the accent of mere appearance. In the social
> calculus of reality representations and test, the former identity
> stands as accidental; the new identity is the 'basic reality'.
> What he is now is what, 'after all', he was all along. [20]

When the store detective stopped Mr Smith, an accusation of theft was implicitly made: Mr Smith was perceived as dishonest. By the time the police officer has arrived, Mr Smith has probably admitted his guilt. At this stage, however, he will see his act of theft as a one-off incident, embarrassing and humiliating, but not a part of his real identity. The involvement of the police changes this self-perception. He is no longer viewed as an honest shopper who has committed an isolated, dishonest act, but is now a 'thief': he has a new identity. The involvement of the police and the routine way that they process him, makes Mr Smith realise that people react to him as a thief and a criminal and do not assume that he is honest.

Garfinkel outlines the conditions for successful degradation ceremonies and these are all satisfied in the arrest of Mr Smith (and other shoplifters). [21] First, the 'denouncer' must be regarded as a publicly known person and must be accepted as speaking on behalf of public morality. Police officers archetypally represent the values of society and are empowered to enforce them. As Gusfield says,

> agents of government are the only persons in modern societies
> who can legitimately claim to represent the total society. In
> support of their acts, limited and specific group interests are
> denied while a public and societal interest is claimed. [22]

Secondly, the witnesses to the ceremony must perceive the event and type of person by referring to a 'dialectical counterpart'; in the case of shoplifting this is provided by the opposites of honest person and thief. Additionally, the event and the perpetrator must be viewed as 'out of the ordinary'. Thirdly, the denounced person must be 'ritually separated from a place in the legitimate order, i.e., he must be defined as standing at a place opposed to it. He must be placed "outside", he must be made "strange". [23] This process is begun in the police station when the shoplifter is arrested and charged, and finalised in the courtroom when he is sentenced.

The effects of arrest by the police, and being searched, fingerprinted, locked in a cell and charged with theft, demonstrate to the shoplifter that what he did was not perceived as an isolated event (certainly by the agents of social control), but an event which was 'typical' of him. His status has now been degraded to that of 'thief'. *He* is changed.

Mr Smith's experience is probably familiar to many shoplifters, but procedures and conditions may vary from police force to police force. For example, if the suspect is a juvenile or a pensioner, treatment will differ. If prosecution by process is being considered, again, practices may vary. In some police stations, the suspect may not be kept in a cell, but may be taken straight to an interview room. The overall pattern of events, however, is how most shoplifters are typically dealt with.

The organisation of police resources in the fieldwork depended to a large extent on the size of the shoplifting problem. Thus, in the four urban police forces studied, where numbers of arrests for shoplifting were high, there were special squads specifically to deal with shoplifters. These squads usually comprised uniformed officers as well as several CID officers, but they generally all wore plain clothes. In the more rural police forces there were no special shoplifting squads, and offences were dealt with as they occurred, the same as any other crime. In only one police force was the uniformed branch responsible for dealing with shoplifters; CID officers were preferred in all the others, although occasionally uniformed officers (who were not in specialist squads) were involved.

In four of the police forces, store detectives had to accompany the arresting police officer and suspect back to the police station, where a written statement was made and any additional questions were elicited. In two of the forces (one urban, one rural) statement forms or 'pro-formas' were given to trusted store detectives, who wrote their statements while waiting for the police to attend, thus obviating the need to attend at the police station. Further details could always be checked at a later date. The two forces concerned were equivocal about this practice, as it was realised that probationary officers gained valuable experience from taking statements, and that 'pro-formas' did not allow facts to be expanded or explained more clearly. Nevertheless, where store detectives were experienced and trusted, it was felt that the saving in time and effort in using 'pro-formas' was justified. It was unusual for store detectives to attend court when the suspect was pleading guilty (though they did when a not guilty plea was entered). In the West End of London, however, it was customary for a store detective to attend the court, but provided that all the suspects pleaded guilty, one store detective could represent the store for a number of offenders.

The suspect's home was routinely searched in only one police force (and that was for adults only). The other police forces would search a suspect's home only when they were suspicious and the situation warranted it.

Police attitudes to store detectives were again ambiguous. All the forces concerned praised the work of the more experienced store detectives, and considered that they had a good rapport with the various stores. Nevertheless, there was an almost universal call for more training for store detectives. On the whole, in-house store detectives were preferred, partly because they were considered to be better trained and partly because they were able to exercise discretion over trivial offences. Agency detectives were often considered to be ill-trained and not as good as the in-house detectives; they were thought to be more concerned with producing 'bodies' to justify themselves. One police force, however, preferred dealing with agency detectives as it believed them to be better trained and more experienced.

Juveniles were normally cautioned, and all the police forces operated a Juvenile Liaison Bureau, whereby an officer would consult with the child's parents, school and social services before making a decision to prosecute. Two police forces (including the Metropolitan Force) did not caution adults over the age of 60; the remainder were more lenient in this matter, and routinely considered pensioners as well as juveniles for a caution.

Overall, with the exception of the Metropolitan Police Force, the ACPO recommendations for prosecutions and cautioning were followed by the police forces, although there was some variation between them with regard to cautioning adults. The general picture then of the treatment of shoplifting by the police broadly corresponds to that recommended in the ACPO report, the exception being the Metropolitan Police.

198

Notes

1. Home Office, *Criminal Statistics. England and Wales* (London: HMSO, 1981).
2. Ibid.
3. See, for example, Barton, M., *The Policeman in the Community* (London: Tavistock, 1964) Holdaway, S., *The British Police*. (London: Edward Arnold, 1979). Manning, P., *Police Work: the Special Organisation of Policing* (London: MIT Press, 1977) Chatterton, M., 'Police in Social Control', in King, J.F.S. (Ed.), *Control Without Custody?* (Cambridge: Institute of Criminology, 1976).
4. Following the Royal Commission on Criminal Procedure, 'The Government has decided to go ahead with plans for an integrated national prosecution system headed by the Director of Public Prosecutions which was outlined in a White Paper published with the Police Bill last October.' *The Guardian,* 29 March 1984.
5. Lidstone, K.W., Hogg, R. and Sutcliffe, F., *Prosecutions by Private Individuals and Non-Police Agencies,* Royal Commission on Criminal Procedure. Research Study No. 10 (London: HMSO, 1980), p. 3.
6. Association of Chief Police Officers, *Shoplifting. Police Policy and Procedure,* Report of a working party appointed by the Association of Chief Police Officers CID Committee.
7. Merseyside, Northumbria, South Yorkshire and West Midlands.
8. Lidstone *et.al., op. cit.,* pp. 104—10.
9. 1978 figures:

Police force	(a) Actual police strength	(b) Recorded shoplifting	Ratio (b):(a)
Metropolitan Police	22,197	25,608	1.1
West Midlands	5,979	11,345	1.9
Greater Manchester	6,390	12,091	1.9
West Yorkshire	4,683	9,759	2.0
Merseyside	4,373	7,351	2.2
South Yorkshire	2,510	5,934	2.4
Northumbria	3,259	7,731	2.4

10. Lidstone *et al., op. cit.,* p. 108.
11. Ditchfield, J.A., *Police Cautioning in England and Wales.* Home Office Research Unit Report No. 37 (London HMSO, 1976), p. 1.

12. Home Office, *op. cit., supplementary tables* (1981).
13. Murphy, D.J.I. and Iles, S.C., 'Dealing with Shoplifters', Home Office Research Bulletin, No. 15 (1983), pp. 25–9.
14. Ibid.
15. More recently, the Metropolitan Police have decided to extend their use of formal cautions. How far this applies to shoplifters of all ages remains to be seen. Note also the Home Office has recently issued consultative guidelines to create more consistent and effective cautions by the police. Cf. *The Guardian*, 27 June 1984.
16. Murphy and Iles, *op. cit.*
17. Oliver, E. and Wilson, J., *Practical Security in Commerce and Industry* (Epping: Gower Press, 1978), p. 105.
18. Goffman, E., *Asylums* (Harmondsworth: Penguin Books, 1961).
19. Garfinkel, H., 'Conditions of Successful Degradation Ceremonies', *American Journal of Sociology,* Vol. 61 (1956), pp. 420–4.,
20. Ibid.
21. Ibid.
22. Gusfield, J.R., 'Moral Passage: The Symbolic Process in Public Designations of Deviance', *Social Problems,* Vol. 15, No. 2 (1968), pp. 175–88.
23. Garfinkel, *op. cit.*

8 Shoplifting and the courts

Introduction

This chapter is divided into two parts: the first examines the structure
of criminal justice in England and Wales and discusses its organisation
and operation in practice. Statistics on shoplifters and their disposal
are also presented. Part two outlines what happens to shoplifters in
court, and is based upon data obtained from observations in two
metropolitan and four provincial magistrates' courts.

PART ONE

The background to the criminal justice system in England and Wales

There are two types of criminal courts in England and Wales: magistrates' courts and crown courts.[1] Magistrates' courts usually consist of a
'Bench' of three magistrates, one of whom acts as chairperson. Magistrates are generally lay people, selected from local worthies who sit on a
part-time, voluntary basis. The clerk of the court is a full-time, paid
official who is responsible for advising magistrates on legal matters, as
well as supervising the administration of the court. In major population
centres, where there is considerable pressure on the courts, stipendiary
magistrates, who are full-time, paid officials, are often appointed, and
these usually sit alone.

   When offenders are under 17 years of age the Bench sits as a juvenile
court and proceedings are far more informal and flexible. For adult

offenders there are generally two modes of procedure: the 'summary trial' and 'committal proceedings'. In a summary trial the magistrate(s) decides whether the offender is guilty or innocent, although most people plead guilty. The magistrates then have to decide upon an appropriate sentence. Committal proceedings occur when the offence is so grave it has to be tried at crown court (e.g. murder), or when one of the parties concerned prefers a crown court trial to summary justice (for certain offences only, the 'triable-either-way' offences: see Chapter I). In committal proceedings the magistrates act as examining justices to determine whether there is sufficient evidence to warrant a crown court trial.

Crown courts are served by High Court and circuit judges and by part-time recorders, who sit with a jury of twelve adults selected from the electoral register. Crown courts deal with offences referred by magistrates' courts 'on indictment', as well as acting as a Court of Appeal for the decisions made in magistrates' courts. Additionally, offenders found guilty by magistrates may be referred to the crown court when magistrates feel their powers of sentencing to be insufficient.[2]

Criminal cases are overwhelmingly heard before magistrates and the percentage of offenders tried at crown court is very small. According to the Central Office of Information (COI), 'about 98 per cent of all criminal cases are finally heard and determined by unpaid lay justices.'[3] Bottoms and McClean's research suggests that 95 per cent of defendants choose a summary trial when the option is available to them: in their study 95 per cent of men and 92.5 per cent of women pleaded guilty.[4] As Laurie says, 'From the layman's point of view, the unexpected corollary of the high guilty plea rate is that the contested trial which we have come to know from innumerable representations in court room dramas, on film and television, is completely atypical.'[5] Far from being an exciting legal confrontation, 'the truth is that, for the most part, the business of the criminal courts is dull, commonplace, ordinary and after a while downright tedious.'[6]

Magistrates, then, are often required to do little more than accept a guilty plea, listen to the details of the offence and offender, and decide upon an appropriate sentence. According to Tarling and Weatheritt, 'the penalties available to magistrates when dealing with male indictable offenders aged 21 and over range from an absolute discharge to sentences of imprisonment of up to six months, or in the case of some or several offences, of up to one year.'[7] Since the Criminal Law Act 1977, magistrates have been able to levy a fine of up to £1,000 per offence (previously £400) and, since February 1984, this has been doubled. Additionally, they can make probation, community service and hospital orders, suspend prison sentences, and give conditional discharges. For young offenders, magistrates can recommend detention centres, supervision and care orders, etc. Where magistrates feel their powers to be insufficient they can refer the offender to the crown court for sentencing.

Courts in practice

The advantages to the prosecution (whether police or other agency) and to the criminal justice system as a whole in a high percentage of guilty pleas are obvious. A guilty plea saves time, effort and resources. Not-guilty pleas, even in magistrates courts, involve considerable work in securing statements, interviewing witnesses, arranging dates and preparing cases. Needless to say, the effort involved in crown court trials is considerably greater. As Bottoms and McClean phrase it, 'the smooth administration of justice essentially [depends] on the cooperation of the mass of defendants' in pleading guilty.[8] 'The truth is,' according to Baldwin and Bottomley, 'that the resources of the system require a very high level of guilty pleas and there are, at almost all stages of the criminal process pressures on defendants to plead guilty.'[9] The decision to plead guilty or not-guilty obviously depends to a large degree on the question of guilt or innocence, but research suggests a number of extraneous factors affect that decision.

Heberling believes that defendants who plead not-guilty risk being remanded in custody, which is distressful in itself, but also jeopardises their employment.[10] There could also be a financial penalty involved in defence costs, especially if they are found guilty. Moreover, defendants who contest their trials and are found guilty risk a harsher sentence. Zander explains this is justified on the tenuous grounds that guilty pleas may be construed as demonstrations of genuine remorse[11] (cf. Baldwin and McConville and their discussion on the 'sentencing discount'[12]).

Contested trials often take months before they are finally heard. In Bottoms' and McClean's research, for example, over 90 per cent of uncontested cases were heard within approximately a month, whereas only 8 per cent of men and 28 per cent of women who contested their charges were dealt with within a similar period. Since their research both periods of waiting time have been considerably extended, particularly in the cities (cf. the Vera Institute study (1979) and Nacro Briefing (1981)).

The anxiety involved in the long delays which can precede court appearances in contested cases, and the strain imposed on defendants and their families, can be imagined. Moreover, contested trials are more likely to attract the attention of the press with the consequent risk of publicity. 'Often the result of such pressure', states Heberling, 'is the "get-it-over" syndrome. The defendant makes a statement to the police and pleads guilty to take the pressure off. This especially happens where the defendant is likely to receive a non-custodial sentence anyway.'[13]

The following extract illustrates the pressures that confront many defendants when they decide how to plead. It is particularly relevant as it involves a case of shoplifting, but the features are generalisable to other offences. Moreover, the defendant in this example does not usually reside in the United Kingdom and it would appear that there are further tensions for such people.

£60,000 Arab says 'I'm not a shoplifter'

A £60,000-a-year postmaster was fined £400 in London yesterday for shoplifting. But last night 45-year-old M. Al-L. said it was all a terrible mistake — that he pleaded guilty on a technicality. The fine was imposed at Marlborough Street Court where he admitted stealing a shirt worth £8.79 from Z's in Oxford Street. 'I don't need to steal a shirt,' said Al-L., who was wearing a £30 Christian Dior tie. 'I could buy all the shirts in Z's if I wanted to. I had taken back a shirt because I had got the wrong size. The only mistake I made was in not asking permission to change it. I have paid £400 for the mistake. I will now make sure that I get a receipt, even for a tin of Coca-Cola.'

Al-L., who comes to Britain every four or five months, said that he brought £15,000 with him in April. That is to last him until September. In addition, he receives a weekly allowance of £210 from [his] embassy. 'I have no need to steal,' he said. 'And I am an honest man. I pleaded guilty because I was told that was the best thing to do. If I had said I was innocent, I would have to go in court after court and go before a jury and it would have taken months. They would have taken my passport away from me and I didn't want to go through all that.' He suggested that many foreigners who appeared in court might plead guilty for the same reasons. Al-L., who is married with three children, said that his wife was very upset by the whole thing. 'It was terrible standing there behind thieves in the court. It has made me feel very sick. I am too embarrassed to tell my embassy about it. When I was taken to the police station, I felt so terrible I just wanted to leave Britain. But I love this country and I will stay. I won't shop in Z's again unless I have to.'[14]

There has been some research into why defendants who later claimed innocence actually pleaded guilty. Blumberg found that of a sample of 700 defendants who had pleaded guilty in the USA, a half maintained their innocence.[15] The desire to get the case over featured significantly in this inconsistent pleading (cf. Dell[16]). In 57 per cent of cases, pressure to plead guilty came from the defendant's own lawyer, not from the police or prosecution. Although the percentage of 'possibly innocent' defendants was much lower in Bottoms' and McClean's study in England (18 per cent), they too believed the pressure to plead guilty stemmed from legal advice. [17]

Most research into plea-bargaining and inconsistent pleading in this country has focused on the crown court (see, for example, Baldwin and McConville [18]). In a study of defendants who changed their pleas at crown court (from not-guilty to guilty), Purves found that there was little evidence of pressure from the prosecution, and further, this sample was unlikely to be bewildered by the court's procedures as most defendants were familiar with the legal process. [19] In a later study, McCabe and Purves concluded that there was little evidence to suggest that the police had pressurised crown court defendants to plead guilty. [20]

Bottoms' and McClean's research, which included the lower courts, found that unrepresented cases had the lowest incidence of inconsistent pleaders, implying that legal advice was associated with the decision to plead guilty. [21] This finding is contradicted by the results of Dell's study of female defendants, where the police were instrumental in influencing defendants' pleas.

> Several girls said that they had been advised to plead guilty in a kindly, even fatherly spirit, the policeman telling them that this was the simplest way to get the case over, and to avoid the risk of publicity, or remands in custody. It was easy to see how those without experience at police stations or courts might gratefully accept such advice, and it was significant that, while only 9 per cent of inconsistent recidivists gave police advice as their reasons for pleading guilty, 64 per cent of the inconsistent first offenders said they had done so in response to police persuasion. [22]

Dell's results might partly be explained by the predominance of public order offences, where the evidence of the police is often critical. The conclusions to be drawn from these various studies are not straightforward but they do serve as a reminder that the decision to plead guilty or not guilty is not merely a question of guilt or innocence but is influenced by other factors, including the venue of the trial, legal representation and the nature of the offence. In addition, it would appear from the evidence presented in Chapter 6 that store detectives also have an influence in persuading shoplifters to plead guilty.

In short, criminal justice in England and Wales is largely a matter of defendants pleading guilty at summary trials and being sentenced. Shoplifting is no exception, as the following figures reveal.

Court statistics for shoplifting

Table 8.1 examines offenders found guilty of shoplifting by type of

Table 8.1: Persons Proceeded Against for Shoplifting, 1981 [23]

Magistrates' courts

1.	Persons proceeded against		M —	48,637
			F —	34,565
				83,202
2.	Persons dealt with summarily	M & F —		77,884[a]
3.	Persons found guilty		M —	42,905
			F —	30,051
				72,956
4.	Percentage found guilty	93.67 per cent		

Crown courts

1.	Persons dealt with		M —	2,492
			F —	1,747
				4,239
2.	Persons found guilty		M —	1,752
			F —	1,125
				2,877
3.	Percentage found guilty	67.87 per cent[b]		

Total persons found guilty at all courts = 75,833

Percentage found guilty at magistrates' courts = 96.2 per cent

Percentage found guilty at crown courts = 3.8 per cent

Notes:

a. Excludes those people referred to crown court, bailed, etc.

b. Acquittal rate of 32.13 per cent (100—67.87%) includes 138 not prosecuted.

court and sex. Figures for findings of guilt and innocence are also presented. From Table 8.1, it is apparent that the majority of offenders are dealt with by magistrates — 77,884 defendants were dealt with summarily and only 4,239 were tried at crown court, a total of 82,123 (approximately 1,000 people who were proceeded against were thus not tried for a variety of reasons — e.g. insufficient evidence, etc.). Consequently, 94.83 per cent of defendants were dealt with by magistrates. Of those persons who were tried summarily, 93.67 per cent were found guilty. The percentage of persons found guilty at crown court was lower at 67.87 per cent, but this reflects the fact that more defendants contest their cases at crown court and most defendants at magistrates' courts plead guilty. Research conducted for the Royal Commission on Criminal Procedure which examined only those defendants prosecuted by retailers, found that 90 per cent of defendants pleaded guilty to charges of shoplifting in magistrates' courts in 1977, and that the overall percentage found guilty was 94 per cent.[24] Looking at the figures for persons found guilty in the two types of court, it transpires that over 96 per cent of such defendants are dealt with at magistrates' courts. Thus, criminal justice for shoplifting defendants is almost entirely magistrates' justice.

Moreover, as with most defendants in the lower courts, the majority of shoplifters who come before magistrates are unrepresented. In Bottoms' and McClean's study, 88 per cent of males and 71 per cent of females charged with shoplifting were unrepresented.[25] Since their study, however, the authors believe that the situation has improved, as magistrates will now usually ensure that defendants are represented when they are considering a custodial sentence.

Table 8.2 examines the statistics on males and females found guilty of shoplifting at magistrates' courts in 1981. The table shows that there is little difference between the age bands of men and women found guilty of shoplifting at magistrates' courts. Indeed, for the age bands over 30, the percentages of male and female offenders are almost identical. Taking males and females together, the largest group of persons found guilty is that aged 17—20 (16.97 per cent). The next largest group is that aged 30—39 (16.2 per cent), but this is obviously a much wider age band. Taken together, male and females aged under 25 found guilty constitute just over 44 per cent of all persons found guilty of shoplifting. Perhaps what is more surprising is that those over 25 make up 56 per cent of all offenders found guilty of shoplifting.

Like most other offences for which people are convicted, younger people tend to be more numerous. What is noticeable with the shoplifting figures is that significant percentages of other age groups are also represented. Table 8.3, looks at these same figures but analyses the percentages differently. It is clear for the 10—13 age group that boys predominate amongst those found guilty of shoplifting, constituting almost three-quarters of such offenders. For the next age band (14—16), males still predominate, but this time only by two-thirds. The next seven

Table 8.2: Persons Found Guilty of Shoplifting in Magistrates'
Courts by Age and Sex, 1981 [26]

Age	Males		Females		Total M & F (and percentage)	
10—13	2,557	(5.95%)	912	(3.03%)	3,469	(4.75%)
14—16	5,882	(13.7%)	3,215	(10.69%)	9,097	(12.46%)
17—20	6,946	(16.18%)	5,438	(18.09%)	12,384	(16.97%)
21—24	3,869	(9.01%)	3,436	(11.43%)	7,305	(10.01%)
25—29	3,690	(8.6%)	3,045	(10.13%)	6,735	(9.23%)
30—39	6,870	(16.01%)	4,949	(16.46%)	11,819	(16.2%)
40—49	5,700	(13.28%)	3,819	(12.7%)	9,519	(13.04%)
50—59	4,834	(11.26%)	3,480	(11.58%)	8,314	(11.39%)
60+	2,557	(5.95%)	1,757	(5.84%)	4,314	(5.91%)
Totals	42,905	(100%)	30,051	(100%)	72,956	(100%)

Table 8.3: Percentage of Persons Found Guilty of Shoplifting
in Magistrates' Courts in Each Age Band by Sex, 1981 [27]

Age	Total Persons in each age band	Male	Female
10—13	3,469	73.71%	26.28%
14—16	9.097	64.66%	35.34%
17—20	12,384	56.08%	43.91%
21—24	7,305	52.96%	47.03%
25—29	6,735	54.79%	45.21%
30—39	11,819	58.13%	41.87%
40—49	9,519	59.88%	40.12%
50—59	8,314	58.14%	41.86%
60+	4,314	59.27%	40.73%
Totals	72,956	58.8%	41.19%

age bands show a remarkably consistent pattern, with males predominating at all ages (slightly less so for those aged 17–20, 21–24, and 25–29). Females found guilty of shoplifting thus constitute approximately 40+ per cent (maximum 47 per cent) for all age bands over 17 years.

The figures for persons found guilty of shoplifting at crown court are shown by age and sex in Table 8.4. Once again, the percentages of males and females in each of the age bands found guilty of shoplifting at crown court are remarkably similar, usually only varying by a percentage point or two. For the 21–24-year-olds, for example, the males found guilty were 16.2 per cent of all males found guilty, and the females were 16.97 per cent of all females. Again, young offenders are significantly represented, with those under 25 constituting over 30 per cent of convicted offenders. There appears, however, to be a greater representation of older offenders, with those between 30 and 40 constituting nearly a quarter of all persons found guilty. This no doubt reflects the tendency of crown courts to deal with the more experienced offenders, and the greater likelihood of previous convictions among these older defendants.

Table 8.5 examines these same figures, but with the percentages calculated differently. Clearly, nothing can be extrapolated from the three juveniles aged under 14 as the numbers involved are too small though it should be noted that crown courts do not normally deal with juveniles, except when they are being prosecuted with an adult, and even here, they are remitted to the juvenile court for sentence if found guilty. The same applies to the next age band (14–16). From age 17 onwards, male offenders consistently are found guilty more often than women. The percentages of males and females found guilty are reminiscent of the figures for magistrates' courts (see Table 8.3): the totals of 60 per cent male and 40 per cent female for each age band appear to apply to both crown and magistrates' courts. There is more variation between the age bands in crown courts, however, with the percentage of women found guilty of shoplifting in each age group falling to approximately a third on several occasions. Nevertheless, there seems to be a remarkable consistency between all four tables, (8.2–8.5).

Having examined the age and sex characteristics of those persons found guilty of shoplifting in both types of court, the sentences those persons received can now be discussed. Figures relate only to magistrates' courts as this is how over 96 per cent of shoplifting offenders are dealt with.

Table 8.6 details the disposal of all persons found guilty of shoplifting in magistrates' courts. It demonstrates that the most frequently used sentence for all persons found guilty of shoplifting is the fine (56.35 per cent) and a similar percentage applies to both male and female offenders. The next most common sentence is the conditional discharge (15.72 per

Table 8.4: Persons Found Guilty of Shoplifting at Crown Court by Age and Sex, 1981 [28]

Age	Males		Females		Total (and percentage) M & F	
10—13	1	(0.06%)	2	(0.18%)	3	(0.10%)
14—16	12	(0.69%)	6	(0.53%)	18	(0.63%)
17—20	262	(14.95%)	178	(15.82%)	440	(15.29%)
21—24	284	(16.21%)	191	(16.97%)	475	(16.51%)
25—29	293	(16.72%)	164	(14.58%)	457	(15.88%)
30—39	424	(24.2%)	291	(25.87%)	715	(24.85%)
40—49	253	(14.44%)	175	(15.56%)	428	(14.88%)
50—59	160	(9.13%)	81	(7.2%)	241	(8.38%)
60+	63	(3.6%)	37	(3.29%)	100	(3.48%)
Total	1,752	(100%)	1,125	(100%)	2,877	(100%)

Table 8.5 Percentage of Persons Found Guilty at Crown Court in Each Age Band by Sex, 1981 [29]

Age	Total persons in each age group	Male %	Female %
10—13	3	33.34%	66.66%
14—16	18	66.66%	33.34%
17—20	440	59.55%	40.45%
21—24	475	59.79%	40.21%
25—29	457	64.11%	35.89%
30—39	715	59.30%	40.70%
40—49	428	59.11%	40.89%
50—59	241	63.39%	33.61%
60+	100	63.00%	37.00%
Total	2,877	60.09%	39.01%

Table 8.6: Disposal of All Persons Found Guilty of Shoplifting in Magistrates' Courts, 1981 [29]

Disposal	Male	Female	Total (and percentage) M + F
Absolute discharge	212 (0.49%)	188 (0.63%)	400 (0.55%)
Recognisance	8 (0.02%)	9 (0.03%)	17 (0.02%)
Conditional discharge	5,682 (12.31%)	5,789 (19.26%)	11,471 (15.72%)
Hospital order	29 (0.07%)	8 (0.03%)	37 (0.05%)
Probation order	2,737 (6.38%)	3,756 (12.05%)	6,493 (8.9%)
Supervision order	1,555 (3.62%)	1,017 (3.38%)	2,572 (3.53%)
Fine	24,149 (56.28%)	16,967 (56.46%)	41,116 (56.35%)
Community service	1,231 (2.87%)	399 (1.33%)	1,630 (2.23%)
Attendance centre	1,247 (2.91%)	141 (0.5%)	1,388 (1.9%)
Detention centre	374 (0.87%)	0 –	374 (0.51%)
Care order	275 (0.64%)	191 (0.64%)	466 (0.64%)
Suspended sentence	2,037 (4.75%)	910 (3.03%)	2,947 (4.03%)
Immediate imprisonment	2,516 (5.86%)	439 (1.46%)	2,955 (4.05%)
Committed for sentence (s. 38)	558 (1.3%)	169 (0.56%)	727 (1.00%)
Committed for sentence (MCA 1980, s. 37.)	123 (0.28%)	47 (0.16%)	170 (0.23%)
Other	172 (0.04%)	21 (0.07%)	193 (0.26%)
Total	42,905 (58.8%)	30,051 (41.62%)	72,956 (100%)

cent), and here the proportion of women is greater than that for men. The same applies to probation orders, where women are twice as likely to receive this sentence than men. If one takes suspended sentences together with immediate imprisonment, the overall rate for both males and females is similar to that of probation orders, but men are more likely to receive sentences of immediate imprisonment. The remainder of the available sentences are used only relatively infrequently.

Table 8.7: Disposal of Persons over 21 Found Guilty of Shoplifting in Magistrates' Courts, 1981 [30]

Disposal	Male	Female	Total (and percentage) M + F
Absolute discharge	129 (0.47%)	140 (0.68%)	269 (0.56%)
Recognisance	6 (0.02%)	8 (0.04%)	14 (0.03%)
Conditional discharge	2,893 (10.51%)	3,660 (17.87%)	6,553 (13.65%)
Hospital order	28 (0.1%)	8 (0.04%)	36 (0.07%)
Probation order	2,095 (7.61%)	2,815 (13.74%)	4,910 (10.23%)
Supervision order	– –	– –	– –
Fine	16,778 (60.97%)	12,407 (60.56%)	29,185 (60.79%)
Community service	803 (2.92%)	268 (1.3%)	1,071 (2.23%)
Attendance centre	1 –	– –	1 –
Detention centre	– –	– –	– –
Care order	– –	– –	– –
Suspended sentence	1,883 (6.84%)	717 (3.5%)	2,600 (5.42%)
Immediate imprisonment	2,366 (8.6%)	358 (1.75%)	2,724 (5.67%)
Committed for sentence (s. 38)	405 (1.47%)	97 (0.47%)	502 (1.05%)
Committed for sentence (MCA 1980, s. 37)	2 –	– –	2 –
Other	131 (0.48%)	8 (0.04%)	139 (0.29%)
Total	27,520 (57.33%)	20,486 (42.67%)	48,006 (100%)

Table 8.7 illustrates the disposal of persons over 21 found guilty of shoplifting, where the range of sentences available to magistrates is more restricted. When persons under the age of 21 are excluded from the figures, it is noticeable that the rate of fining is increased, as is the rate of imprisonment (though only marginally). Again, there is little difference in the percentage of males and females who are fined, but disparities between male and female imprisonment rates are more marked,

particularly for immediate imprisonment.

Table 8.8 examines the amount of fines levied on all offenders found guilty of shoplifting (N= 41,116), remembering that this includes approximately 12,000 persons under the age of 21, who are more likely to be treated leniently. Looking at Table 8.8, there appears to be little consistency in the amount of fine levied. Clearly, the large fines for shoplifting which feature so prominently in the newspapers are not representative, with only 4 per cent of offenders receiving fines over £100 and only 1 per cent being fined over £200. The most common amounts levied are £20—£30 and £40—£50, with 17 per cent of offenders receiving fines of £70—£100. Persons receiving fines of between £500 and £1,000 are so statistically small as not to register in these statistics.

Previous research has examined the disposal of shoplifters, among other offenders. For example, Tarling and Weatheritt examined the sentences given in 30 magistrates' courts to males over 21 and found that fines for shoplifters were the most popular punishment (67.4 per cent), followed by imprisonment (immediate and suspended — 14.8 per cent).

Table 8.8: Offenders Fined at Magistrates' Courts for Shoplifting by Amount of Fine, 1981 [31]

Amount fined	Percentage of all offenders fined
£10 and under	9%
£11 to £20	12%
£21 to £30	22%
£31 to £40	9%
£41 to £50	22%
£51 to £70	5%
£71 to £100	17%
£101 to £200	3%
£201 to £500	1%
£501 to £1,000	negligible
£1,000 +	"

Total number of offenders fined = 41,116

Table 8.9:   Percentage of Persons Found Guilty of Shoplifting

Petty sessional division or London court [a]	Total found guilty (=100%)	Absolute or conditional discharge	Probation or supervision order
Marlborough St. M.C.	3669	9.5	2.4
Birmingham	1586	11.7	6.7
Manchester	1465	28.2	5.8
Liverpool	1216	15.5	10.9
Leeds	1034	10.3	10.1
Teesside	912	9.8	6.0
Horseferry Rd. M.C.	862	15.7	3.0
Newcastle upon Tyne	858	4.8	7.6
Bristol	807	10.8	9.4
Nottingham (City)	749	13.4	9.2
Sheffield	722	10.7	6.8
Cardiff	676	10.5	4.7
Kingston upon Hull	651	10.1	5.7
Croydon	643	12.4	8.1
Bradford	623	12.2	10.1
Southampton	610	13.3	8.9
Plymouth	580	8.3	5.7
Marylebone M.C.	573	16.6	5.8
Leicester (City)	552	7.2	8.5
South Western M.C.	550	14.9	5.6
Brighton	541	9.6	7.2
Coventry	514	19.6	7.4
Greenwich M.C.	494	22.3	6.5
West London M.C.	478	19.9	5.0
Knowsley	474	6.3	5.5
Tottenham M.C.	458	10.5	8.3
Total	22297	12.8	6.4
Other PSDs in England and Wales	37724	13.4	8.5
Total England and Wales	60021	13.2	7.7

Notes:
a. PSDs/courts with 500 or more persons proceeded against for shoplifting (excluding juvenile
b. Includes detention centre, care order, committal to the crown court for sentence.

The figures quoted are subject to the inaccuracies of all large data collection systems and are not

Fine (£)	Imprisonment		Otherwise dealt with.[b]	Median fine (£)
	Suspended	Immediate		
81.7	3.0	1.1	2.3	75
67.5	4.9	6.9	2.2	40
49.4	5.9	7.0	3.8	10
63.7	3.0	3.1	3.8	25
65.0	5.0	7.1	2.5	25
72.7	2.6	4.5	4.4	20
69.6	4.2	5.3	2.2	50
74.6	1.5	4.2	7.3	45
66.8	4.6	5.8	2.6	50
59.0	6.0	8.0	4.4	20
75.2	1.4	2.6	3.3	25
65.1	11.1	5.6	3.0	20
74.0	5.1	2.9	2.2	25
68.4	4.2	3.9	3.0	50
67.4	3.9	4.3	2.1	40
58.9	6.1	9.8	3.1	25
64.0	7.6	8.8	5.7	25
64.0	7.0	3.5	3.1	40
74.8	2.4	4.3	2.7	40
61.6	10.9	4.4	2.5	30
62.5	9.6	8.1	3.0	50
64.2	2.7	3.9	2.1	25
61.1	5.3	3.2	1.6	25
53.8	9.2	4.8	7.3	30
83.1	2.1	1.7	1.3	25
69.9	3.3	3.5	4.6	75
68.3	4.7	4.6	3.2	30
67.3	4.3	3.4	3.1	30
67.7	4.4	3.9	3.1	30

courts).

necessarily accurate to the last digit shown.

Conditional and absolute discharges together accounted for 12.7 per cent of sentences given to males over 21.[32] The general trend of these statistics follows those of 1981, but is accentuated by considering only males over 21 for imprisonment rates. The proportion fined appears somewhat higher than in 1981 (these figures are comparable because there is no sex bias in fining adult shoplifters).

Table 8.9 is reproduced from a survey conducted by the Home Office Statistical Department and examines the disposal of 37 per cent of all shoplifters convicted at magistrates' courts in 1978. The data are based on the records of 26 courts. Again, the fine was the penalty most often imposed and is higher here (at about 70 per cent) than in Tarling or Weatheritt or the 1981 statistics, presumably due to the courts selected for the sample (ignoring possible fluctuations from year to year).

Table 8.9 demonstrates how the level of fine fluctuates with each court, but even in Marlborough Street, where £1,000 fines are regularly reported, the median fine is only £75. In the 26 courts studied, absolute or conditional discharges were given to approximately 13 per cent of offenders, while 8 per cent received terms of imprisonment (immediate and suspended).

Table 8.9 is useful in demonstrating the variation between magistrates' courts in the types and level of sentences imposed. These statistics help put the following cases quoted in the press into perspective.

£400 Fine for Shoplifting

A Lebanese architect who was said by police to be earning £100,000 a year was fined £400 with £20 costs at Marlborough Street yesterday for shoplifting.

A.B., 38, visiting London and staying at Mayfair, admitted stealing clothing worth £35.22 from a West End store. He said he did not earn as much as had been stated.[34]

Although £400 was the maximum fine at the time, it could be imposed several times if more than one offence were involved.[35] For example,

Girl Shoplifter Fined £600

Miss I.C., 17, on holiday in [a] school party from Spain [was] fined £600 today after admitting stealing 40 items, mainly toys and games worth a total of £54.69 from *three* stores in West End.[36]

As part of the 'moral panic' about shoplifting (cf. Chapter 2), attention was focused on the level of the financial penalty which could be imposed by magistrates. The maximum fine was subsequently increased to £1,000, and it was soon utilised.

First £1,000 Fine for Shoplifting

A Persian doctor's wife became the first shoplifter to be
fined the new maximum of £1,000 when she appeared at
Marlborough Street during the weekend. Mrs F.H., 34,
who admitted stealing a £9.99 nightdress from an Oxford
Street store, said: 'This is not justice, it's robbery.' Mrs H.
who had £2,976 on her when she was arrested, is on a six-
month visit.

Under the Criminal Law Act, 1977, the maximum fine for
shoplifting was increased from £400 to £1,000 last Monday.[37]

The following press cutting illustrates both that a maximum fine can
be imposed several times for different offences, and, perhaps more
interestingly, the almost bizarre variation in sentences (and the ideology
behind them) that can occur.

£3,000 in Fines for Iraqui Woman Shoplifting

Fines totalling £3,000 were imposed yesterday on an Iraqui
woman tourist caught shoplifting in the West End. She has
only £4 left in this country and will have to serve an alternative
sentence of 28 days in prison unless she can raise the money.
The £3,000 is the most so far that one person has been required
to pay at one time for offences of this nature. 'This was obviously
a deliberately planned shoplifting expedition,' Mrs E.D., Chair-
man of the Bench in Marlborough Street Court, said to Miss R.A.R.
'You stole 48 items from three different stores.' Miss R., 38, who
was staying in Paddington, missed her flight home with her
brother because of the case. She admitted three offences of
stealing jewellery and other items together valued at £73.09
from three West End stores and was fined the maximum
£1,000 on each, plus £30 costs.

Previously, shoplifters have been fined the maximum £1,000
but never on three separate counts at once. The penalty was
raised from a maximum of £400 on July 17 under the Criminal
Law Act 1977.

Later Mrs D. fined a Persian woman civil servant £2,000 with
£30 costs or 30 days' imprisonment for stealing cosmetics and
a pullover valued at £17.55 from two stores. Miss S.B., 42,
on holiday and staying in Mayfair, admitted stealing the goods
while shopping with £1,155 on her.

In a different court room at Marlborough Street, Mr J.H.,
the magistrate, conditionally discharged a Polish couple who
shoplifted while on honeymoon. The magistrate, who heard
the couple had been robbed of £100 in London, said: 'I think

they were suddenly confronted by an array of consumer goods which they don't see at home.' A.B., 30, an artist, and his wife, K., 23, staying at West Ealing, admitted stealing goods valued at £71 from three stores.[38]

Finally, before moving to part two and the courtroom observations, the biggest fine imposed for shoplifting:

The biggest fine ever imposed for shoplifting, £7,200, was paid on the spot by an Arab woman who handed the money to court officials from her purse.[39]

PART TWO

On being prosecuted

This section focuses on how shoplifters are dealt with in magistrates' courts. During fieldwork, a total of 85 complete cases of shoplifting were observed with an additional few which had been remanded for social enquiry reports. Many features of shoplifting trials are common to the prosecution of other offences, and, reciprocally, much of what has been written on magistrates' justice applies also to shoplifting. As was shown in part one of this chapter, shoplifting is a typical offence in that the majority of defendants are not represented and plead guilty. In what follows, a number of shoplifting cases are first discussed to demonstrate how magistrates' courts operate. Then, some particular aspects of shoplifting hearings will be examined.

Carlen has written perceptively about proceedings in magistrates' courts. She argues that far from the idealised version of adversaries standing as equals before the law, justice is subjugated to considerations of organisational efficiency, and that defendants are manipulated to promote rapid processing. It is clear that adversary justice does not particularly obtain in magistrates' courts, but this may be a function of the high percentage of guilty pleas rather than any other factors. Whether the staging of magistrates' justice is deliberately geared to maximise organisational efficiency to the exclusion of other considerations is a moot point. However, much of what Carlen says about the presentational aspects of proceedings in magistrates' courts is persuasive.[40]

Courtrooms for adults in magistrates' courts are stark places. At one end, there is the magistrates' 'bench', raised above the rest of the court. Opposite or sometimes to the side of the magistrates' dais, is the defendants' dock, with symbolic rails around the top. Between the magistrates and the defendants in the well of the court, sit the prosecution, the police, probation officers, reporters, defence solicitors and the clerk of the court. The defendants' platform is raised above the rest of the court, though is not as high as the magistrates' bench, often with the public benches behind. Acoustically, most courts are badly designed, and the difficulties defendants experience in hearing the magistrate or clerk are exacerbated by the continuous 'whisperings' of solicitors and police officers, and the almost continuous arrival and departure of lawyers, defendants, witnesses and the public.

The following two cases exemplify how shoplifting offences are typically dealt with in magistrates' courts.

Case 29: This is the first case to be heard. The police inspector has already called the defendant who now stands in the dock. Normally defendants will be called into the dock from the public gallery, but where they have been remanded in custody, they will be accompanied from the cells by a police officer. The magistrates enter, and the clerk says, 'Stand, please'. Everybody stands until the three magistrates are seated, then they too sit. In this case the prosecution is carried out by a solicitor acting for the retailer. He asks for a summary trial, to which the magistrates agree. The clerk of the court then explains to the defendant that she has a choice of being tried there or at crown court, but the magistrates retain the right of referring the case to the crown court, if the defendant is found guilty. 'The magistrates have decided that the case is best dealt with here, if you consent and are found guilty, the magistrates considering your previous character and antecedents may commit you to crown court for sentence.'[41] The defendant opts for summary trial.

The clerk of the court next reads out the charge: 'You are charged that on the 16th of August 1979, you stole four vests and three sweaters to the total value of £16.50, the property of M., contrary to section 1 of the Theft Act, do you plead guilty or not guilty?' The defendant replies, 'Guilty. I'm terribly sorry.' The defendant is told to sit down by the clerk and the prosecuting solicitor stands and says:

'Your honour, the brief facts of the case are these. The defendant was seen to select a sweater and put it into a bag. She paid for some goods, and then proceeded to roll up four vests and put them into her bag. When stopped she produced two more sweaters and said, "I will pay, I can afford them." She had £267 on her at the time.'

The solicitor asks for costs and sits down.

The police inspector stands and reads out the defendant's antecedents taken at the police station.

'She is a married woman, aged 37 years, of previous good character. She lives in Cairo with her husband, a civil engineer, and three children. She is a housewife. She arrived in this country on the 14th of August for a holiday and brought £300 with her. She has to pay a hotel bill of £50 and £30 for a coach trip to Paris where she will meet her husband.'

The defendant is told to stand and is asked if she has anything to say. Now crying, the defendant replies, 'I owe money for hotel and food. I am very sorry, it is all correct. I do apologise to the court and the police for the trouble I've caused. I am terribly ashamed. I do not know what has happened.'

After a few moments of deliberation and consultation with his two colleagues the magistrate sentences the defendant to a £100 fine, plus costs of £30. The defendant is shown out of the dock to the office to pay the fine. The whole case has taken less than ten minutes.

Case 59 was observed in a different court and involved two women who needed the assistance of an interpreter. All statements, questions and instructions were relayed to the women via the interpreter.

Case 59: The magistrates are already seated and the police call for the two defendants, who are led into the dock. The police ask for a summary trial and the magistrate agrees. The clerk of the court offers the defendants a choice of venue for the proceedings, with the usual rider that if found guilty, the magistrates may commit them to crown court. The defendants opt for a summary trial. The charge is read out: 'You are charged that on Thursday 26th of July you stole 1 shirt, 1 sweater, 1 nightdress to the total value of £12.90, the property of C.'s.' The defendants are asked how they plead, to which they reply 'Guilty', and are then told to sit down.

The police inspector relates the details of the case.
'On Thursday the 26th July at 11.30 a.m. the defendants were on the ground floor of C's. They are mother and daughter. The mother was holding a shirt which she was seen to push into a Harrods bag she was carrying. They proceeded to another department where they selected and examined a black sweater. They took it off the hanger and the mother draped it over her arm. When they moved to the blouses she pushed it into the Harrod's bag. Her daughter bought a blouse. On the first floor, the daughter selected two night-dresses, kept one and gave the other one to her mother. In the coat department, the daughter paid for her nightdress

and the mother was seen to push her nightdress into a bag. They left the store. When they were stopped, the items were found with their tags torn off incorrectly. When arrested the daughter said, 'Yes, I know why we are here. We have done wrong.' She had £23.93 at the time and her mother had £25.95.'

The officer proceeds to read out the background antecedents. 'They are on a tour of Europe and arrived in this country on the 25th of July. They live in Tehran. The husband/father is a retired civil servant. They have no details of their financial situation except that all bills have been paid. They are due to return to Iran today. The daughter is a single woman, aged 23 years. She is unemployed, has no savings, and is supported by her family.'

The defendants are told to stand up. They have no questions and nothing to say. The magistrate fines the mother £200 plus £30 costs, and the daughter is fined £200. An alternative sentence of 14 days' imprisonment is given if the defendants cannot pay the fine.

Although specific details may vary from case to case, the above two examples describe the general features of shoplifting cases heard in magistrates' courts. The defendants are generally unrepresented, they opt for summary trials and plead guilty. Magistrates and the prosecution are similarly eager to consider the case in the lower court. The charge is read out. The prosecution, usually represented by the court police sergeant or inspector (or solicitor acting for the retailers in London), reads out the 'brief details of the case'.

The police officer relates the defendants' antecedents, to provide the magistrates with a personal background to the case, and the defendants are asked if they have anything to say. Having considered the details of the case, the defendants' background and any pleas of mitigation, the magistrate finally imposes sentence. The whole proceedings are routine and semi-automatic to the court personnel, and usually take little more than ten minutes. Often the speed and routinisation of the proceedings affects the defendant as much as the sentence imposed.

The following examples will be used to illustrate particular features of court proceedings: the plea, the circumstances of the offence, antecedents, mitigation and sentence.

Most shoplifters, like most other offenders, plead guilty. In this study it was not feasible to interview defendants after the hearing and so it was not possible to ascertain the number of 'guilty but innocent' defendants. It is likely that shoplifters are as prone to the extraneous pressures to plead guilty discussed in the previous section as other defendants. In two cases, during the fieldwork, a hasty change of plea was observed.

Case 41 involved a man from the USA who was charged
with stealing an imitation spitoon, valued at £4.40. He was
asked whether he pleaded guilty or not guilty and replied
that he had forgotten to pay. The clerk then instructed the
defendant that he could not accept a plea of guilty in this
case as he was saying that he had no intent to steal and
therefore the case would have to be put back. The defendant
explained that he had to leave the country in a week and could
not afford to delay further. The clerk reiterated what was
involved in a guilty plea — that it was an acknowledgment of
a dishonest act with intention. The defendant subsequently
pleaded guilty and was fined £100 with £20 costs, and was
allowed to leave.

In Case 48, the defendant was a visitor from Pakistan, who
was even more explicit about his reasons for pleading guilty
to stealing a £4 T-shirt. When asked whether he was guilty
or not, he declared that he did not intend to steal the shirt
but was pleading guilty because he had to go home the next
day. The clerk refused to accept that as a guilty plea, explaining that if the defendant did not intend to steal the proper
plea would be not guilty, and the case would be put back to
a later date for trial. After a few moments deliberation, the
defendant changed his mind and declared that his intention
was to steal. The clerk accepted this as a guilty plea, and the
magistrate fined him £200 plus £20 costs.

In both of these cases, immediate planned departure dates appeared
instrumental in determining the defendants' eventual pleas. Moreover,
for visitors on a fixed budget, the prospect of several weeks or months
wait for a trial might be prohibitively expensive and act as a powerful
factor in pleading guilty. This report is not the place to discuss general
changes in the Magistrates' Courts' Acts, but it does seem that some
consideration should be given to defendants who might plead not-guilty
if they were not due to depart.

After the charge has been read out and the defendant's plea has been
established, the prosecution reads out the 'brief details of the case'.
Despite the fact that the defendant has in all probability pleaded guilty,
the rationality of the defendant's actions are stressed in the account.
This may partly be due to a desire on the prosecution's (and store detective's) part to emphasise the correctness of their actions and the
appropriateness of their decision to bring the case to court. It may also
be used as an opportunity to demonstrate to the magistrates that the
defendant was acting intentionally, thereby pre-empting mitigating pleas
of absent-mindedness. Cases 79 and 60 are typical examples of how the

'facts' are presented.

> Case 79: The prosecuting solicitor says, 'The defendant was seen to *select* a cardigan, fold it and *look around* before putting it into her bag. She was seen to pick up two boy's cardigans, *fold them* and put them into her bag. *She was very watchful and kept looking around.* She spoke to some friends at the front of the shop before leaving. When she was stopped outside, she said, "I pay now." '

> Case 60: The prosecution says, 'The defendant was seen in M.'s. *She selected* a cardigan, draped it over her arm and then put it into her bag. She went to a counter and picked up a total of four tops, which she *pushed* into her bag. She also *selected* two pairs of trousers and put them into her bag. She purchased a pair of trousers and some food. She then *selected* a cardigan, tried it on, *looked around* and *concealed* it behind the bags she was carrying. When stopped by store detectives she said, "I can pay now." '

Both cases illustrate that the defendants 'selected' the goods, implying rational choice and preference and forestalling pleas of absent-mindedness. Similarly when defendants 'look around' or are 'watchful', the prosecution cites this as instances of intent: the defendants are implicitly looking to see if they are being watched before stealing — the acts of careful, rational people who intend to steal. An absent-minded person would not look to see if they were being observed. The way defendants fold articles may be construed as having significance, especially if there is a three-way process of selection/draping or folding/'concealment'. Goods are rarely 'put' into bags, they are usually 'concealed', occasionally they may have to be forcefully and deliberately 'pushed' into bags — hardly the act of a forgetful person. Finally, the words uttered by the defendant when stopped by store detectives are often cited, as these can be used as evidence that the defendant has not paid and that the goods have been taken (though not necessarily stolen). The overall purpose, then, of the presentation of the 'brief facts' is to demonstrate that the defendant was acting rationally and intended to steal the articles.

In their pleas of mitigation, defendants or their solicitors will try to present the facts of the case from a different perspective. Whilst usually accepting that they have stolen (by pleading guilty) they attempt to provide an account for their behaviour. Solicitors present mitigations in a professional manner, but the various tactics they use are often employed by unrepresented defendants, albeit in a more amateurish fashion.

King outlines a number of tactics used by defence lawyers. For example, they may correct any misinterpretations the prosecution may have given. They may blame others for their client's presence in the court. They will try to provide an account of the case which puts their client in a more favourable light.

> For example, whenever possible, defence lawyers will pursue an episodic rather than a dispositional interpretation of their client's behaviour stating, e.g. the offence was quite out of character. Where inappropriate they will typically offer an explanation in terms of their client's personal pathology, and at the same time will resist the suggestion that this pathology be defined as a moral failure. Rather than being 'evil', 'dishonest', 'aggressive' or 'exploitative', they prefer to describe their clients as 'immature', 'easily led', 'lacking self-control', 'over-excitable' or 'subject to bouts of depression'. [42]

Finally, it is good practice to apologise to the court and the police for taking up their time and to demonstrate contrition and repentance.

The following cases illustrate how solicitors (professional mitigation presenters) describe their clients, and then how defendants account for their own actions.

In Case 82, a 59-year-old man had been remanded on bail for social enquiry reports, during which period he had committed a second offence. He had five recent convictions for theft and had pleaded guilty. His defence solicitor presented his case thus:

> Mr P. spent many years in the army where he says he was a social drinker. He was married but has not seen his wife for eight years or his married daughter. At one stage he became such a heavy drinker he received medical treatment at W.P. hospital for alcoholism. He has been 'dry' for some time, but it is suspected that he now drinks beer instead of spirits. His physical health is not too good — in the past ten years he has crushed his right leg, broken his left one, fractured his arm and broken his shoulder. A probation order was recommended. As you have been kind enough to indicate that you are considering making a probation order I have nothing further to say.

The magistrate then asked the defendant if he understood what a probation order entailed and whether he was willing to accept it. The defendant agreed and was given a probation order for two years.

Case 42 involved a woman who readily admitted shoplifting with numerous previous convictions for theft. She was detained in custody after being arrested because, as the police officer explained to the magistrate, 'We tried to find a surety, but were unable to do so. The defendant does have previous convictions and has failed to surrender to bail before.' The defending solicitor described his client as:

> Miss D. has led an unhappy life so far. She suffers with both
> mental and physical difficulties. She is ill-equipped to cope
> with the demands placed upon her by society, although she
> is nearly twenty-four. Previous punishment appears to have
> had little effect. Society needs to be protected from her
> activities. I have explained the idea of a suspended sentence
> to her and she understands. She is able to hold down a job,
> and is capable of keeping out of trouble. I believe one goes
> hand in hand with the other, she does have a job waiting for
> her.

Miss D. was subsequently sentenced to three months' imprisonment
which was suspended for twelve months.

In both cases the defending solicitors were at pains to point out the
physical and mental problems of their clients. In addition, social problems such as divorce, excessive drinking and the inability to maintain
gainful employment are also emphasised. The overall effect is to present
the clients as objects of pity, rather than as determined, professional
thieves. Similar tactics were also used by unrepresented defendants.

> Case 21: A man of previous good behaviour had pleaded
> guilty to stealing goods valued at £22.47. In mitigation he
> said: 'I cannot understand why I did it, I am under a lot of
> strain mentally. My daughter is anorexic, my wife is about
> to go into hospital for an operation. My uncle, who I treat
> as a father is about to die. I am very sorry, I just don't know
> why I did it.' The magistrate responded to this plea with:
> 'What you did didn't help the situation. Fines are usually
> very high for this offence, but what you have told us has
> helped to abate the fine in your case.'
>
> The defendant was subsequently fined £50 and £30 costs,
> with seven days to pay.

Stress in the defendant, then, appears to be a factor taken into consideration by magistrates when deciding sentence.

Depression also features quite extensively in pleas of mitigation. In
the following example, it is even referred to by the prosecution.

> Case 1: Mrs B., aged 39, had pleaded guilty to stealing two
> pairs of briefs, pants, necklaces, etc., from B.'s to the value
> of £16.12, and was further charged with stealing a packet
> of Lillets, shorts, Femfresh, an ironing-board cover, a suspender-
> belt, self-tanning cream, two flannels and a packet of hand-
> kerchiefs from W.'s to the value of £35.70.
>
> The prosecution related the details of the case and amplified

the background circumstances of Mrs B.: 'She stole things she couldn't pay for. She is under treatment for depression. Monetary and domestic problems may have contributed. All the property was returned. She has no previous convictions.'

In mitigation, Mrs. B said she was 'just under depression, not getting on with my husband. Can't do the housework, can't go on holiday since they've sold the car.' The clerk asked her when her last treatment was and she replied, 'Last went to hospital in January, see the doctor regularly and take Valium. Everything came to a head.' Mrs B. was fined £100 in each case, plus £30 costs.

Contrition and repentance are also effective pleas as illustrated by the following example:

Case 65: A young woman pleaded guilty to stealing a pair of earrings valued at £1.95 from S. 'The defendant was seen to select the earrings walk away, drop them into her bag and leave the store. When stopped, she said, "What more can I say other than I'm sorry?" She is a single woman aged 23 years, of previous good character. She is a drama student living with her parents. She is employed for the summer vacation by British Airways and earns £50 per week. She has no savings.'

In mitigiation, the defendant said, 'It was a stupid reckless act, and I shall never do anything like it again. I am sorry for the trouble caused to this court, and for the anguish caused to my parents.'

The magistrate responded, 'You are right in saying it was a ridiculous thing to do. We have considered your case and will give you a conditional discharge for two years and £30 costs.'

Pleas of migitation do not necessarily have to be routine as this case exemplifies:

Case 73: A man of 22 pleaded guilty to stealing a continental quilt valued at £105.95. He had one previous offence of shoplifting which had occurred two years previously. The defendant explained his actions:

'It is all true. If I am not wasting the court's time I would like to offer an explanation on why someone like myself would put themself into such a situation. Less than a week ago my girl friend told me she was having an affair with another man. She wanted a quilt. This man worked for a bedding company and was going to give her a quilt. I know it was a ludicrous way to try and save a relationship. My motives were to give her something of a better quality than he could. That's the only explanation I can offer.'

The magistrate asked what the defendant had previously taken and was informed that it was a briefcase. The Bench retired for a few minutes' discussion. [The magistrate informs the clerk that the Bench will retire, the clerk instructs the court to stand, and the magistrates retire.] Upon their return they fined the defendant £100 with £30 costs.

In some cases, medical conditions provided as mitigation may even lead to the charge being dropped, as the following extract illustrates.

Charge Dropped

A shoplifting charge against A., 62, a JP, was dropped at Marylebone Court yesterday after the magistrate read a medical report that she suffered from debility and nervous exhaustion.[43]

Absent-mindedness may often be used in mitigation, but it is difficult to establish as grounds for a not guilty plea. Nevertheless, absent-mindedness is a legally acceptable defence against a shoplifting charge though often difficult to prove.[44]

Unless the magistrate decides to refer the case to a higher court or to ask for further reports, sentence is usually passed once the pleas of mitigation have been heard. The variety of sentences available to magistrates was discussed in part one of this chapter, and the different sentences imposed for shoplifting indicated. Ideally, the sentence imposed should take into account the severity of the offence, the defendant's character, circumstances, etc., and pleas of mitigation. The following cases illustrate the variety of sentences imposed in some of the prosecutions which were observed, together with the background circumstances of the cases.

Cases 51 and 74 demonstrate the high financial penalties which may be attached to prodigious shoplifting expeditions. In Case 51, a 42-year-old woman pleaded guilty to stealing 7 pairs of tights, 3 bras, 1 nightdress, 2 children's nightdresses, a half-slip, 1 full slip, 1 girdle, 11 pairs of pants and one duvet cover, total value of £97.78 from M.'s (n.b. only one offence of shoplifting); she was fined £1,000 with £30 costs. In Case 74, a married woman with previous convictions for shoplifting, pleaded guilty to stealing 3 pairs of earrings, value £2.69 from D.'s, 2 pairs of pants, value 98p from B.'s, 1 bra, value £4.90 from E.'s, and 1 mug, value £3.45 from L.'s, all on the same day. She was fined £250 on each charge and £30 costs, a total of £1,030 with an alternative of 30 days' imprisonment.

Magistrates are not always so severe, however, as Case 27, which occurred in the same court as Cases 51 and 74 shows. A single, 25-year-old woman of previous good character pleaded guilty to stealing 1 bra, 1 half-slip and 7 pairs of briefs, total value of £13.29, the property of M.'s. When asked if she had anything to say, she began crying. The magistrate consoled her saying, 'Do not distress yourself', and fined her £50 with £30 costs and seven days to pay.

Other cases were observed that in retrospect hardly deserved the full weight of the criminal justice system. In Case 9, a French girl student aged 18, of previous good character, pleaded guilty to stealing chocolate and chewing gum, valued at 47p, the property of W.'s. In mitigation, she said that friends in France had told her it was very easy to steal in England and so she tried it. She was fined £50.

Thefts of small amounts were treated differently in other courts, though it is apparent that the pleas of mitigation were more convincing. In Case 15, a housewife had pleaded guilty to stealing 1 packet of cheese and 1 packet of biscuits valued at 94½p the property of L.'s. The case had been adjourned for social enquiry reports and the defendant was not at first represented. The defendant said that she thought she was guilty. She had put the goods in her bag and walked out, but it was not premeditated. Her solicitor pointed out that there were doubts whether she should plead guilty as her concentration often drifted because she was suffering from multiple sclerosis. The defendant was given a conditional discharge.

Case 17 was of a similar nature and outcome to Case 15. A housewife of previously good character had pleaded guilty to two offences of shoplifting involving property valued at 29p from a small shop and a joint of pork valued at £2.25½p from S.'s. She had been remanded for social enquiry reports and was now represented. Her solicitor presented the circumstances as follows:

> 'She is of previously good behaviour and then does two silly
> things. She succumbed to temptation. There is a background
> of financial difficulty, unemployment and rent arrears. I can
> only assume she had difficulty in making ends meet. Every-
> thing was on open shelves and she just succumbed to temp-
> tation. She is sorry. Her appearances in court have warned
> her and are sufficient punishment. The social enquiry report
> recommends a conditional discharge. There is little likelihood
> of return.' The defendant was given a conditional discharge.

On one occasion (Case 7), the magistrate did not consider his powers of sentencing to be sufficient or appropriate and referred the defendant to the crown court. The case involved a woman who pleaded guilty to stealing goods valued at £29 from S.'s, £2.90 of goods from W.'s and goods valued at £7.02 from C., on the same day. Her only income was

228

supplementary benefit and she had already been imprisoned for shop-lifting. She had 71 previous offences, mostly for shoplifting. She had been given a probation order for three years on the condition that she resided in a alcohol unit for a year, but the order had been breached. The social enquiry reports could not suggest any course of action. By way of mitigation the defence solicitor summarised his client's circumstances:

> 'From birth, she has had a most appalling life and the offences result from this. The offences are not the result of greed. She was brought up by her mother as a shoplifter. She is not cold or callous. When she came out of prison she was very under-weight. She is generous and helps out at the Simon Hostel. Things are looking up for her. Her common-law husband is not drinking and there is a chance of accommodation. If she is sentenced custodially, then it should be short and suspended for a short time. She has had umpteen psychiatric reports and there is no point in any more.'

The magistrates could not decide on a suitable (or perhaps severe enough) sentence and remanded her in custody for sentence at the crown court.

Only one charge was acquitted in the course of the fieldwork and this concerned a female academic. There was no denial of the physical taking of goods, what was disputed was the dishonest intent. The rather confusing details of the case were related to the magistrates. The woman was seen to select a blue cashmere jumper, take it off the hanger and drape it over her arm. In her bag were two brown jumpers for which she had already paid. The defendant wished to obtain a refund for one of the brown jumpers and exchange the other for a different coloured one. She selected a beige jumper and held it with the blue cashmere. She then approached an assistant at the till, and exchanged one of the brown jumpers for the beige one and asked for a refund on the other. She was given a docket to take to the refund counter on the floor below. She placed both blue and beige jumpers in her bag, went to the basement, cashed her refund and left, whereupon she was stopped by a store detective.

The defendant conducted her own defence. She pointed out that she was carrying three bags, some of which contained goods she had just purchased from the store, a handbag and a umbrella. She said that she had chosen the blue cashmere jumper with the intention of buying it if she could not find a cheaper one. She became confused when conduct-ing the exchange and refund and placed all the jumpers in one bag, and then forgot about the blue cashmere for which she had not paid.

The magistrates left the Bench to consider the case. When they return-ed the chairperson announced that it was not impossible to take things without intending to steal (cf. Regina vs. Ingram 1975), and that there was some doubt in the present case. The woman had purchased a number of goods and there was some doubt as to why she should take the cashmere if she had money to pay. The woman was of good char-acter, she had been in the shop for some time, paying for the various items quite properly. Only one item had been taken (implying that more items would have reduced the possibility of absent-mindedness). Critically, there was no evidence of furtive behaviour and the woman had put the sweater in her bag in front of the assistant (not the act of a deliberate thief). The magistrate concluded by saying he thought there was an element of doubt and therefore he dismissed the case.

For many defendants, the shame and degradation does not finish with the magistrate's sentence. As King says, 'a far worse consequence of conviction by the magistrates than any formal penalty which the court may impose is the possibility of the papers getting hold of the story'.[45]

Chance factors also play a part in determining how much detail of the matters revealed in the courtroom find their way into print. In some cases it may be no more than a name, address and details of the sentence. At other times, however, the newspaper report may seize upon some epithet or choice phrase and use it in the report.

> By selecting these cases which are likely to be of interest to their readers, the press may be seen as enhancing the status passage objectives of the court, for those defendants who attract the stigma of the community either through their heinous offences or through their high social status are the ones most likely to have their cases reported.[46]

One sad example of this was that of Lady Isobel Barnett, the well-known television personality and JP, for whom the publicity attendant upon her prosecution was a far more serious penalty than the fine imposed by the judge, and which was closely followed by her suicide.

Lady Barnett found Guilty

Former television personality Lady Isabel Barnett was 'shattered' last night after being convicted of shoplifting. A jury at Leicester Crown Court unanimously found her guilty of stealing a carton of cream and a tin of tuna fish worth 87 pence from a village store. They had heard that she hid the goods in a secret pocket pinned inside her coat. Lady Barnett, aged 62, of the White House, Cossington, Leicestershire, was fined £75 and ordered to pay £200 towards the prosecution costs. Judge James Blythe told her it was always sad when someone appeared in the dock for

the first time for dishonesty, particularly when it was a
person like her, who had enjoyed public esteem as a well-
known figure and had contributed a great deal in the com -
munity as a magistrate and in many other ways. 'No sentence
I can pass can match the punishment you have already suffered by way of the anxiety you have experienced awaiting
this trial and now the disgrace of the finding of guilty,' said
the Judge. 'But shoplifting is an offence which is all too
prevalent and people who enjoy public esteem and acclaim
should really set an example.'

Lady Barnett, a lecturer and broadcaster, who starred in the
BBC's 'What's My Line?' quiz programme in the 1950s, had
chosen trial by jury. Lady Barnett was said to have stolen
the cream and the fish during one of her regular visits to the
store in Rothley, Leics., in June, hiding the goods in a 'poacher's
pocket', a 16 x 12in cloth bag pinned inside her coat. She told
the court that she had put the items there because she needed
both hands to reach for a packet of biscuits. She had forgotten
about them. Prosecution counsel, called this a cock-and-bull
story. He submitted that it was a calculated theft and not
simply absent-mindedness.[47]

A few days later, Lady Barnett committed suicide. The first thing to
point out is that having denied her guilt, there was little alternative but
to take the case to court. The storekeeper had made an accusation of
theft and if he had not called the police he could have been sued for
false arrest, etc. The police could not consider the possibility of a
caution, as the offence was denied. The repercussions of an 87 pence
theft, however, were horrendous.

A few months before this incident the Attorney General highlighted
the position of OAPs who stole, but was rebuked by Baroness Phillips.

Old Age 'No Excuse for Shoplifting'

Sir Michael Havers, the Attorney-General, has come under
criticism for suggesting that favourable consideration should
be given to old people who face prosecution for shoplifting.
Baroness Phillips, Director of the Association for the Prevention of Theft in Shops said: 'The Attorney-General should
be more circumspect in what he says. This statement could be
taken as an encouragement to older people to steal.' Sir Michael
made the suggestion in the House of Commons after an 83-year-
old man accused of shoplifting committed suicide. The
Attorney-General said that the Director of Public Prosecutions
should be consulted before very old people were prosecuted for
shoplifting.[48]

A number of alternatives for dealing with shoplifters will be discussed in the conclusion: for the moment, all that needs to be said is that given the present system cases like Lady Barnett and the 83-year-old man will persist.

Various models of the criminal justice system have been presented by theorists (e.g. King, [49] Carlen[50]). Most of these advance some version of Packer's two concepts of 'crime control' and 'due process'.[51] Bottoms and McClean favour the 'liberal bureaucratic model' as a device for understanding English justice: 'The liberal bureaucratic model holds that the protection of individual liberty, and the need for justice to be done and to be seen to be done, must ultimately override the importance of the repression of criminal conduct.'[52]

Certainly, the cases of shoplifting which were observed being prosecuted had little of the due process model and much of the bureaucratic about them. In addition, the status degradation described by Garfinkel[53] and elaborated by Carlen[54] was often apparent, though it was difficult to determine whether this was a deliberate function of the legal process or a by-product. It seems likely that different models of criminal justice apply to different offences of shoplifting. What can be said is that appearances in court are seldom pleasant events and for the majority of offenders mark the end of an extremely distressing, and often traumatic incident in their lives, the memory of which stays forever. Indeed, for many, the prosecution and sentence are less important than the shame and humiliation which accompany their public disgrace, particularly when this is publicised in local and national newspapers.

Notes

1. For historical and political reasons, Scotland has a different system of criminal justice to England and Wales.
2. COI, *Criminal Justice in Britain* (London: HMSO, 1975); Bottoms, A.E. and McClean, J.D., *Defendants in the Criminal Process* (London: Routledge & Kegan Paul, 1976).
3. COI, *op. cit.*
4. Bottoms, and McClean, *op. cit.,* p.106.
5. Laurie, P., 'Negotiations Between the Defendant and the Police', in *Criminal Justice,* ed. Baldwin, J. and Bottomley, A.K. (London: Martin Robertson, 1978), pp. 91—4.
6. Bottoms, and McClean, *op. cit.,* p. 226.
7. Tarling, R. and Weatheritt, M., *Sentencing Practice in Magistrates' Courts.* Home Office Research Study No. 56 (London: HMSO, 1979), p. 2.
8. Bottoms, and McClean, *op. cit.,* p. 6.
9. Baldwin, J. and Bottomley, A.K. (eds.), *Criminal Justice.* (London: Martin Robertson, 1978), p. 73.
10. Heberling, J.L., 'Plea Negotiation in England', in ibid., p. 101.
11. Zander, M., 'Saving Time — and Money', *The Guardian* (23 February 1976).
12. Baldwin, J. and McConville, M., 'The Influence of the Sentencing Discount in Inducing Guilty Pleas', in Baldwin and Bottomley (eds.), *op. cit.,* pp. 116—28. See also Vera Institute of Justice, *Waiting Times in Magistrates' Courts An Exploratory Study* (December 1979); and NACRO, *'Delays in Coming to Trial',* Nacro Briefing (January 1981).
13. Heberling, *op. cit.*
14. *Daily Mail,* 4 August 1977.
15. Blumberg, A.S., *Criminal Justice* (Chicago: Quadrangle Books, 1967), pp. 90—104.
16. Dell, S., 'Inconsistent Pleaders', in Baldwin and Bottomley (eds.), *op. cit.,* pp. 106—15.
17. Bottoms, and McClean, *op. cit.,* p. 121.
18. Baldwin, J. and McConville, M., *Negotiated Justice* (London: Martin Robertson, 1977).
19. Purves, R.F., 'That Plea-Bargaining Business: Some Conclusions From Research', *Criminal Law Review* (1971), pp. 470—5.
20. McCabe, S. and Purves, R.F., *By-Passing the Jury* (Oxford: Basil Blackwell, 1972).
21. Bottoms, and McClean, *op. cit.,* p. 128.
22. Dell, *op. cit.*
23. Home Office, *Criminal Statistics. England and Wales* (London: HMSO, 1981).

24. Lidstone, K.W., Hogg, R. and Sutcliffe, F., *Prosecutions by Private Individuals and Non-Police Agencies,* Royal Commission on Criminal Procedure (London:HMSO, 1980), pp. 99—111.
25. Bottoms, and McClean, *op. cit.,* p. 140.
26. Home Office, *Criminal Statistics. England and Wales. Supplementary Tables* (London HMSO, 1981).
27. Ibid.
28. Ibid.
29. Ibid.
30. Ibid.
31. Ibid.
32. Tarling and Weatheritt, *op. cit.,* p. 14.
33. Home Office, 'Persons Found Guilty of Shoplifting by Petty Sessional Division and Result', Statistical Division I (1980).
34. *Daily Telegraph,* 24 March 1977.
35. Any number of goods taken from one shop constitutes *one* offence of shoplifting. Two articles, however, taken from two different shops count as two offences. Anomalous situations can thus arise with many items from one store counting as one offence, but a few goods (relatively) from several shops counting as multiple offences.
36. *Evening Standard,* 4 April 1977.
37. *Daily Telegraph,* 24 July 1978.
38. Ibid., 15 August 1978.
39. Ibid., 31 August 1981.
40. Carlen, P., *Magistrates' Justice* (London: Martin Robertson, 1976).
41. Although defendants understand what is being said, Carlen (ibid.) and Bottoms and McClean *(op. cit.)* believe that the significance of the choice is lost on many defendants.
42. King, M., *The Framework of Criminal Justice* (London: Croom Helm, 1981), p. 88.
43. *Daily Mail,* 13 January 1979.
44. *The Times,* 17 April 1975.
45. King, *op. cit.,* p. 92.
46. Ibid., p. 115.
47. *The Guardian,* 16 October 1980.
48. *Daily Telegraph,* 14 April 1980.
49. King, *op. cit.*
50. Carlen, *op. cit.*
51. Packer, H., *The Limits of the Criminal Sanctions* (Stanford: Stanford University Press, 1969).
52. Bottoms, and McClean, *op. cit.,* p. 228.
53. Garfinkel, H., 'Conditions of Successful Degradation Ceremonies', *American Journal of Sociology,* Vol. 61 (1956), pp. 420—4.
54. Carlen, *op. cit.*

9 Summary and conclusions

This final section is in two parts; the first summarises the main arguments of the book, the second relates them to the wider questions of control and treatment of shoplifters.

Summary

The first chapter traced developments in criminology. In the nineteenth century, crime was seen as a social malaise and statistics on offending were viewed as measuring the moral health of society. There were two major problems with these criminal statistics: the first involved around questions of representativeness, the second around validity. It was realised that officially recorded statistics of crime were but a sample of an unknown number of offences and offenders, and thus many criminologists attempted to measure how representative were these criminal statistics. 'Dark figure' research, as it came to be known, was conducted in two ways: self-report studies, and victim surveys. Although both these methods had methodological and theoretical flaws, they were useful in demonstrating that there was considerably more 'crime' occurring than ever appeared in police records.

   The validity of criminal statistics proved to be a more intractable problem. Exponents of the 'institutional approach' perceived criminal statistics as objects in their own right: they recorded the activities of various agencies, be they the police, the courts or the prisons. On the other hand, they were not representative of an unknown but theoreti-

235

cally knowable amount of offending. On the contrary, attempts to 'fix' the size of the crime problem ignored the constitutive aspects which went into the production of an 'offence', and were thus invalid, as well as being a waste of resources. Attention was focused on how criminal statistics were produced, which for most offences meant investigating police activity. Police involvement in the detection and apprehension of shoplifters, however, is minimal; consequently, any examination of shoplifting entails researching the agents who do control shoplifting in its context of the shopfloor, and these were mainly store detectives.

The literature on shoplifting was reviewed in Chapter 2 and this reflected the concerns of the previous chapter. Studies of convicted shoplifters were considered flawed because they failed to take into account the different selection procedures which determined which offenders were prosecuted (probably much greater than for other offences). Although 'dark figure' research on shoplifting was prone to the same weaknesses as other offences, it was useful in demonstrating that a majority of respondents admitted to shoplifting at some stage in their lives. The surveys of shoplifters apprehended but not necessarily refer - red to the police also showed the generally low value of the items taken.

A new approach to the study of shoplifting was found in 'following exercises'. While these were criticised on the grounds that they were investigating 'taking' but not necessarily stealing, they were useful in demonstrating the proportion of shoppers who took goods without paying and who were seldom detected by store personnel. Little systematic research, however, had been conducted into the activities of store detectives and their operating practices on the shopfloor, the context in which they attempt to control shoplifting. This was the starting point, then, adopted in this research.

How the research was conducted was described in Chapter 3. A variety of methods was used, depending upon the circumstances. For the main part of the study — the investigation of store detectives — a form of participant observation was adopted, corresponding to what Gold terms 'observer-as-participant',[1] and what Schatzman and Strauss call 'limited interaction'.[2] In this way, it was possible to examine the operating practices of store personnel on the shopfloor.

That shoplifting is not a new offence but is rooted in history was established in Chapter 4. Here too the law which underpins shoplifting and its control was discussed; the importance of the intent or *mens rea* aspect of the offence was emphasised; and the powers of the store detective to arrest suspects were shown to be no more than those of any citizen. The extent of shoplifting was discussed: shoplifting offences accounted for 14 per cent of all offences of theft and handling, and approximately 7 per cent of notifiable offences. On average, thefts from shops involved low-value goods.

In Chapter 5 the interviews with chief security officers were analysed. Among other things, what emerged was that most stores viewed store detectives as the best means of controlling shoplifting and so their training was investigated. It was apparent that the intensity of training, both formal and on the shopfloor, varied enormously between retailers.

The operating practices of store detectives provided the focus for Chapter 6. Three models of store detective activity were outlined: the 'law-enforcer', the 'peace-keeper' and the 'moral entrepreneur'. It was argued that the law-enforcer model corresponded closely to the traditional conception of police activity. The first stage of this model was 'exclusion': potential troublemakers were not permitted entry — a policy which was only minimally pursued. The next step was 'screening' — the ways in which store detectives selected suspects for investigation. How store detectives apprehended suspects and the problems they had to overcome in doing so was the third stage of the model. Next came the interview with the suspect — how it was conducted and its purpose. Finally, came 'disposal', which usually entailed police referral unless the suspect fell into one of the categories where leniency was exercised.

The peace-keeping model followed the first two stages of the law-enforcement model ('exclusion' and 'screening'); the arrest stage, however, was eschewed in favour of 'manipultion whereby the would-be 'thief' was converted into a legitimate 'customer'. The peace-keeping role might be adopted by the law-enforcers where the apprehension of the suspect would be inappropriate or undesirable; and only a minority of retailers followed the peace-keeping model by preference, arresting suspects when all else had failed.

Store detectives also act as 'moral entrepreneurs', particularly when dealing with adolescents and gangs of children. More usually, this model was adopted in conjunction with the law-enforcer or peace-keeping model, and was especially used to reinforce the anxiety of apprehension when the police were not called. Critically, these three roles were not mutually exclusive; the store detective might adopt one in preference to another as the circumstances changed.

The role of the police in controlling shoplifting was discussed in Chapter 7. Shoplifting is a significant offence for the police not least because it has a considerable positive effect on the 'clear-up' rate of offences detected, even though police involvement in detecting shop-lifters is minimal, their role generally being that of 'processers'.

Three different procedures for prosecuting shoplifters were outlined: private prosecution, arrest by police, and summons by police. Most police forces follow the policy of arrest by police, or summons by police in special circumstances. The Metropolitan Police District, however, deal with shoplifters as private prosecutions, that is to say, the retailers in their area are responsible for the prosecution of the suspects. As 12 per cent of shoplifters were processed by the MPD, the overall picture of mode of prosecution is consequently skewed.

Similarly, the rates of cautioning shoplifters were affected by the MPD's decision not to caution adults for this offence except in extreme circumstances. As over 50 per cent of offences involved goods worth less than £5, and 83 per cent less than £25, it was argued that police cautions should be considered for the 70 per cent of women and 50 per cent of men who are first-time offenders. In this way, they would avoid the trauma of arrest and prosecution in the courts, with all its attendant humiliation and degradation.

Chapter 8 examined how the majority of shoplifters were dealt with when they came to court. For most shoplifters, criminal justice is magistrates' justice: 95 per cent of shoplifting offenders were dealt with by magistrates, and 93 per cent were found guilty (most of them in fact pleaded guilty). A fine was the most common sentence awarded, particularly when the under-21s were excluded. Even when a defendant pleaded guilty, the prosecution often stressed the rationality of their actions and consequently most pleas of mitigation emphasised the offender's feelings of depression or stress ('I don't know what came over me.')

For the majority of shoplifters, the experience of being apprehended by a store detective, treated as a criminal by the police and publicly sentenced in court, was the most anxious and degrading of their lives.

Conclusions

The Home Office Standing Committee on Crime Prevention has recently reviewed the recommendations made by the Working Party on Thefts from Shops. The following were considered by the Standing Committee:

i)   The introduction of a civil complaint of 'taking goods from a shop without authority and without making payment', as an alternative to a criminal charge of theft.

ii) The introduction of a preliminary procedure before a court hearing for dealing with cases of alleged shoplifting in a more humane way, especially where the person concerned is ill or elderly and has no previous convictions.

iii) An extension of the cautioning procedure, so that police could offer a caution to a first offender accused of a relatively trivial or apparently 'not-deliberate theft', whether there is an admission of guilt or not.

iv) A prohibition of press reporting of the names of persons accused of shoplifting for the first time, or where their previous convictions are 'spent' under the Rehabilitation of Offenders Act. [3]

The Standing Committee rejected the first two recommendations as they believed that they would act to bring marginal cases before the courts and would prolong the anxiety involved in being charged with an offence.

> We particularly do not find i) an attractive proposition as it seems to us that, apart from anything else, such a procedure might well increase rather than decrease distress caused to those suspected of shoplifting since it would have the effect of bringing before the courts some of those people whose borderline cases are not proceeded with. The same sort of consideration applies, we think, to suggestion ii) which would in many cases merely serve to prolong the distress caused to those accused.[4]

Recommendation iv) was also rejected because the Committee was not in favour of extending the very restricted limitations on press reporting of court proceedings, and in any case could not justify it for shoplifting alone, without also including other forms of theft.

The Standing Committee did not consider the possibility of decriminalising petty shoplifting, as is the case in Denmark for thefts of items up to 500 Kr. (£36.00). Such a policy is not even on the agenda at the present time. This leaves iii), and here the position of the Standing Committee is confused. The role of cautioning was not considered in depth because it was being considered elsewhere in the Home Office. However, because the suggestion to extend cautioning was linked to 'apparently not-deliberate theft, whether there is an admission of guilt or not'[5] much of its relevance was negated. The Standing Committee rightly pointed out that cautions are substitutes for prosecution and they cannot be administered to a person who denies guilt. The only place for dealing with a person who pleads not guilty is in the courts. Similarly, they rejected the idea of not-deliberate theft, rightly pointing out that this is contradictory — an offence of theft, by definition, must include intent; if it is 'not deliberate', it is not theft. However, they missed the opportunity to consider extending cautioning (subject to the usual provisions) for relatively trivial offences. This is unfortunate.

The Home Office later issued a consultative document on Cautioning by the Police.[6] This distinguished between young and adult offenders. All things being equal, it was agreed that cautioning was the most appropriate way of dealing with juveniles, and that prosecution was appropriate for the majority of adult offenders, except for young adult offenders, the elderly and other special cases.

> We believe that in the majority of cases the public interest will require that adult offenders should be prosecuted although we feel that there is a particularly strong case for sympathetic

consideration of a lesser disposal in respect of certain groups of adult offenders. With regard both to its diversionary and deterrent elements we believe that the formal caution will continue to have its greatest value in relation to juvenile offenders, although we would certainly wish to encourage cautioning in appropriate cases of adult offending.[7]

Despite the evidence that variations between the cautioning policies of different police forces are being reduced and that the Metropolitan Police now intend to caution more adults, it is unlikely that adult shoplifters will be included in these 'appropriate cases of adult offending'.

This study has two clear messages for the control of shoplifting. The first is that the majority of shoplifters take items of small value and are of previously good character. If police cautioning were extended not only to the ill, old and young, but to all offenders of previously good character who admitted their offence and took only low-valued goods, thousands of offenders would never appear in the courts. The Home Office already accepts that a caution is as an effective deterrent for juveniles. It is likely also that the trauma of being arrested, taken to the police station and given a formal caution would be sufficient to deter most amateur adult shoplifters. If they repeated their offence, they could then be prosecuted in the usual way. By extending the limits for a caution, pressure on the courts would be reduced; money would be saved; amateur offenders of previously good behaviour would not have to endure the anxiety of public prosecution; and the public interest in general would be served.

The second message to come from this study is that there are essentially two methods for controlling shoplifters on the shopfloor: 'law-enforcement' and 'peace-keeping'. It is obvious that the numbers of suspects who are handed to the police differ dramatically according to which model is being pursued. The peace-keeping model is the preferred one of a few retailers who acknowledge the temptation to steal which modern marketing techniques create and they accept the responsibility to convert ordinary shoppers who have succumbed to this temptation. Retailers who pursue the law-enforcement model would criticise the peace-keeping model for being an insufficient deterrent to shoplifters, and the Home Office Standing Committee supports their position: 'A reminder to pay without fear of penalty is no deterrent, and in effect would mean that the thief could not lose.'[8] However, the research clearly demonstrates that all stores on occasions use this method to control shoplifting. The relative merits of either method are beyond the remit of this book. The point made here is that there are methods of controlling shoplifting which do not involve the criminal justice system and these should be given more public discussion.

This report has examined shoplifting as it occurs on the shopfloor, at the police station, and in the courts. It has traced the control of shop-lifters from the 'screening' stage to the sentence at court. In the process, it has demonstrated by means of a wealth of ethnographic and statist-ical data that shoplifting and its control is a massively sophisticated and subtle operation. In addition, it has highlighted two approaches for treating shoplifters, and argues that these require more discussion and research.

Notes

1. Gold, R.L., 'Roles in Sociological Field Observations', in McCall, G.J. and Simmons, J.L., *Issues in Participant Observation* (Reading, Mass.: Addison-Wesley, 1969).
2. Schatzman, L. and Strauss, A.L., *Field Research: Strategies for a Natural Sociology* (New Jersey: Prentice-Hall, 1973).
3. Home Office, *Shoplifting and Thefts by Shop Staff.* A review by the Home Office Standing Committee on Crime Prevention (London: HMSO, 1983), p. 5.
4. Ibid., p. 5.
5. Ibid.
6. Home Office, *Cautioning by the Police. A Consultative Document* (London: HMSO, 1984).
7. Ibid., p. 13.
8. Home Office, *op. cit.* (1983), p. 6.

Glossary of terms

ACPO	Association of Chief Police Officers
APTS	Association for the Prevention of Thefts in Shops.
'Bad Bag'	Bag with the store's logo, repeatedly folded and used, in which shoplifters secrete stolen merchandise to give the impression of legitimate purchases. Cf. 'Booster Bag'.
Banning	Process applied to persons found shoplifting (or suspected of it) by which they are forbidden future entry to the store.
'Boosters'	Commercial shoplifters who steal merchandise to sell it. May also be involved in other offences.
'Booster Bag'	Cf. 'Bad Bag'.
'Booster Box'	Parcel or box, often wrapped in paper or string, with a hidden, spring-trap for placing over articles and secreting them.
'Booster Drawers'	Ladies voluminous knickers, with tight elastic at knees, especially designed to hold stolen goods secreted through an elasticated waistband.
'Bulker'	A low-living person; a petty-thief; one who lives among thieves and beggars.
CCTV	Closed circuit television.

'Crotching'	Usually practised by women in loose dresses. Goods are hidden beneath the dress and held tightly between the upper thighs.
Early warning system	System in which a group of shops in a street or precinct warn their immediate neighbours of suspected shoplifters.
Exclusion	System whereby potential shoplifters or other undesirables are not allowed into the store. Particularly applied to drunks, vagrants, drug addicts and gangs of youths.
'Fagin syndrome'	System, named after the Dickens' character. An adult is accompanied by a child, often below the age of criminal responsibility, who does the actual stealing, while the adult supervises.
Fence	Person who buys and sells stolen merchandise, often to order.
'Foilers'	Vagabonds or petty thieves.
'Ghosting'	A security officer who is suspicious of a shopper but does not have sufficient evidence to arrest, will put exactly the same goods as the suspect in her or his basket and make it obvious to the shopper that they are being watched.
Gondola	A display unit or counter with goods arranged for selection. Often low-lying.
'Heels'	Professional shoplifters who are rarely involved in other offences.
'Hoisting'	See 'Lifting'.
IPSA	International Professional Security Association (formerly Industrial Police and Security Association).
'Lifts'/'Lifting'	Cf. 'Marker' and 'Santar'. Often first of a gang of three. A person who 'lifts' the article with the intention of stealing it. Traditionally applied to shoplifters/lifting.
'Markers'	Cf. 'Lift' and 'Santar'. The 'lift' who takes the article, passes it to the 'marker', who in turn, gives it to the 'santar' to take away.
MPD	Metropolitan Police District.
'Palmers'	One who 'palms' or conceals goods in the hand by sleight of hand.
Price-tag 'switchers'	People who change or 'switch' the price-tags from cheaper items to more expensive ones and then attempt to purchase the expensive item at the reduced price.

244

'Refunders'	People who steal items from one branch of a chain store and then attempt to obtain a money refund for them in another branch.
'Santars'	Cf. 'Lift' and 'Marker'. The 'santar' waits outside the shop to receive the stolen goods from the 'marker'.
To/A 'Screen'	Something or someone interposed so as to conceal the activities of a shoplifter from view.
'Screening'	To sift through customers in order to identify potential shoplifters.
'Senelco'	A brand-name for a 'tagging' system, which sounds alarms if the activating devices are not removed or neutralised from goods before leaving.
'Snitch'	A pilferer. An opportunist/amateur shoplifter.
To/A 'Stall'	A decoy. A pickpocket's or shoplifter's helper who distracts the attention of the victim.
'Star-Glazing'	Victorian method of shoplifting practised by small boys. Adhesive is attached to a small pane of glass, the glass is broken, and then removed so that a hand can be passed through to reach the goods inside the shop.
'Tagging'	Cf. 'Senelco'.
'Troupe'	A gang or group of shoplifters (often three) consisting of the 'lifter', the 'screen' and the 'santar'.

Bibliography

Adley, R., *Take It or Leave It.* Report of a Study Group on Shoplifting (1978).

Antilla, I., 'The Criminological Significance of Unregistered Criminality', *Excerpta Criminologica,* 4 (1964), pp. 411—14.

Arboleda-Florez, J., Durie, H. and Costello, J., 'Shoplifting — An Ordinary Crime?', *International Journal of Offender Therapy and Comparative Criminology,* Vol. 21, No. 3 (1977), pp. 201—7.

Arieff, A.J. and Bowie, C.G., 'Some Psychiatric Aspects of Shoplifting', *Journal of Clinical Psychology,* Vol. 8 (January 1947), pp. 565—76.

Association of Chief Police Officers, *Shoplifting. Police Policy and Procedure,* Report of a Working Party Appointed by the Association of Chief Police Officers CID Committee (1975).

Astor, S.D., 'Shoplifting: Far Greater than We Know?', *Security World,* Vol. 6, No. 11 (1969), pp. 12—13.

Astor, S.D., 'Shoplifting Survey', *Security World,* Vol. 8, Part 3 (1971), pp. 34—5.

Atkinson, J.M., 'Societal Reactions to Suicide: The Role of Coroners' Definitions', in *Images of Deviance,* ed. Cohen, S. (Harmondsworth: Penguin Books, 1977), pp. 165—91.

Atkinson, J.M., *Discovering Suicide: Studies of the Organisation of Sudden Death* (London: Macmillan, 1978).

Badonnel, R., 'Le Vol Dans Les Grands Magasins', *Chronique de Criminologie Clinique.* Vol. 92, 11 (1968), pp. 103—6.

Baker, L.L., *They Always Come Back* (Bognor Regis: New Horizon, 1979).

Baldwin, J. and Bottomley, A.K., *Criminal Justice* (London: Martin Robertson. 1978).

Baldwin, J. and McConville, M., *Negotiated Justice* (London: Martin Robertson. 1977).

Baldwin, J. and McConville, M. 'The Influence of the Sentencing Discount in Inducing Guilty Pleas', in *Criminal Justice*, ed. Baldwin, J. and Bottomley, A.K. (London: Martin Robertson, 1978), pp. 116—28.

Banton, M., *The Policeman in the Community* (London: Tavistock, 1964).

Barbera, V., 'Electronics Application Pioneers for Retailers: Article Surveillance Comes into its own as a Working and Practical Deterrent', *Security World*, Vol. 11, Part 8 (1974), pp. 34—6.

Beattie, R.H., 'Problems of Criminal Statistics in the United States', in *The Sociology of Crime and Delinquency*, ed. Wolfgang, M.E., Savitz, L. and Johnston, N. (London: Wiley, 1962), pp. 37—43.

Becker, H.S., *Outsiders: Studies in the Sociology of Deviance* (New York: Free Press, 1963).

Becker, H.S. and Geer, B., 'Participant Observation and Interviewing', in McCall, G.J. and Simmons, J.L., *Issues in Participant Observation* (Reading, Mass.: Addison-Wesley, 1969), pp. 322—31.

Belson, W.A., *Juvenile Theft: The Causal Factors* (London: Harper & Row, 1975).

Bennett, H. M., 'Shoplifting in Midtown', *Criminal Law Review* (1968), pp. 413—25.

Bickman, L., 'Bystander Intervention in a Crime: The Effect of a Mass-Media Campaign', *Journal of Applied Social Psychology*, Vol. 5, No. 4 (1975), pp. 296—302.

Bickman, L., 'Attitude Toward an Authority and the Reporting of a Crime', *Sociometry*. Vol. 39, No. 1 (1976), pp. 76—82.

Bickman, L. and Green, S., 'Situational Cues and Crime Reporting: Do Signs Make a Difference?', *Journal of Applied Social Psychology*, Vol. 7, No. 1 (1977), pp. 1—18.

Bickman, L. and Helwig, H., 'Bystander Reporting of a Crime', *Criminology*, Vol. 17, No. 3 (November 1979), pp. 283—300.

Biderman, A.D., 'Surveys of Population Samples for Estimating Crime Incidence', *The Annals of the American Academy of Political and Social Science*. Vol. 374 (1967), pp. 16—33.

Biderman, A.D., 'Time Distortions of Victimisation Data and Mnemonic Effects', unpublished paper for the Bureau of Social Science Research Inc.

Biderman, A.D. and Reiss, A.J., 'On Exploring the Dark Figure of Crime', *Annals of the American Academy of Political and Social Science*, No. 374 (1967), pp. 1—15.

Bittner, E., 'The Police on Skid Row: A Study of Peace-Keeping',

American Sociological Review, Vol. 32 (October 1967), pp. 699—715.

Bittner, E., 'The Concept of Organisation', in *Ethnomethodology*, ed. Turner, R. (Harmondsworth: Penguin Books, 1974), pp. 69—81.

Black, D.J., 'Production of Crime Rates', *American Sociological Review*, Vol. 35 (1970), pp. 733—48.

Blackmore, J., 'The Relationship Between Self-Reported Delinquency and Official Convictions Amongst Adolescent Boys', *The British Journal of Criminology*. Vol. 14, No. 2, (1974), pp. 172—5.

Bleakley, R., 'Stock Losses in Retail Stores', in *Studies in Shoplifting*, ed. Challinger, D. (Australian Crime Prevention Council, 1977).

Blumberg, A.S., *Criminal Justice* (Chicago: Quadrangle Books, 1967).

Bottomley, A.K. and Coleman, C.A., 'Criminal Statistics: The Police Role in the Discovery and Detection of Crime', *International Journal of Criminology and Penology*, Vol. 3 (1975), pp. 1—9.

Bottomley, A.K. and Coleman, C.A., 'Police Effectiveness and the Public: The Limitations of Official Crime Rates', in *The Effectiveness of Policing*, ed. Clarke, R.V.G. and Hough, M. (Aldershot: Gower, 1980).

Bottoms, A.E. and McLean, J.D., *Defendants in the Criminal Process* (London: Routledge & Kegan Paul, 1976).

Box, S., *Deviance, Reality and Society* (London: Holt, Rinehart & Winston, 1981; 2nd edn).

Cameron, M.O., *The Booster and the Snitch.Department Store Shoplifting* (Glencoe, Ill.: Free Press, 1964).

Carlen, P., *Magistrates' Justice* (London: Martin Robertson 1976).

Central Office of Information, *Criminal Justice in Britain* (London HMSO, 1975).

Chapman, D., *Sociology and the Stereotype of the Criminal* (London: Tavistock, 1968).

Chatterton, M., 'Police in Social Control', in *Control Without Custody*, ed. King, J.F.S., papers presented to the Cropwood Round Table (1975), pp. 104—22.

Chesney, K., *The Victorian Underworld* (Harmondsworth: Pelican Books, 1970).,

Cicourel, A.V., *The Social Organisation of Juvenile Justice* (London: Heinemann, 1976).

Cohen, L.E. and Stark, R., 'Discriminatory Labeling and the Five-Finger Discount', *Journal of Research in Crime and Delinquency* (January 1974), pp. 25—39.

Cohen, S., *Folk Devils and Moral Panics* (London: Martin Robertson, 1972).

Cohen, S., 'Mods, Rockers and the Rest: Community Reactions to Juvenile Delinquency', in *The Sociology of Crime and Delinquency in Britain*, ed. Carson, W.G. and Wiles, P. (London: Martin Robertson, Vol. 1, 1975), pp. 261—73.

Cohen, S. and Young, J., *The Manufacture of News, Deviance, Social Problems, and the Mass Media* (London: Constable, 1973).

Cox. A.E., 'Shoplifting', *The Criminal Law Review* (1968), pp. 425–30.

Davidson, R.N., 'The Ecology of Shoplifting', paper presented to the Institute of British Geographers (Reading, 1975).

de Rham, E., *How Could She Do That? A Study of the Female Criminal* (New York: Clarkson N. Potter, 1969).

Dean, J.P. and Whyte, W.F., 'How Do You Know if the Informant is Telling the Truth?', in McCall, G.J. and Simmons, J.L., *Issues in Participant Observation* (Reading, Mass.: Addison-Wesley, 1969), pp. 105–14.

Dean, J.P., Eichhorn, R.L. and Dean, L.R., 'Establishing Field Relations', in McCall, G.J. and Simmons, J.L., *Issues in Participant Observation* (Reading, Mass.: Addison-Wesley, 1969), pp. 68–70.

Decker, S.H., 'Official Crime Rates and Victim Surveys: An Empirical Comparison', *Journal of Criminal Justice*, Vol. 5 (1977), pp.47–54.

Dell, S., 'Inconsistent Pleaders', in *Criminal Justice*, ed. Baldwin, J. and Bottomley, A.K. (London: Martin Robertson, 1978)., pp.106–15.

Dertke, M.C., Penner, L.A., and Ulrich, K., 'Observers' Reporting of Shoplifting as a Function of Thief's Race and Sex', *The Journal of Social Psychology*, Vol. 94 (1974), pp. 213–21.

Dickens, B.M., 'Shops, Shoplifting and Law Enforcement', *The Criminal Law Review* (September 1969), pp. 464–72.

Dickenson, S., 'Theft and the Retailer', *Security World* (April 1970), pp. 171–4.

Dingle, J., 'Youth and Shoplifting', in Challinger, D., *Studies in Shoplifting* (Australian Crime Prevention Council, 1977).

Ditchfield, J.A., *Police Cautioning in England and Wales*, Home Office Research Unit Report, No. 37 (London: HMSO, 1976).

Ditton, J., *Part-Time Crime. An Ethnography of Fiddling and Pilferage* (London: Macmillan, 1977).

Ditton, J., *Contrololology* (London: Macmillan, 1979).

Douglas, J.D., 'Understanding Everyday Life', in *Understanding Everyday Life*, ed. Douglas, J.D. (London: Routledge & Kegan Paul, 1971), pp. 3–44.

Draper, H., *Private Police* (Harmondsworth: Penguin Books, 1978).

Economist Intelligence Unit, *'Store Security'*, Special Report, No. 3, *Retail Business*, Vol. 161 (July 1971).

Edwards, L.E., *Shoplifting and Shrinkage Protection for Stores* (Springfield, Ill.: Charles C. Thomas, 1958).

El-Dirghami, A., 'Shoplifting Among Students', *Journal of Retailing*, Vol. 50, No. 3 (1974), pp. 33–42.

Ennis, P., *Criminal Victimisation in the United States: A Report of a National Survey* (Chicago: National Opinion Research Center, 1967).

Farrington, D.P. 'Self-Reports of Deviant Behaviour: Predictive and Stable?', *The Journal of Criminal Law and Criminology*, Vol. 64, No. 1 (1973), pp. 99—110.

Fear, R.W.G. 'An Analysis of Shoplifting', *Security Gazette* (July 1974), pp. 262—3.

Francis, D.B. *Shoplifting: The Crime Everybody Pays For* (New York: Elsevier/Nelson, 1980).

Garfinkel, H. 'Conditions of Successful Degradation Ceremonies', *American Journal of Sociology*, Vol. 6 (1956), pp. 420—4.

Gelfand, D.M., Hartmann, D.P., Walder, P. and Page, B., 'Who Reports Shoplifters? A Field-Experimental Study', *Journal of Personality and Social Psychology*, Vol. 25, No. 2 (1973), pp. 276—85.

Gibbens, T.C.N., 'The Causes of Shoplifting', *New Society*, No. 23 (7 March 1963).

Gibbens, T.C.N. and Prince, J., *Shoplifting*, (London: ISTD, 1962).

Goffman, E., *Asylums* (Harmondsworth: Penguin Books, 1961).

Goffman, E., *Stigma: Notes on the Management of Spoiled Identity* (Harmondsworth: Penguin Books, 1968).

Gold, M., 'Undetected Delinquent Behaviour', *Journal of Research into Crime and Delinquency*, Vol. 3 (1966), pp. 27—46.

Gold, R.L., 'Roles in Sociological Field Observations', in McCall, G.J. and Simmons, J.L., *Issues in Participant Observation* (Reading, Mass.: Addison-Wesley, 1969), pp. 30—8.

Griew, E., *The Theft Acts 1968 and 1978* (London: Sweet & Maxwell, 1978; 3rd.edn).

Griffin, R.K. 'Shoplifting: A Statistical Survey', *Security World*, Vol. 7, Part 10 (1970), pp. 21—5.

Griffin, R.K. 'Behavioural Patterns in Shoplifting', *Security World*, Vol. 7, Part 10 (1971), pp. 21—5.

Griffin, R.K. 'Shoplifting Policy for Retailers', *Security World*, Vol. 10, Part II (1973), pp. 34—6, 41—4.

Gusfield, J.R., 'Moral Passage: The Symbolic Process in Public Designations of Deviance', *Social Problems*, Vol. 15, No. 2 (1968), pp. 175—88.

Harris, B., 'What is a Shoplifter?', *The Magistrate*, Vol. 35, No. 9 (September 1979), pp. 134—5.

Hastings, G.B., 'Customer Attitudes Towards Security Devices in Shops and Preparedness to Report Shoplifting', *Abstracts on Criminology and Penology* (1980), pp. 639—42.

Hawkins, R.O., 'Who Called the Cops? Decisions to Report Criminal Victimisation', *Law and Society Review*, Vol. 17 (1973), pp. 427—44.

Heberling, J.L., 'Plea Negotiation in England', *Criminal Justice*, ed Baldwin, J. and Bottomley, A.K. (London: Martin Robertson, 1978), pp. 95—105.

Hiew, C.C., 'Prevention of Shoplifting: A Community Action Approach', *Canadian Journal of Criminology,* Vol. 23, No. 1 (1981), pp. 57—65.

Hindelang, M.J., 'Decisions of Shoplifting Victims to Invoke the Criminal Justice Process', *Social Problems,* Vol. 21, No. 4 (1974), pp. 580—93.

Hindelang, M.J., Dunn, C.S., Sutton, L.P. and Aumick, A.L., *Source Book of Criminal Justice Statistics.* (Washington, D.C.: Government Printing Office, 1975).

Holdaway, S., *The British Police* (London: Edward Arnold, 1979).

Hole, R.R., 'Shoplifting Apprehensions Can Be Made to Stick'., *Security World,* Vol. 9, No. 1 (1972), pp. 32—46.

Homan, R., 'The Ethics of Covert Methods', *British Journal of Sociology,* Vol. 31, No. 1 (March 1980), pp. 46—59.

Home Office, *Criminal Statistics. England and Wales* (London: HMSO) published annually.

Home Office, *The Theft Act* (London: HMSO, 1968).

Home Office, *Judges' Rules and Administrative Directions to the Police,* H. O. Circular No. 89 (London: HMSO, 1978).

Home Office, *Shoplifting and Thefts by Shop Staff. Report of A Working Party on Internal Shop Security* (London: HMSO, 1973).

Home Office, *The Private Security Industry, A Discussion Paper* (London: HMSO, 1979).

Home Office, *Shoplifting and Thefts by Shop Staff,* A Review by the Home Office Standing Committee on Crime Prevention (London: HMSO, 1983).

Home Office, *Cautioning by the Police,* A Consultative Document (London: HMSO, 1984).

Hood, R. and Sparks, R., *Key Issues in Criminology* (London: Weidenfeld & Nicolson, 1978).

Hough, M. and Mayhew, P., *The British Crime Survey* (London: HMSO, 1983).

Institute of Grocery Distribution, *Report of a Working Party on Shrinkage* (n.d.).

Johnson, J.M., *Doing Field Research* (New York: Free Press, 1975).

Justice of the Peace and Local Government Review, 'Shoplifting' (10 June 1967), pp. 357—8.

Keeton, G.W. 'The Hand in the Till', *Justice of the Peace* (22 October 1977), pp. 623—5.

Kellam, A.P., 'Shoplifting Treated by Aversion to a Film', *Behaviour Research and Therapy,* Vol. 7 (1969), pp. 125—7.

King, M., *The Frame-Work of Criminal Justice* (London: Croom Helm, 1981).

Kitsuse, J.I. and Cicourel, A.V., 'A Note on the Use of Official Statistics', *Social Problems,* Vol. 11 (1963), pp. 131—9.

Klockars, C.B., *The Professional Fence* (London: Tavistock, 1974).

Kraut, R.E., 'Deterrent and Definitional Influences on Shoplifting', *Social Problems*, Vol. 23 (1976), pp. 358—68.

Latané, B. and Darley, J.M., 'Bystander "Apathy" ', *American Scientist*, Vol. 57 (1969), pp. 244—68.

Laurie, P., 'Negotiations Between the Defendant and the Police', in *Criminal Justice*, ed. Baldwin, J. and Bottomley, A.K. (London: Martin Robertson, 1978), pp. 91—4.

Lehr, K., 'Shoplifting by a Gang', *Kriminalistik*, Vol. 23 (1969), pp. 433—6.

Levine, J., 'The Potential for Crime Over-Reporting in Criminal Victimisation Surveys', *Criminology*, Vol. 14 (1976), pp. 307—30.

Lidstone, K.W., Hogg, R. and Sutcliffe, F., *Prosecutions by Private Individuals and Non-Police Agencies*, Royal Commission on Criminal Procedure, Research Study, No. 10 (London: HMSO, 1980).

Locke, H.J., 'Are Volunteer Interviews Representative?', *Social Problems* (April 1954), pp. 143—6.

Lodge, T.S., 'Criminal Statistics', reprinted from *Journal of the Royal Statistical Society*, Series A, Vol. CXVI, Part III (1953), pp.283—97.

Lundman, R.J., 'Shoplifting and Police Referral: A Re-Examination', *The Journal of Criminal Law and Criminology*, Vol. 69, No. 3 (1978), pp. 395—401.

McCabe, S., and Purves, R.F., *By-Passing the Jury* (Oxford: Basil Blackwell, 1972).

McCabe, S. and Sutcliffe, R., *Defining Crime: A Study of Police Decisions*, published for Oxford University Centre for Criminological Research (Oxford: Basil Blackwell, 1978).

McCall, G.J., 'Data Quality Control in Participant Observation', in McCall, G.J. and Simmons, J.L., *Issues in Participant Observation* (Reading, Mass.: Addison-Wesley, 1969), pp. 128—41.

McCall, G.J. and Simmons, J.L., *Issues in Participant Observation* (Reading, Mass.: Addison-Wesley, 1969).

McClintock, F.H., 'The Dark Figure', *Report of the Sixth Conference of Directors of Criminological Research Institutes* (Strasbourg: Council of Europe, 1968), pp. 9—34.

McIntosh, M., *The Organisation of Crime* (London: Macmillan, 1975).

Manning, P.,*Police Work: The Special Organisation of Policing* (London: MIT Press, 1977).

Mapes, G.,'Campus Shoplifting', *Security World* (May 1968), pp. 29—32.

Marks, D.A.,'Retail Store Security in Ireland', *Top Security* (September 1975), pp. 204—6.

Martin, J.P.,*Offenders as Employees*, Cambridge Studies in Criminology (London: Macmillan, 1962).

Mawby, R.,*Policing the City* (Farnborough, Hants: Saxon House, 1979)

May, D.,'Juvenile Shoplifters and the Organisation of Store Security: A Case Study in the Social Construction of Delinquency', *International Journal of Criminology and Penology,* Vol. 6 (1978), pp. 137—60.

Mayhew, P.,'Crime in a Man's World', *New Society,* Vol. 40, No. 560 (16 June 1977).

Meek, V., *Private Enquiries* (London: Duckworth, 1967).

Merrick, B., 'Shoplifting: A Microcosm', *The Criminologist,* Vol. 5. No. 18 (1970), pp. 68—81.

Meyer, S.M., 'A Crusade Against Shoplifting', *Police Chief* (June 1974), pp. 34—6.

Meyers, T.J.,'A Contribution to the Psychopathology of Shoplifting', *Journal of Forensic Science,* Vol. 15, Part III (1970), pp. 295—310.

Morris, T.,*The Criminal Area* (London: Routledge & Kegan Paul, 1957).

Morris, T.,*Deviance and Control. The Secular Heresy* (London: Hutchinson, 1976).

Morrison, W.,'The Interpretation of Criminal Statistics', *Journal of the Royal Statistical Society,* Vol. LX, Part I (1897), pp. 1—24.

Murphy, D.J.I., 'Theft From Stores by Employees and the Public — An Everyday Perspective', *Abstracts on Criminology and Penology,* Vol. 19, No. 3 (1979), pp. 243—8.

Murphy, D.J.I. and Iles, S.C., 'Dealing with Shoplifters', *Home Office Research Bulletin,* No. 15 (1983), pp. 25—9.

NACRO, *'Delays in Coming to Trial'* Nacro Briefing, January, 1981.

National Deviancy Conference/Conference of Socialist Economists, *Capitalism and the Rule of Law* (London: Hutchinson, 1979).

Neustatter, W.L., 'The Psychology of Shoplifting', *Medico-Legal Journal,* Vol. 22 (1954), pp. 118—30.

Oliver, E. and Wilson, J., *Practical Security in Commerce and Industry* (Epping, Essex: Gower Press, 1978, 3rd edn).

Ordway, J.A., ' "Successful" Court Treatment of Shoplifters', *Journal of Criminal Law, Criminology and Police Science,* Vol. 53 (March 1962), pp. 344—7.

Oxford English Dictionary, (Oxford University Press, compact edn, 1971).

Packer, H., *The Limits of Criminal Sanctions* (Stanford: Stanford University Press, 1969).

Pearce, F., *Crimes of the Powerful. Marxism, Crime and Deviance* (London: Pluto Press, 1978).

Polsky, N., *Hustlers, Beats and Others* (Harmondsworth: Penguin Books, 1967).

Post, R., *Combating Crime Against Small Business* (Springfield, Ill.: Charles C. Thomas, 1972).

Purves, R.F., 'That Plea-Bargaining Business: Some Conclusions from

Research', *Criminal Law Review* (1971). pp. 470—5.

Redding, R.G., 'The Social Evil', *Justice of the Peace* (10 January 1976), pp. 17—18.

Retail Review, 'Video Recordings as Evidence', *The Newsletter of the Industrial Police and Security Association* (January 1977), p. 9.

Robertson, R. and Taylor, L., *Deviance, Crime and Socio-Legal Control* (London: Martin Robertson, 1973).

Robin, G,D., 'Patterns of Department Store Shoplifting', *Crime and Delinquency,* Vol. 9 (1963), pp. 163—72.

Robin, G.D., 'The Corporate and Judicial Disposition of Employee Thieves', in *Crimes Against Bureaucracy,* ed. Smigel, E.O. and Ross, H.L. (New York: Van Nostrand, Reinhold, 1970), pp. 119—42.

Roshier, B., 'The Selection of Crime News by the Press', in Cohen, S. and Young, J., *The Manufacture of News, Deviance, Social Problems and the Mass Media* (London: Constable, 1973), pp. 28—39.

Rouke, F.L., 'Shoplifting. Its Symbolic Motivation', *Crime and Delinquency,* Vol. 3 (1957), pp. 54—8.

Russell, D.H., 'Emotional Aspects of Shoplifting', *Psychiatric Annals,* Vol. 3 (1973), pp. 77—86.

Sapsford, R., *Crime and its Growth* (Milton Keynes: The Open University Press, 1980).

Schatzman, L. and Strauss, A.L., *Field Research: Strategies for a Natural Sociology* (New Jersey: Prentice-Hall, 1973).

Scheff, T.J., 'Negotiating Reality: Notes on Power in the Assessment of Responsibility', *Social Problems,* Vol. 16 (Summer 1968), pp. 3—19.

Scott, M. B and Lyman, S.M., 'Accounts, Deviance and Social Order', in *Deviance and Respectability,* ed. Douglas, J.D. (New York: Basic Books, 1970).

Schwartz, M.S. and Schwartz, C.E., 'Problems in Participant Observation', in McCall, G.J. and Simmons, J.L., *Issues in Participant Observation* (Reading, Mass.: Addison-Wesley, 1969), pp. 89—104.

Sellin, T., 'The Significance of Records of Crime', in *The Sociology of Crime and Delinquency,* ed. Wolfgang, M.E., Savitz, L. and Johnston, N. (London: Wiley, 1962), pp. 59—68.

Sellin, T. and Wolfgang, M.E., *The Measurement of Delinquency* (New York: John Wiley, 1964; reprinted 1978).

Short, J.F. and Nye, F.I., 'Reported Behaviour as a Criterion of Deviant Behaviour', in *The Sociology of Crime and Delinquency,* ed. Wolfgang, E.M., Savitz, L. and Johnston, N. (London: Wiley, 1962), pp. 44—9.

Skogan, W.G., 'Measurement Problems in Official and Survey Crime Rates', *Journal of Criminal Justice,* Vol. 3 (1975), pp. 17—32.

Skogan, W.G., 'Citizen Reporting of Crime', *Criminology,* Vol. 13, No. 4 (February 1976), pp. 535—49.

Smigel, E.O., 'Public Attitudes Towards Stealing as Related to the Size of the Victim Organisation', *American Sociological Review*, Vol. 21 (1956), pp. 320—7.

Smigel, E.O. and Ross, H.L., *Crimes Against Bureaucracy* (New York: Van Nostrand, Reinhold, 1970).

Smith, J.C., *The Law of Theft* (London: Butterworth, 1979; 4th edn).

Sohier, J., 'Shoplifting: A Rather Ordinary Crime', *International Criminal Police Review*, Vol. 24, No. 229 (1969), pp. 161—5.

Sparks, R.F., Genn, H., and Dodd, D.J., *Surveying Victims* (London: Wiley, 1977).

Steffensmeier, D.J., 'Levels of Dogmatism and Willingness to Report "Hippie" and "Straight" Shoplifters: A Field Experiment Accompanied by Home Interviews', *Sociometry*, Vol. 38, No. 2 (1975), pp. 282—90.

Steffensmeier, D.J. and Steffensmeier, R.H., 'Who Reports Shoplifters? Research Continuities and Further Developments', *International Journal of Criminology and Penology*, Vol. 5 (1977), pp. 79—95.

Steffensmeier, D.J. and Terry, R.M., 'Deviance and Respectability: An Observational Study of Reactions to Shoplifting', *Social Forces*, Vol. 51 (1973), pp. 417—26.

Steiner, J.M., Hadden, S.C. and Herkomer, L., 'Price-Tag Switching', *International Journal of Criminology and Penology*, Vol. 4 (1976), pp. 129—43.

Strauss, A. *et al.*, 'Field Tactics', in McCall, G.J. and Simmons, J.L., *Issues in Participant Observation* (Reading, Mass.: Addison-Wesley, 1969), pp. 70—2.

Sudnow, D., 'Normal Crimes: Sociological Features of the Penal Code', *Social Problems*, Vol. 12 (1965), pp. 255—70.

Sudnow, D., *Passing On. The Social Organisation of Dying* (New Jersey: Prentice-Hall, 1977).

Sutherland, E.H., *The Professional Thief — By A Professional Thief* (Chicago: Chicago University Press, 1937).

Tarling, R. and Weatheritt, M., *Sentencing Practice in Magistrates' Courts*, Home Office Research Study No. 56 (London: HMSO, 1979).

Taylor, I., Walton, P. and Young, J., *The New Criminology* (London: Routledge & Kegan Paul, 1977).

Taylor, L.B., *Shoplifting* (New York: Franklin Watts, 1979).

Terry, R.M. and Steffensmeier, D.J., 'The Influence of Organisational Factors of Victim Store on Willingness to Report a Shoplifting Incident: A Field Experiment', *Sociological Forces*, Vol. 6 (1973), pp. 27—45.

Thorsen, J.E., 'The War on Shoplifting', *Security World* (November 1975), pp. 22—34.

Vera Institute of Justice, *Waiting Times in Magistrates Courts. An Exploratory Study* (December 1979).

Verill, A.H., 'Reducing Shop Losses', in *Combating Crime Against Small Business* ed. Post. R. (Springfield, Ill.: Charles C. Thomas, 1972).

Versele, S.C., 'Study of Female Shoplifters in Department Stores', *International Criminal Police Review* (March 1969), pp. 66–70.

Viditch, A.J. and Shapiro, G., 'A Comparison of Participant Observations and Survey Data', in McCall, G.J. and Simmons, J.L., *Issues in Participant Observation* (Reading, Mass.: Addison-Wesley, 1969), pp. 295–302.

Wallerstein, J.S. and Wyle, C., 'Our Law-Abiding Law-Breakers', *Probation* (April 1947), pp. 107–12.

Wallin, P., 'Volunteer Subjects as a Source of Sampling Bias', *The American Journal of Sociology*, Vol. 54 (1949), pp. 539–44.

Walsh, D.P., *Shoplifting: Controlling a Major Crime* (London: Macmillan, 1978).

Wax, R.H., 'Reciprocity as a Field Technique', *Human Organisation*, Vol. 11 (3) (1952), pp. 34–7.

Wheeler, S., 'Criminal Statistics: A Reformulation of the Problem', *Journal of Criminal Law, Criminology and Police Science*, Vol. 58, No. 3 (1967), pp. 317–24.

Wiles, P., 'Criminal Statistics and Sociological Explanations of Crime', in *The Sociology of Crime and Delinquency in Britain*, ed. Carson, W.G. and Wiles, P. Vol. I (London: Martin Robertson, 1975), pp. 198–219.

Wisher, C., 'Teenage Shoplifting: Who, Where, When, How?', *Security World*, Vol. 5, Part 10 (1968), pp. 16–20.

Won, G. and Yamamoto, G., 'Social Structure and Deviant Behaviour: A Study of Shoplifting', *Sociology and Social Research*, Vol. 53, Part I (1968), pp. 44–55.

Zander, M., 'Saving Time — and Money', *The Guardian*, 23 February 1976.

Zimmerman, D.H. and Pollner, M., 'The Everyday World as a Phenomenon', in *Understanding Everyday Life*, ed. Douglas, J.D. (London: Routledge & Kegan Paul, 1971), pp. 80–103.

Zola, E., *L'Assomoir* (Harmondsworth: Penguin Books, 1974; first published 1876.

Index